'Alice Loxton is … d
*UPROAR!* is a ser… ut
as one of the brig… popular history'
**Dan Jones, author of *Powers and Thrones***

'A rollicking ride through late eighteenth century Britain in all its effervescent rudeness and hilarity. Hugely entertaining'
**Dr Linda Porter, author of *Mistresses***

'Alice Loxton's analysis of Georgian England is razor sharp, witty and engaging. An appropriately "laugh out loud" history of the age of satire'
**Helen Carr, author of *The Red Prince***

'Alice Loxton heads the charge of an exciting new generation of historians – this is an exuberant, iconoclastic and, yes, uproarious debut'
**Jessie Childs, author of *The Siege of Loyalty House***

'As wittily subversive and deeply entertaining as the material it details, Alice Loxton's *UPROAR!* is a delightful romp through the colourful and controversial eighteenth century. Loxton has built a time-machine in a book, and invited us all along for a ride. I would suggest you hop in!'
**Dr Joanne Paul, author of *The House of Dudley***

'Loxton writes with a terrific sense of time and place. She delivers Georgian Britain in a bold modern manner, with plenty of bounce'
**Franny Moyle, author of *Desperate Romantics***

'Alice Loxton's *UPROAR!* is a delight: an energetic and highly enjoyable exploration of the careers and the turmoil of the social and political world of the leading caricaturists of the great age of satire, Thomas Rowlandson, James Gillray, and Isaac Cruikshank. So rich is her research and so vivid is her prose that we emerge from reading this book feeling that we have argued, laughed and drunk punch with these men and felt the fierce brilliance of their minds and their art – which shines bright still today'

**Jeremy Musson, author of *The Country House: Past, Present, Future***

'As vivid and vibrant as any Rowlandson print – bawdy, beautiful, and brilliant'

**Kate Lister, author of *A Curious History of Sex***

'Loxton plunges us headfirst into the tumultuous world of London's eighteenth-century printmakers in this lively, riveting and pacy account'

**Charlotte Mullins, author of *A Little History of Art***

'A gripping, energetic and easy to follow deep dive into the raucous satire revolution of late Georgian Britain. Alice has created a diamond of a debut book'

**Tristan Hughes, author of *The Perdiccas Years, 323–320 BC***

# UPROAR!

## SATIRE, SCANDAL & PRINTMAKERS in GEORGIAN LONDON

ALICE LOXTON

Published in the UK and USA in 2024 by
Icon Books Ltd, Omnibus Business Centre,
39–41 North Road, London N7 9DP
email: info@iconbooks.com
www.iconbooks.com

Sold in the UK, Europe and Asia
by Icon Books,
39-41 North Road,
London, N7 9DP or their agents

Distributed in the UK, Europe and Asia
by HarperCollins Publishers,
Westerhill Road, Bishopbriggs,
Glasgow, G64 2QT

Distributed in the USA & Canada
by Independent Publishers Group,
814 N. Franklin St.,
Chicago, IL 60610

Distributed in India
by Penguin Random House India Pvt. Ltd.
No: 04-10 to 04-012, 4th Floor,
Capital Tower-I, Meherauli Gurgaon
Road, Sikanderpur, Sector-26,
Gurugram-122002, Haryana

Distributed in Australia
by Peribo Pty Limited,
58 Beaumont Road,
Mt Kuring-Gai, NSW 2080

Distributed in Singapore
by Times Distribution Pte. Ltd,
1 New Industrial Road, Times Centre,
Singapore 536196

Distributed in South Africa
by Jonathan Ball,
Office C4, The District,
41 Sir Lowry Road, Woodstock, 7925

Distributed in Malaysia
by Times Distribution (M) Sdn Bhd,
Level 1 Tower 2A, Avenue 5
Bangsar South
No. 8 Jalan Kerinchi, 59200
Kuala Lumpur, Malaysia

ISBN: 978-178578-955-7



Map rights details: Rocque, J., Pine, J. & Tinney, J. (1746) A plan of the cities of London and Westminster, and borough of Southwark, with the contiguous buildings. London, John Pine & John Tinney. Retrieved from the Library of Congress, https://www.loc.gov/item/76696823/.

Portrait of James Gillray on p.v, Charles Turner, 1819, mezzotint after Gillray's self-portrait, National Portrait Gallery, London.



Typeset in LTC Caslon Pro by Marie Doherty

Printed and bound by CPI (UK) Ltd, Croydon CR0 4YY

*For James Gillray*

*'Laughter is a bodily exercise, precious to health.'*

– ARISTOTLE (SO THEY SAY)

# Contents

# *Author's Note*

London at the close of the eighteenth century was a circus: port-pickled politicians wept over the brilliance of classical oratory; duchesses pranced through butchers' shops in a flutter of lace and ribbons; and every vagabond and countess, scoundrel and bishop gossiped with glee over the Royal Academy's placement of a fig leaf.

But right in the heart of this pantomime was a force, a magnetism, so strong it kept the entire city in check. This force was not imposed by king or law, but the electric creativity emanating from a set of visionary artists. Their satirical prints were so acerbic, so insightful, that every Londoner's folly and foible was fair game. Earls and rakes, fishwives and barbers were kept awake at night. Life-long reputations were destroyed in an instant. No one was safe.

Yet, this story is unknown by all but a few enthusiasts and academics. *UPROAR!* seeks to change that.

A word of guidance, though. The following pages are not for the faint-hearted. We are about to journey through some of the most dramatic and thrilling moments in British history. We will encounter madness and cruelty, revolution and war.

But it is also a story to inspire and delight. Prepare to come face-to-face with some of the greatest visionaries this country has ever seen. As we follow their journey and peer over their shoulders, we will glimpse dazzling sparks of genius. Sunglasses are advised.

We'll pry into the most intimate moments of our ancestors' lives – see them sneeze and yawn, hear them giggle and snort. In turn, you might find we're probing deep into the secrets of your own character, too. Be prepared to be shocked. Be prepared to weep. And definitely be prepared to laugh.

So, hold on to your hats. It's going to be a rollicking ride. Welcome to the world of *UPROAR!*

*Alice Loxton*
*Covent Garden*
*September 2022*

# *Map and Timeline*

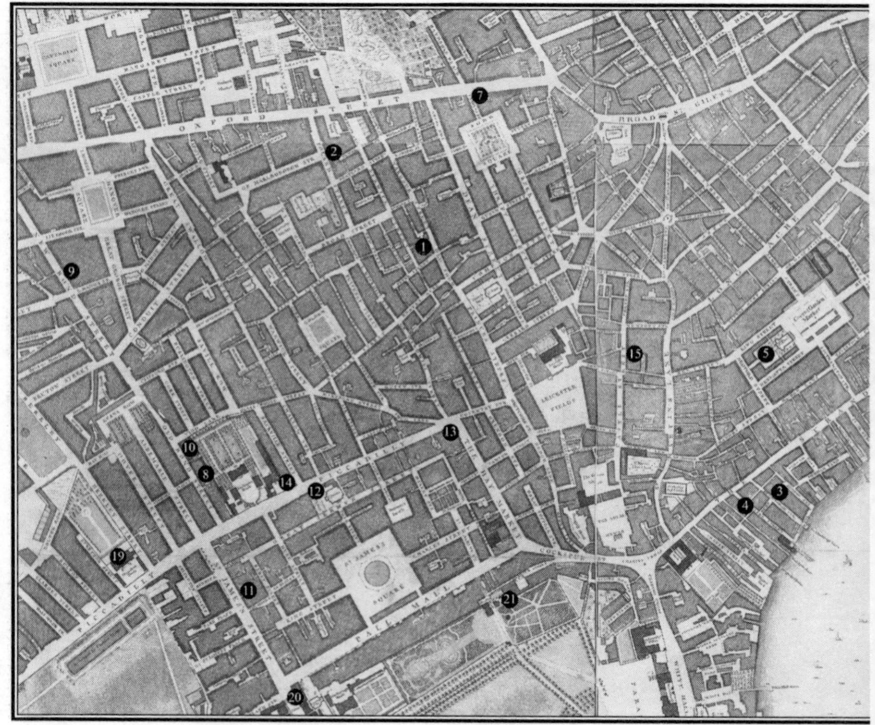


## Key to map

1. 103 Wardour Street, where Rowlandson stayed with Aunt Jane until 1786
2. 50 Poland Street, the home of Rowlandson's Aunt Jane from 1786
3. 2 Robert Street, Rowlandson's 'dismal' basement lodgings, where he lived 1792–*c.* 1795
4. 1 James Street, Rowlandson's final lodgings
5. St Paul's Church, Covent Garden, where Rowlandson is buried
6. 66 Drury Lane, William Holland's early print shop
7. 50 Oxford Street, William Holland's Laughing Lounge print shop
8. 18 Old Bond Street, Hannah Humphrey's print shop (1779–83 and 1790–94)
9. 51 Old Bond Street, Hannah Humphrey's print shop (1783–9)
10. 37 New Bond Street, Hannah Humphrey's print shop (1794–7)
11. 27 St James's Street, Hannah Humphrey's print shop (1797–1817)
12. St James's Church, Piccadilly, where Gillray was buried
13. 3 Piccadilly, Samuel Fores' print shop until 1796
14. 50 Piccadilly, Samuel Fores' print shop from 1796

15 St Martin's Court, the Cruikshanks' early lodgings
16 117 Dorset Street, where the Cruikshanks' lived later on
17 St Bride's Church, where Isaac Cruikshank is buried
18 Somerset House, home to the Royal Academy from 1771
19 Devonshire House, home of Georgiana, Duchess of Devonshire
20 St James's Palace
21 Carlton House, the notorious building project of Prince George
22 Rudolph Ackermann's print shops (96 Strand 1795–7, 101 Strand 1796–1827)
23 111 Cheapside, Thomas Tegg's Apollo Library

NB: This map dates from the 1740s, giving us an idea of what London looked like when the artists were born. There wasn't a great deal of change in the following decades, so it can be used as a rough guide for the city plan during their lives, too. Major developments included the Adam brothers' Adelphi complex, where Rowlandson lived.

## GENERAL HISTORIC DATES

**25 October 1760**
George III becomes king, succeeding his grandfather George II

**10 December 1768**
Royal Academy of Arts founded

**1768–1771**
Captain James Cook leads his first expedition to the Pacific

**January 1770**
Lord North becomes Prime Minister

**1771**
Britain's first cotton mill opens, beginning the 'Factory Age'

**16 December 1773**
Tensions heighten in North American colonies with the 'Boston Tea Party'

**2–11 June 1780**
'Gordon Riots' break out in protest against the Catholic Relief Act

**19 October 1781**
Americans defeat the British army at Yorktown, Virginia

**December 1783**
William Pitt the Younger becomes Prime Minister, aged 24

**November 1788–February 1789**
George III's illness sparks a regency crisis

**29 April 1789**
The formerly enslaved Olaudah Equiano publishes his autobiography

**14 July 1789**
French Revolution begins with the storming of the Bastille

1750s | 1760s | 1770s | 1780s

**13 August 1756**
James Gillray born

**13 July 1757**
Thomas Rowlandson born

**5 October 1764**
Isaac Cruikshank born

**6 November 1772**
Rowlandson begins study at the Royal Academy Schools

**1778**
Gillray begins study at the Royal Academy Schools

**1783**
Cruikshank moves to London

## *UPROAR!* DATES

**1 January 1801**
Act of Union creates the United Kingdom

**2 December 1804**
Napoleon crowns himself Emperor at Notre Dame

**21 October 1805**
Royal Navy defeats a French and Spanish fleet at the Battle of Trafalgar

**1806**
Death of William Pitt the Younger and Charles James Fox

**25 March 1807**
Britain abolishes the slave trade

**1808**
British West Africa Squadron is formed to suppress slave trading

**28 January 1813**
Jane Austen's *Pride and Prejudice* published

**18 June 1815**
Napoleon defeated at the Battle of Waterloo

**1816**
The 'Year Without a Summer'

**1816**
Lord Elgin sells the Parthenon marbles to the British government

**16 August 1819**
Eleven die at the Peterloo massacre in Manchester

**29 January 1820**
George III dies and is succeeded by George IV

**27 September 1825**
World's first steam locomotive passenger service begins

**13 April 1829**
Parliament grants Catholic emancipation

**26 June 1830**
George IV dies and is succeeded by his brother William IV

| 1790s | 1800s | 1810s | 1820s |
|---|---|---|---|

**27 September 1792**
Birth of George Cruikshank

**1793**
William Holland imprisoned for seditious libel

**1797**
Gillray lodging with Hannah Humphrey

**January 1803**
Creation of 'Little Boney'

**February 1805**
Gillray's *Plumb-pudding* published

**1808**
Rudolph Ackermann starts publishing 'The Microcosm of London'

**April 1811**
Death of Isaac Cruikshank

**1 June 1815**
Death of Gillray

**February 1818**
Death of Hannah Humphrey

**21 April 1827**
Death of Rowlandson

# *Act I*

# 1

# *A Bench of Artists*

## A SOBER, DILIGENT PERSON OVER THE AGE OF TWELVE

6 November 1772.[1] A fifteen-year-old whippersnapper named Tom scurried through the grimy backstreets of eighteenth-century London. As the bells of St Paul's tolled out to herald a new day, he tripped and skipped and darted across potholes, broken glass and horse dung. He overheard tavern keepers evict sleeping drunks and caught snippets of gossip from dutiful maids as they carried out their early-morning errands. The November sunlight pierced through dusty windows of ale houses and coffee shops, and the city erupted into life once again.

Stumbling out of this labyrinth, Tom burst out into the wide-open space of one of central London's most fashionable streets: the Strand, a playground for the super-rich. Tom might have glanced through the shopfronts to gaze upon curious delicacies from across the globe: coffee from Arabia, silks from Madras or furs from New York. He probably passed No. 216, where the tearooms of Thomas Twining emitted the tantalising scent of finely blended tea. Or the bookshop at No. 34, where Samuel Johnson could often be spied, poring over the vast collection of titles. As he trotted westward, Tom was vigilant to dodge the obstacles of the street: the wide, square hoops of fashionable ladies in sack-back gowns, or the hordes of labourers, toiling to complete the latest building schemes of Robert Adam, the great neoclassical architect of the day.

In the early 1770s, Britain was on the brink of transformation. In 1771, the inventor Richard Arkwright opened the first cotton mill at Cromford, Derbyshire, marking the start of Britain's Factory Age. Meanwhile, up and down the country, thousands of curious punters gathered to listen to the electrifying words of Methodist preacher John Wesley. And across the Atlantic Ocean, long-growing tensions in the American colonies, in which calls for 'No taxation without representation' were reaching boiling point, would soon erupt with the Boston Tea Party in 1773. It was on such issues as these that 34-year-old King George III – in the twelfth year of his reign by 1772 – would have consulted his prime minister, Lord North.

Nowhere was the change more apparent than in London, a city which was swelling at incredible pace. It was a thriving metropolis, flooded by thousands of young people each year eager to make something of themselves. In 1700, the city's population numbered about half a million. By 1800, it would double to 1 million, the first city in Europe to do so since Ancient Rome.[2] The streets were buzzing with horse-drawn hackney coaches and trading carts bouncing over the cobblestones, and sedan chairs and pedestrians in their thousands.

All of these were easily avoided by our young friend Tom as he picked his way down the Strand. And today, he was bursting with excitement. For he was heading for the Royal Academy Schools to begin his first day of study. This was the start of his great career to become Britain's Next Top Artist.

Tom knew these streets like the back of his hand: he was a Londoner born and bred. His family, the Rowlandsons, were of Huguenot extraction. His grandparents still lived in silk-weaving Spitalfields (then green fields to the east). But Thomas' parents, William and Mary Rowlandson, were based in the beating heart of the City of London, on Old Jewry. It was here that Thomas Rowlandson was born on 13 July 1757.

The family made a respectable living by trading wool and silk. But it wasn't an easy ride. When young Tom was a toddler, his father's business hit the rocks. 'The elder Rowlandson,' it would be recorded in Tom's obituary, 'who was of a speculative turn, lost considerable sums experimenting upon various branches of manufactures, which were tried on too large a scale of his means; hence his affairs became embarrassed.'[3] On 16 January 1759, William Rowlandson was declared bankrupt, and to hammer home the humiliation, it was printed in the *Gentleman's Magazine* for the world to see.

Creditors seized the family house. William and Mary upped sticks and hurried north to Richmond, Yorkshire. Luckily, William's brother, James, had made less of a hash of things. He was a prosperous Spitalfields silk weaver, happily married to a generous Frenchwoman named Jane. Having no children of their own, they took in young Tom, allowing him to remain in London.

But tragedy struck in 1764. Uncle James died of fever. Aunt Jane sold the business and moved to rooms on Church Street, Soho. She sent Tom to Dr Barwis' school on Soho Square, 'the first academy in London'.[4] In language befitting an Ofsted report, the school was said to attain 'an extraordinary degree of excellence'.[5]

The school's founder, Martin Clare, had described himself as 'M. Clare, School-Master in Soho Square, London. With whom Youth may Board, and be fitted for business.'[6] Clare was the author of two utilitarian books: *Youth's Introduction to Trade and Business* and *Rules and Orders for the Government of the Academy in Soho Square*. For just £30 a year, plus a sprinkling of paid-for extras, parents could expect their sons to excel in French, drawing, dancing and fencing, and get a decent grounding in morality, religion and philosophy, too.

When Tom enlisted, in the 1760s, the school was run by Rev. Cuthbert Barwis, who added a dash of theatrics to the mix. Under his thespian leadership, the Soho School became famed for the masterful array of Shakespeare plays performed by the pupils. His eccentricity was not lost on an impressionable cast of schoolboys, who turned out to be an impressive bunch: the actors Joseph Holman, John Liston and Jack Bannister, as well as the artist J.M.W. Turner, all passed through Dr Barwis' doors.

Tom was popular with his peers, who dubbed him 'Rowly'.* It was in these boisterous classes where Tom, struggling to engage his mind with competing theories of trade and economics, began doodling. The margins of his books were soon black with scribblings of 'humorous characters of his master and many of his scholars'.[7] In Tom's fifteenth year, these sketches were considered worthy of more than just textbook marginalia. Probably with the encouragement of Barwis – keen for some more sparkle to add to his list of alumni – Tom was put forward to apply for the brand-spanking-new Royal Academy Schools.

The Academy Schools were part of the Royal Academy of Arts, itself less than four years old after being founded in 1768. It had been launched by the Instrument of Foundation, a scheme signed off by King George III. In a pompous and unimaginative declaration, it claimed to be a 'well-regulated School or Academy of Design, for the use of students in the Arts, and an Annual Exhibition, open to all artists of distinguished merit'.[8]

So, this was the official establishment of the hub of British creativity. And the chosen lexicon was … 'well-regulated'. The British art scene kicked off in a haze of procedure and red tape. How thrilling! How wild! How shockingly subversive! When George III trawled through the 27 clauses relating to membership, government, officers, schools, professors, servants, exhibitions, library, admin, red tape, procedure and admin, his unbridled enthusiasm for this new arm of

* There was probably some double entendre here. 'Old Rowley' was well-known as the lustful stallion of King Charles II – a nickname that was also given to the King himself, and probably hinted at his many mistresses and illegitimate children.

top brass was duly noted next to a signature: 'I approve of this plan; let it be put in execution.'[9]

Despite a muted beginning on paper, the Royal Academy was founded with good intentions. It sought to provide a standard of excellence to a hitherto unregulated and unprofessional art scene. In affiliation with the Royal Academy came the Academy Schools, at which Tom became a student. Originally based in defunct auction rooms in Pall Mall, in 1771 the school moved to extensive space in the old Somerset House in the Strand. This comprised a lecture room, a library, a room for life drawing, known as the Life Room, and a hall filled with casts of classical sculpture called the Plaister Academy.

The entry requirements were tough. Prospective students were expected to be pretty clued up already, having 'An acquaintance with Anatomy (comprehending a knowledge of the Skeleton, and the Names, Origins, Insertions, and Uses of, at least, the external layers of Muscles)'.[10]

To separate the wheat from the chaff, candidates were invited to the premises to be tested. Tom had been put through his paces at his interview. He was brought for inspection to the Keeper of the Schools, George Michael Moser, an elderly Swiss-born artist, who had once been a drawing-master to the King, and a specialist in ornamental enamels.*

Moser was happy enough with Master Rowlandson's submitted samples, but still needed convincing. Tom was sent to the Plaister Academy. For several long, nerve-wracking days, he toiled away on a further set of drawings: marking out every tiny detail, triple-checking his angles and trying to steady his shaking hand. Tom knew that his whole career rested on these studies, and he spent every waking minute working them up to perfection.

* Tiny paintings on a white enamel canvas.

The endeavour paid off. His application was approved by the council, and a letter of admission dispatched by Francis Newton, the secretary of the Academy. He was in!

But would Tom suit the 'well-regulated' demands of this prestigious institution? He had all the ingredients to become a great artist – a technical ability beyond his years, an unwavering self-belief, a sharp mind bursting with ideas, and a quick wit to charm his way through polite society.

He was admitted on the condition that he 'behave with that respect which is due to an Institution subsisting under the gracious protection of the Sovereign'.[11] But in truth, Tom didn't often observe such rules of the room – he was better known for his 'social spirit'. He was a young lad 'who sought the company of dashing young men; and, among other evils, imbibed a love for play'.[12]

It was perhaps following such indulgence that Tom pranced down the Strand and finally stepped foot inside the walls of the Academy Schools on that sunny November morning in 1772.

## AN ACQUAINTANCE WITH ANATOMY

It must have been a thrilling moment for Tom when he first tiptoed through the Academy drawing rooms, squeezing his skinny frame past the back-of-house clutter and classical casts. His pulse must have raced as he hunted for a seat in the Life Room: he edged along the rounded benches, careful not to knock the shaded candleholders on each desk, and unpacked his bag. Only now he noticed the walls were covered from floor to ceiling with shelves, overflowing with classical casts, dusty figurines and other backroom knick-knacks.

Hugging the walls of the room were long rows of tables and benches, tiered and curved to create an amphitheatre-like space – meaning that every desk would have an uninterrupted view of the central platform. Here posed a living, breathing model, with every bulge and twist of their naked body illuminated by a single oil lamp suspended from the ceiling. To keep within the bounds of propriety, the rules were strict: 'No Student under the Age of twenty shall be admitted to draw after the female model, unless he be a married man.'[13]

*Drawing from Life at the Royal Academy, Somerset House*, Thomas Rowlandson and Augustus Pugin, 1808.
Royal Academy of Arts, London

In the Life Room (sometimes called the School of Living Models), Tom would be taught to understand the secrets of classical grandeur, the grace of the human form, and sensible ideas of 'taste'. It was a syllabus created by a 49-year-old ear-trumpet-wielding vicar's son from Devon: the president of the Royal Academy, Joshua Reynolds. The teaching was led by a series of visiting artists, known as Academicians, who were elected to teach for one month each, on rotation. During term time the life classes ran for two hours every evening, and in the summer students were booted out to make way for the Academy's annual Summer Exhibition.

The earliest surviving sketch from Tom's days at the Academy tells us that he got the hang of drawing pretty quickly. But the image is not one of the Academy's languishing nude models placed in a classical recline. Tom had been looking elsewhere. He'd been busy sketching seven fellow students on the opposite side of the room. 'A Bench of Artists,' reads the annotation, 'Sketched at the Royal Academy in the Year 1776–'.

Squashed together with just enough elbow room and with pairs of legs sprawling out from the bench like those of a centipede, here are the future stars of the art world, some daydreaming, some smirking, some diligent, some anxious.

Taking centre stage is 23-year-old William Beechey, who would become the leading English portraitist of his day. Think of a famous name and Beechey would one day paint them: George III, George IV, William IV, young Queen Victoria, Nelson, Wellington, actresses, politicians – the works. The student on Beechey's left appears to be slouching, but this dark-haired artist was the 24-year-old Charles Reuben Ryley, who had a 'weakly constitution' and was 'deformed in figure'.[14] Unlike Rowlandson, Ryley is diligently concentrating on drawing the life model, his great bushy brows raised in magnificent arches.

*A Bench of Artists*, Thomas Rowlandson, 1776.
Tate. Purchased as part of the Oppé Collection with assistance from the National Lottery through the Heritage Lottery Fund 1996.

Students also developed their understanding of anatomy through the study of plaster casts. The Plaister Gallery, which provided an informal setting to study and form friendships, was open from Monday to Saturday, 9am to 3pm. It was available throughout the year apart from four weeks in September, two weeks from Christmas Eve to Epiphany, and 46 days in April and May. Rules were to be strictly obeyed. Students were forbidden from touching, let alone moving, the valuable casts:

> There shall be Weekly, set out in the Great Room, One or more Plaister Figures by the Keeper, for the Students to draw after, and no Student shall presume to move the said Figures out of the Places where they have been set by the Keeper, without his leave first obtained for that Purpose.[15]

Regulations were even required to prevent students nabbing each other's drawing spots, declaring that 'when any Student hath taken possession of a Place in the Plaister Academy, he shall not be removed out of it, till the Week in which he hath taken it is expired'.[16]

The room displayed the Academy's collection of busts, figures and ornamental reliefs. Here, students could learn how the great artists and craftsmen from Ancient Rome, Renaissance Florence and Bourbon France had moulded flesh from marble. Unlike the life models, who often moved to itch a crooked nose or stretched only to return to a different position, the plaster casts captured the ideal of mankind's beauty, unmoving and unblemished.

The casts were made from gesso, a mixture of chalk, gypsum and white pigment – a mixture that remains largely unchanged for artistic study today. Students were encouraged to cultivate a light source using candles and mirrors, creating a deeper eye socket or furrowed brow. How did the flicker of a flame splay out Newton's spectra of colour? How did this expose new forms of the gesso physique?

With the guidance of Academicians, Tom began to unpick the secrets of his profession. As he replicated the graceful swirls of drapery of the *Apollo Belvedere*, he noticed how they articulated the body to both reveal and conceal the torso and limbs. He discovered how figures posed in the *contrapposto* stance – where the weight falls more heavily on one foot, swaying the hips and relaxing the shoulders – made the sculpture seem to come alive.

Finally, he understood what Pliny and Vitruvius had meant when they wrote of 'the ideal beauty'. All of these tributes to the human form had been developed from mathematical ratios. As the students sketched away in the shadows of dancing fawns and Greek goddesses, they were reminded of great lessons of the past: 'It's coming along, Tom, but this angle under the chin isn't quite right. The collarbone is too short. Remember the words of Leonardo: the length of the outspread arms is equal to the height of a man.'

Tom and his fellow students were also given permission to draw from the cast collection at the Duke of Richmond's private sculpture gallery at Whitehall. Admission cards were provided, much like the library cards university students have today. These were about the size of a passport and emblazoned with a large red wax seal marked: 'ROYAL ACADEMY, LONDON'.

A letter from Aunt Jane on 25 November 1772 was required to assure the assistant secretary at the Academy that her nephew would behave himself:

> The bearer Master Thomas Rowlandson being Desirous of becoming a student in his Grace the Duke of Richmond's Gallery – the recommendary figure delivered you by him being his own performance and it being necessary to find security for his good behaver in admission I humbly offer myself for that Purpas and am with much respects.
>
> Your mo: ob: servant,
>
> J. Rowlandson[17]

*The Antique School at New Somerset House*, Edward Francis Burney, *c.* 1780.
Royal Academy of Arts, London

## HIS TWELFTH GLASS OF PUNCH

Whether Aunt Jane was confident in her unruly nephew's behaviour – and whether Tom lived up to these promises – is hard to know. But it wouldn't matter for long. By 1774, in 'his sixteenth year', he was whisked away on a Royal Academy 'study abroad' scheme, at the Académie Royale de Peinture et de Sculpture in Paris. Here he would acquire a taste for French methods and fashions, build contacts with collectors and, as Aunt Jane probably hoped, grow up a bit.

As Tom caught a coach down to Dover for the passage across the Channel, he picked up 'an Englishman of the name of Higginson', also heading off to study at the Académie Royale.[18] Higginson had hundreds of contacts in Paris, so Tom realised he was well worth sticking with.

These two teenage Brits arrived 'immediately after the death of Louis the Fifteenth at the moment of the putting on of public mourning'.[19] Incredibly, King Louis had ruled since 1715, a reign of 59 years, so the boys arrived to find a city that was in a pensive mood.

Rowlandson's Parisian study was sponsored by Jean-Baptiste Pigalle, one of the wealthiest and most respected sculptors in France. Not only could Pigalle fashion innate lumps of stone into contorted human flesh, he had a network full of star-studded names. The sculptor had enjoyed the patronage of the cherry on top of the *crème de la crème*: Louis XV's mistress, Madame de Pompadour. To meet Pigalle as a young artist, let alone be sponsored and probably taught by him, was the opportunity of a lifetime. If joining the Royal Academy under Sir Joshua Reynolds was the chance to get a five-minute interview on *The One Show*, studying with Pigalle in Paris was the equivalent of being sent to Hollywood.

At this point, Paris was a 'ridiculous jumble of shells, dragons, reeds, palm-trees and plants', according to the neoclassical painter Merry-Joseph Blondel.[20] For these were the final years of France's love affair with Rococo – a style which luxuriated in elegant extravagance and frothy decoration, and a time when men and women were decked in frills, ruffles, bows and lace. Artists of the Rococo didn't bother to lay down weighty political metaphors or comment on the grinding poverty of the French farmer. They preferred to paint a window into a chocolate box world of love, classical myths, youth and playfulness.

Pigalle's classically inspired portrait busts and full-size sculptures indulged in this era of light-hearted mischief. He pricked the pomposity of noble heroes by giving them a human edge. In 1753, he made a sculpture of a young boy leaning over to buckle his sandals. Was this an ice-cream-wielding child on a Cornish beach, holding up the entire family as they strapped up their jelly shoes? Not quite. This was Mercury, the mighty messenger of Roman Gods.

How about Pigalle's ode to Voltaire, the pillar of the French Enlightenment. Would he be decked in grand robes of ancient times, befitting his status as a great thinker? Pigalle didn't bother to clothe him at all. There he is, completely starkers, saved only by some convenient drapery. When King Gustavus III of Sweden saw the portrait, his first reaction was supposedly to offer to buy Voltaire a coat.

Although the coat never materialised, art historians have since dressed Pigalle's work up with some erudite but predictable analysis (we are told to admire his 'truth of form, expression, and gesture').[21] But the real point is that while Pigalle was a highly competent artist, his lumps of stone captured the subtleties of human expression and betrayed a real, living character.

It was to be an important lesson for young Tom Rowlandson, had he visited Pigalle's workshop, based at the Rue Saint-Lazare, in extensive grounds below the hill of Montmartre. Much like *X Factor* starlets staying at Simon Cowell's LA mansion, Pigalle's students caught a glimpse of the mega wealth artists could acquire.

On 11 May 1775, two months short of his eighteenth birthday, Tom was listed in the register of the school of the Académie Royale de Peinture et de Sculpture as the '*protégé par Jean-Baptiste Pigalle*'.[22]*

Meanwhile, Paris was descending into turmoil. Riots over wheat prices erupted into a Flour War and thousands of troops stormed Paris' streets to keep the peace. And a few months later, there was the terrible burning of Palais de la Cité, the royal residence in Paris. It was a city in which tensions seemed to erupt into violence at the slightest provocation. Tensions that would see regicide committed on the streets within two decades.

Blissfully unaware of the looming bloodbath and electrified by the thrill of public disorder, Tom lived in the 'midst of its ever-varying gaieties'[23]: the capital was a place where the yearly average wine intake for a man was 300 litres. It was by good chance that he bumped into another young Londoner, Henry Angelo, who had been sent to Paris to refine his French and master the sword. Fresh out of Eton, Henry was the son of Domenico Angelo, the famous fencing master of Soho; Angelo senior seemed to be chums with 'almost

* Unfortunately, his name was misspelled as 'Rolanson'.

every artist of eminence, foreign as well as native, who practiced [in London] during the latter half of the last century'.[24]

In Henry, Tom found a kindred spirit. Together, they threw themselves into the closing act of Bourbon Paris: they 'mixed in all societies; and [Tom], speaking French fluently, made himself acquainted with the habits of thinking, as well as those of acting, in that city, where everything, to an English eye, bore the appearance of burlesque'.[25]

Such bonhomie was shared by Henry's landlord, Charles Leviez, whose house on the Rue Battois became a bohemian hub for artists. Here, Tom was no doubt fast to pick up tips and titbits about the art world. Leviez had once been a much-admired dancer on the London stage and ballet-master on Drury Lane. Now he was a socialite, art dealer and full-time eccentric. He was known to dress up as Apollo, arrange nine chairs in a circle, pretending these were the Nine Muses of Greek Mythology, and perform his fiddle to them, 'with the most extravagant grimaces'.[26]

While he wasn't serenading his furniture, Leviez commissioned, collected and dealt in prints. And what's more, many artists 'frequently passed the evening at his house', including Johann Georg Wille, Jacques Philippe Le Bas and Claude-Joseph Vernet.[27] Even his wife, Madame Leviez, had modelled for Roubiliac commemorations in Westminster Abbey.

For Tom, the French capital provided a kaleidoscope of models displaying all forms of foible and incongruity: 'Paris, as viewed under the old *régime*, opened a prolific source for his imitative powers. Nothing can exceed the fun and frolic which his subjects display, picked up amongst every class, from the court down to the *cabaret*.'[28]

One episode was a particular source of mirth. Remember Higginson,* the fellow student Tom picked up at Dover? He had taken a hotel on the Rue Battois, next to Charles Leviez's house,

* There is no record of Higginson's first name. I'd take a guess at Philip.

where Henry was lodging. Higginson was another young Englishman who initially seemed like a good egg – until one incident: Suitgate.

Higginson sent a valet over to ask Henry whether he could borrow a black suit, 'which he knew would fit him to a T'.[29] Henry, being the decent sort of chap that he was, 'readily consented', on the agreement that it would be returned later that evening.

Higginson appeared 'a pleasant companion, but, as it fell out, one who seemed to live upon his wits'. To Henry's despair, Higginson went AWOL with the suit. 'Rowlandson lost sight of him for two days and nights; on the morning of the third day he returned'.[30] At this news, Henry barged into Higginson's apartment. He was surprised to find Higginson was 'seated under the frosting powder-puff of a French friseur, having his hair frizzled and powdered, à la mode'. As his hair was being curled, he threw a nonchalant 'Ah! *mon amie*, is it you?' to his inquisitor.[31]

And to Henry's astonishment, not only was this a flagrant, unacceptable disregard for the offence already caused, as Higginson sat in this cloud of powder, he was still 'in my mourning suit'.[32]

Tom, an onlooker to this spectacle, found great mirth in Suitgate, capturing it in a couple of drawings. And the indignation of his drinking companion uncovering the criminal red-handed was no doubt retold at any mention of the name Higginson thereafter.

Although the drawings are lost in the mists of time, they were described in Henry's memoirs with fond musings and an astute perception into the artists' progress. It was episodes such as this, abundant in hilarity and the folly of real life, that spurred Tom to experiment artistically, to break out from the considered methods of Academy teaching. He started to scribble down 'subjects of real scenes' in an 'original, rapid manner'.[33]

Rowlandson's trip to Paris was important. His eyes were opened to the swirling lines of the Rococo, the workshop of the greatest artist of the time and the day-to-day workings of the print trade. He 'made rapid advances in the study of the human figure … and occasionally indulged that satirical talent, in portraying the characteristic of that fantastic people [the French] whose *outré* habits, perhaps, scarcely demanded the exaggerations of caricature.'[34]

But the Parisian excursion also gave Rowlandson a chance to grow up, to live without home comforts and make lifelong friends. Far from the gaze of Aunt Jane or the rules of the Academy, Rowlandson, with his new accomplice Henry Angelo, was free to indulge his personal desires and artistic curiosities.

## A MODERN BOCCACCIO

By the end of 1776, Rowlandson was back on home turf in London. He'd grown into a tall, muscular, striking young man: 'His person was a noticeable one; his features were regular and defined, his eye remarkably full and fearless, his glance being described as penetrating and suggestive of command; his mouth and chin expressed firmness and resolution.'[35]

His friendship with Angelo flourished in the playground of London; unsurprisingly, they had parted ways with Higginson. At the onset of Rowlandson's twentieth birthday, two important changes occurred. The first was progressive to his education at the Academy: Tom was deemed eligible to enter life classes with female models. The other change was somewhat regressive to study: his friendship with Jack Bannister.

Jack, another import from Dr Barwis' School, was the son of an acclaimed actor and singer, and as such his childhood had been spent between the stages of Covent Garden and Drury Lane. This exposure to theatrics was evident in his study at the Academy, where he was renowned for playing the fool. Jack was that loud one of the group, the first on the dance floor, the one who was terrific at accents and whose party trick was ridiculous impersonations. He could mimic anyone on request and had an 'unaffected hilarity in conversation'.[36] 'Thomas Rowlandson, John Bannister, and myself...

were inseparable companions,'[37] recalled Henry Angelo, 'the tales of these two gossips, told in one of those nights, each delectable to hear, would make a modern Boccaccio.'[38*]

The three bonded over a serious devotion to schoolboy tomfoolery. Their conversation was peppered with cheeky side-glances, ridiculous anecdotes and saucy double entendre. They were 'the mutual advisers of each other's studies, more frequently the prompters of each other's tricks, to the great annoyance of poor old George Michael Moser, the keeper of the Academy'.[39] The layout of the life classes set the scene to perfection. The artists, bunched together on curved benches, had every opportunity to indulge in an elbow nudge or roll their eyes at each other.

'My friends Bannister and Rowlandson,' Angelo recalled, 'were students at the Royal Academy, at this period; and both being sprightly wights,[†] the [librarian] kept a watchful eye upon their pranks.'[40] As Rowlandson made comic sketches, Bannister stirred the pot through comic performance: 'The one was apt to engage the attention of the fellow disciples, by caricaturing the surly librarian; never forgetting to exaggerate his mulberry nose; whilst the other, born to figure in the histrionic art, a mimic by nature, used to divert them, in his turn.'[41]

Endeavour intended for the noble study of classical form was directed towards frightening teachers with 'tragedy tricks'.[42] On one occasion, most likely encouraged by his accomplices, Tom smuggled a pea-shooter into one of the life classes, which he fired at the female

* Boccaccio was a fourteenth-century Italian author, most famous for *The Decameron*, a story of seven young women and three young men who escape to a secluded villa just outside Florence to escape the Black Death. They each tell ten of the juiciest stories they can think of, dotted with practical jokes, tales of wit and, most notably, erotic love. *The New Yorker* considered it 'probably the dirtiest great book in the Western canon' – so it would have been well received by Rowlandson and his gang, no doubt.

† A 'wight' meant an ordinary living human being, although it's now used more in the realm of fantasy to describe a mythical, immortal being.

model to startle her out of her pose. While most of the room was consumed with mirth, Rowlandson narrowly escaped expulsion.

Bannister only lasted a couple of years at the Academy, his heart being in the world of theatre. This was a great relief to more diligent students, whose 'joy arose avowedly from their being freed from an encumbrance on their grave pursuits'.[43] And soon it was Rowlandson's turn to wave goodbye to his student days. He stood at the crossroads of life, and a path needed to be chosen.

Rowlandson toyed with sculpture, following in the footsteps of Pigalle. He had potential here: he had been awarded a silver medal from the Academy for a clay replica of a bas-relief. And it could be lucrative, as portrait busts were all the rage with the *belle monde* of Georgian England.

But it was Rowlandson's drawings that marked him out from the others. His 'studies from the human figure at the Royal Academy, were made in so masterly a style' that they were said to rival his teachers' work.[44] The pen, the burin and the etching needle were to be his weapons of choice.

And yet, there was an elephant in the sketching room. Sure, Rowlandson was capable. He was 'indulged by the most eminent of the Royal Academicians and the French professors' and his work was displayed 'on the walls of the Royal Academy Exhibition without a break'.[45] But his natural flair just didn't cut the mustard in the Royal Academy's world of prescribed tastes and established conventions. Although the Academy's founder, Joshua Reynolds, claimed to be a rule breaker, writing that 'every opportunity should be taken to discountenance that false and vulgar opinion, that rules are the fetters of genius', his own stranglehold on the Academy simply replaced the old doctrine with a new one.

Rowlandson probably would have agreed with previous students who found the Academy a wash of 'eternal blazonry, and tedious repetition of hackneyed, beaten subjects, either from the Scriptures, for the old ridiculous stories of heathen gods'.[46] It was no place for a creative chap.

Like Jack Bannister, the master of mimicry, Rowlandson couldn't help but see animation and vitality wherever he looked. While the rest of the world saw a diligent student focusing on work, Tom saw the perfect opportunity for a devilish prank. When Tom was instructed to sketch classical heroes from alabaster casts, he preferred to imagine them sneezing, hiccupping or snoring. Everywhere he looked, he saw a pantomimic panorama of life.

The 'fecundity of [Rowlandson's] invention' with 'his fancy so rich', was producing ideas so surprising that 'every species of composition flowed from his pen'.[47] Perhaps Tom was inspired by his tutor, John Hamilton Mortimer, a leading figure in the Society of Artists. Mortimer's work seemed to leap from the page, his subjects expressed through deft, sharp pen outlines, explosions of spiky dots and vibrant zigzag shading to create a cocktail of texture. Soon this energy was darting around the sketchbooks of his brilliant student, Tom Rowlandson.

But Rowlandson's *joie de vivre* and energy of line didn't sit happily in the rule of the Royal Academy. Tom's 'misfortune' was that he was too imaginative, he had 'too ready an invention … this rare faculty, strange as it may seem, however desirable to the poet, often proved the bane of the painter'.[48]

But this was no true misfortune. This would be the secret to Rowlandson's success. No one could control his spirit, nor suppress his creative impulse. Once he had the confidence to break free from Reynolds's rule book, Rowlandson and his accomplices would produce art in a more unhinged, wild, raucous, deliberate manner than had ever been seen before.

## A SPOT OF FISHING

How Tom progressed next can perhaps best be explained through an episode entirely of my own imagination – but it is entirely possible, nonetheless.

Maybe, dear reader, you are lying in bed, an awkward crick in your neck as you strive to read this book. Perhaps you're on the lido deck of a cruise ship in the western Mediterranean. Perhaps you're on a packed train, pushed up against another sweaty commuter. Wherever you are, it's time to leave the realms of your current reality. I'm taking your hand; there are now pink swirls of smoke filling your vision. Xylophone scales fill your ears to herald that we are stepping back in time to 1778.

As the smoke clears, we find ourselves in the Old Bell on Fleet Street, a pub built a century before by Christopher Wren for his masons working at St Paul's. It's pretty dingy, but the mood is jolly. The tolls of Wren's church bells are muffled by guffaws of laughter and frank conversation thrown backwards and forwards between the wooden piers, which support the low, beamed ceiling. A spaniel sniffs around the scuffed boots on the uneven stone floor. Stop fretting! No one will see you in your swimming costume. We're just spectres, you see, invisible. Now, pay attention to those two young men taking a pew furthest from the door. These are our friends Thomas Rowlandson and Jack Bannister:

> 'Hang on a sec, Rowly,' pipes up Bannister. 'Who's that chap?'
>
> Rowlandson guffaws. 'Oh! That sour-looking fellow in the corner? Let's call him over,' he says with a mischievous wink: 'Good day, sir, pull up a chair over here!'
>
> 'I've got business to attend in—' the stranger replies.
>
> 'I say! I know who you are. You're one of the new intake, aren't you! I saw it on the lists today, nine new students and at the bottom read Gilly or Gillweed or Gulliver or something strange. And then "21 next August", with a big swirly signature of Sir J. I'm right, aren't I! Am I right? Am I, Gillyweed?'
>
> 'Quite right, I'm afraid. My name is Gillray. James Gillray.'
>
> 'Go on, then, Gilly, which bit of the Academy are you in?'

'I'm not quite sure yet. I submitted quite a shabby drawing of a plaster cast, which the committee seemed to think was all right, and now I'm down for etching.'

'An etcher, then, Gillweed.'

'Gillray – actually – Gillray. It means "ruddy-faced". It's a Highland term.'

'You're Scottish then? Oh, Charlie, can we have another of these ales – and one for Master Gillray.'

'I've always lived in London, but my father was from a hamlet just south of Edinburgh. Lanarkshire, beautiful rolling, wild hills around there, you know? He was a blacksmith, working with his hands and all, but enlisted like they all do. A private he was, in the royal cavalry. He lost his right arm fighting at Fontenoy and it must have been – let's see – 1746 when the muster roll would have marked him joining the Chelsea Hospital. Then a couple of years later, along I came.'

'Hang on a minute, don't sound so bleak about it all. Jolly noble to have fought at Fontenoy.'

'It's not bleak, it's just the truth. It's hard not to be bleak when your parents are Moravians.' At the blank expressions of his companions, he continues. 'The Moravian Brotherhood is one of the strictest Protestant sects. From the age of five, I was sent to Bedford to be cocooned from the corrupting influences of the world – from places like this tavern. Damn nasty place, that school. When my brother died, they all celebrated, because it meant that he was to join the Saviour. It means I've been trained to see depravity and guilt wherever I look.'

'And now you're at the Academy, staring at naked flesh all day and indulging in the evening. What would all those Moravian brothers say to that?'

'—or what would they say to last night, eh? Henry Angelo falling in the river?'

'—or when we hijacked that sedan chair on Fleet Street!'

'—and fell out in a tumble of lace!'

While Rowlandson and Bannister have been batting their stories of misdemeanour and anecdote back and forth, they've failed to notice that their new acquaintance James Gillray has slipped away. All that is left is a sketch, on Henry's copy of the *Tatler*, just below details of the daily orders of Queen Charlotte.

'Look at that, Rowly! He was sketching us all along. That's you, knocking the stool over. The likeness is uncanny – he's captured the way your lip curls up.'

'Yes, and look he's given you a bulbous nose – it seems even more like you than you are yourself,' retorts Bannister.

The sketch is indeed of Rowlandson and Bannister in animated conversation. There's no mistaking the identity of the sitters. But the lines spiral and zigzag and cross and dart to warp them in a comic contortion. And in a neat, serifed hand, the young men notice it is labelled.

'And look here, Rowly, a caption: *UPROAR!*'

Reader, we have indulged long enough. I must tear you away from this cosy scene to return through that pink dreamlike haze back to the sun deck of *Symphony on the Seas*, or the delights of the London Underground escalator queue.

It might have been a surprise to Rowlandson to know that it was Gillray, this sheepish, reclusive first-year student, who would be his greatest ally and, one day, outshine him. Although they seemed to be polar opposites in nature, creatively they would tread very similar paths. The insuppressibly creative spirit of these fellows would produce art in a more wild, raucous, deliberate manner than had ever been seen before. These Piccadilly Mad Men were to become an acerbic and dangerous tool to outwit and outmanoeuvre the Royal Academy itself.

# 2

# *Putrid Masquerades and Twittery*

## BRIGHT WAS THEIR STEEL

Just north of London's Trafalgar Square is St Martin's Lane. Today, it's the heart of Theatreland, throbbing with thesps hurrying between stage doors, rickshaws blasting out music, and tourists with a programme in one hand and a cocktail in the other. But this was once home to the great hub of London's artistic scene: Old Slaughter's Coffee House. Old Slaughter's was the haunt of architects, painters, poets and sculptors, where Hogarth, Gainsborough and Roubiliac were part of the throng. For the price of a penny, you could drink coffee, learn the news of the day, and gossip over a game of chess, draughts or whist.

By 1780, Old Slaughter's was still a centre for students and teachers of the Royal Academy – Thomas Rowlandson and James Gillray may well have dropped in on the way to lectures. A fly on the wall may have spied 23-year-old Gillray, with his ink-stained hands and bag of sketching tools, picking up one of the seventeen newspapers published in London every week.

Among the murmur of coffee-fuelled conversation, Gillray might have scanned the *Westminster Chronicle*, inked to the seams in lines and lines of Caslon font. He may have flitted over reports of a young sea captain, Horatio Nelson, sailing the seas from Jamaica in command of the 28-gun HMS *Hinchinbrook*, two brigs, three sloops, the transport *Penelope* and a tender, the *Royal George*. Or, had Gillray perused the *British Mercury*, he may have turned to the letters page, where epistolaries were frothing with despair at the Tory prime minister, Lord North – would he stand in the elections the coming autumn? Some columns might touch on the latest from the Protestant Association, arguing against the new laws that would enable Catholics to join the British Army and plot treason – a bubbling anger that would soon erupt in the violence of the Gordon Riots later that summer. And if Gillray had picked up the *London Magazine*, he might have darted over the latest write-ups from the theatre at Drury Lane, describing a sparky debut from Joseph Grimaldi, who would one day become the most popular comic entertainer in England.

But one piece of news would have particularly dilated the pupils of young James: the announcement of the twelfth Summer Exhibition of the Royal Academy of Arts to be held in the new exhibition space in Somerset House. Coffee-house lizards could have guessed this piece of news would pique interest in Gillray: he was so obviously a second-year student from the Academy. The tell-tale signs were there: satchel, pencils, ink-stained fingers, and notebook at hand, ready to be whipped out to sketch unsuspecting caffeine addicts. But while this specimen, insular and alone, seemed to blend in seamlessly with the London coffee house scene, his roots lay far from St Martin's Lane. James Gillray had ended up in London by mistake.

The Gillray story began on 11 May 1745 in a muddy field outside Belgium: a bloodbath known as the Battle of Fontenoy. This was a major engagement in the War of the Austrian Succession, where an allied force of English, Austrian and Dutch soldiers were crushingly defeated by the French. Out of the 100,000 men who started the day on the field, by sunset, a fifth were dead or wounded. The Irish poet, Thomas Osborne Davis, captured the moment in verse:

Bright was their steel, 'tis bloody now, their guns are filled
with gore;
Through shattered ranks and severed files the trampled flags
they tore;
The English strove with desperate strength, paused, rallied,
staggered, fled–
The green hill-side is matted close with dying and with dead.[1]

One of the staggering troops fighting under England's banner was a blacksmith named James Gillray, a Calvinist from Edinburgh assigned to the Queen's Dragoons. He'd got away lightly: he only lost his right arm *and* lived to tell the tale. But it was the end of his army career. On 15 March 1746, he ended up at the only place he could find help: the Royal Chelsea Hospital where he would join the Chelsea Pensioners. At this time, Chelsea was a small village on the north bank of the Thames, about two miles south-west of central London.

And so it was that this one-armed Scotsman began his next chapter. He found a loving wife, Jane Coleman, from Longhope, Gloucestershire, and together they settled into London life.

Get involved with the community, they say, when you move to a new area. Get stuck in. Make a few friends. Have a bit of *fun*. But this one-armed Scotsman didn't heed such advice. James and Jane Gillray moved into a terraced cottage at 26 Milman's Row, which backed on to the Moravian chapel, where Mr Gillray became a sexton. He had joined the most depressing gang in town: the local Moravian Church on Fetter Lane.

The Moravians were an earnest bunch. If they came to a party, they would reliably kill the vibe. For them, the glass was always half empty, never half full. For a pillar of Moravian faith was one depressing belief: the essential, unavoidable, terrible depravity of mankind. Mr and Mrs Gillray, as devout Moravians, regarded the world with acute cynicism (they would have been good at risk assessments), to the extent that they considered life on earth as worthless. They taught their children to welcome death as a glorious release from earthly bondage, to desire passionately to *not* recover from illness. When one son, Johnny, became ill with a fatal fever, his dying words were: 'Pray don't keep me! O let me go, I must go!'[2]

The death of a young child was to fall upon the Gillray family four times. Only one reached maturity: James, the 23-year-old student now sitting in Old Slaughter's Coffee House.

In 1762, when he was just five, young Gillray was sent to a Moravian boarding school in Bedford. He stayed for a couple of years until the school closed, at which point he was probably brought back to Chelsea, where his parents led a strict regime. This only child was banned from playing games and obligated to live a life of introspection. Despite their rather serious outlook on life, the Moravians were firm believers in a rigorous education: James grew up to be 'an extremely well-informed and widely read man', who was familiar with classical allegory and political theory.[3]

It was clear from the start that James had artistic prowess. At the age of nine, he made a beautiful sketch of a goldfinch, labelled: 'James Gillray. The first bird he did draw and paint.' At fourteen, he was sent to work as an apprentice for Henry Ashby, engraving buttons and business cards.

Here, Gillray was taught the techniques of etching: 'Many a choice specimen of penmanship was copied by young Gillray, in sweeping flourishes on the copper.'[4] A fellow apprentice considered 'the early part of [Gillray's] life might be compared to the spider's, busied in spinning of lines'.[5] But it was a stifling environment, where only 'rich curving lines' were allowed.[6] Any 'ornamental knots and sprigs' were strictly out of the question. It is hard to imagine any arty teenage boys being excited by 'this mechanical drudgery'.[7] Indeed, like Rowlandson doodling away in his school textbooks, Gillray left us 'certain humorous scraps which he sketched on the borders of the examples of round hand and text'.[8]

*Bird nestling*, James Gillray.
By permission of the British Library, London. Ref. BL7283261.

By his late teens, James Gillray packed the apprenticeship in. Perhaps it was living with his strict parents. Perhaps it was the prospect of a career drawing lines on business cards. Perhaps it was London itself. His thirst for life, adventure and excitement was close to bursting. This was his moment of teenage rebellion. A time to loiter around gin shops, or dabble in cockfighting, or visit a few of the Soho brothels – just because he could. The story goes that he ran away with a few of the other apprentices to join a troupe of strolling players.*

* A group of actors who went from place to place performing plays.

Like many gap years, it's a mystery what happened in these months. But he clearly got some teenage angst out of his system. In 1778, he returned to London with a foot wedged in the heavy door of the Royal Academy Schools. He took classes in anatomy, drawing, painting and engraving from prestigious artists such as Benjamin West, Giovanni Cipriani and Francesco Bartolozzi.

It was the Italian artist Bartolozzi whose work piqued Gillray's interest. Brilliant Bart was considered a real trailblazer: a man who tore up the rule book. While the engraving world worked with black inks, brazen Bart had worked with red, orange and brown, creating softness and shading. And what's more, this wild Italian didn't work in line, as was de rigueur, he created engravings using his 'stipple technique'. Like the Pointillists after him, blazing Bart used delicate dots to create the illusion of shading.

Under Bart's wing, Gillray worked towards a career as a serious engraver, reproducing the great portraits and history paintings of the day. Gillray's 'eccentric humour displayed itself; for during his studies in that school of *super-Italian* softness and elegance, verging on beautiful insipidity, did he display the rudiments of that daring species of dramatic design, that extraordinary graphic hyperbole, which almost met in its highest flights the outposts of the creations of Michael Angelo.'[9]

## TWO PENNY WORTH OF CABBAGE LEAVES

By 1780, Gillray was well integrated in Reynolds's educational scheme. And as he perused the papers in Old Slaughter's, a few snippets of chit-chat may have made their way through the haze of caffeine: 'The new space is absolutely tip-top you know … it's going to be the best one yet … I've heard Sir Joshua is over the moon …'

The summer of 1780 was indeed a watershed moment for the Royal Academy: they had a swanky new venue. There had been a growing perception that London had no great public buildings, that important societies and departments were hidden away, dotted in alleys and lanes that didn't befit their importance. It was Edmund Burke, an Irish-born Whig MP, who led the campaign for some sort of 'national building', and in 1775 Parliament passed an act for 'erecting and establishing Publick Offices in *Somerset House*'.[10] Sir William Chambers set to work on this plot of land between the Strand and the Thames, and it wasn't long before a grand tribute to the Palladian style sprung up. This was for the use of, among other things, the Salt Office, the Stamp Office, the Tax Office, the Navy Office, the Navy Victualling Office, the Publick Lottery Office, the Hawkers and Pedlar Office and the Royal Academy of Arts.

The Royal Academy made its new home in the North Wing of Somerset House. The Exhibition Room was at the top of a steep winding staircase. The 32-feet high, top-lit, purpose-built room was considered 'undoubtedly at the date, the finest gallery for displaying pictures so far built'.[11]

*Exhibition Room, Somerset House*, Thomas Rowlandson, 1808.

As the Academicians prepared to open the 1780 Summer Exhibition, they dotted a few classical casts around the rooms, usually used for teaching. So, the first visitors to the 1780 exhibition, hauled up the great marble stairs, were a motley group of alabaster copies of the *Farnese Hercules* and the *Apollo Belvedere*. But, to the surprise of the Academicians, this sent London into uproar.

Within a week of opening, a letter, addressed to Joshua Reynolds, was published in the *Morning Post*:

> Sir, I always understood you were a man of delicacy as well as taste, and therefore was the more astonished to find that, as President of the Royal Academy, you could admit the several statues in their present shameful state of nudity, to the terror of every decent woman who enters the room.[12]

The letter, signed from 'Peeping Tom', continued to argue that if no fig leaves were available to maintain modesty of the exhibits, 'two penny worth of *cabbage leaves* will fully answer the purpose'.

On 15 May 1780, the *Morning Post* reported:

> In the second room antique, Apollos, Gladiators, Jupiters, and Hercules's all as naked, and as natural as if they were alive!! ... Many ladies, and those married ones, who are equally above the imputation of prudery and of false delicacy, have turned short of this temple of Priapus, and have been obliged to forego their desire of seeing that best part of the whole fabric, the lecture room.[13]

The Academicians, lacking both fig leaves and backbone, bent to the demands of public outrage. By 25 May 1780, the readers of the *Morning Post* were treated to this humble apology from the Royal Academy.

> Mr Editor, I congratulate you in the name of decency on the reformation you have wrought among the brawny statues of

> the Royal Academy exhibition, the vine-leaf addenda are properly applied agreeable to your intimation, and therefore pray tell the Ladies that they may now traverse the whole suite of those magnificent apartments without meeting any thing that can raise a blush on the cheek of Modesty.[14]

The Academicians had learnt their lesson. The council minutes for the following year instructed 'the Figures be covered', and £50 awarded to an Italian sculptor for the job of creating the plaster fig-leaf additions.[15] Crisis over.

This PR disaster must have been a source of great mirth for the Academy's visitors – especially the likes of Thomas Rowlandson, who delighted in the ridiculous. Despite this early hiccup, the exhibition was a great success. A record-breaking 61,381 visitors flocked to Somerset House to glimpse the 489 exhibits. The main attractions were Reynolds's new portraits of King George III and Queen Charlotte.

There was also an entry from 'T. ROWLANDSON 103 Wardour Street, Soho'. Until now, Rowlandson had occupied himself with penwork only, sometimes adding grey wash for shadows. But now, he was using watercolour too, known as a 'stained' or 'tinted' drawing. One of his comic pastoral scenes had been selected by the hanging committee, and now hung in the anteroom. The exhibition catalogue marked it as '373. Landscape and Figures', and there were good reviews: 'Landscape and Figures by Mr Rowlandson,' the *Morning Chronicler* reported, 'where much humour is displayed.'[16]

Both James Gillray and Thomas Rowlandson may well have taken interest in entry number 475: 'Hyde Park. H.W. Bunbury, Esq; H.' It was a chaotic equestrian scene that would sit happily in a Thelwall cartoon: horses are dancing and prancing and refusing to budge, humiliating the riders in the process. The amateur artist, Henry Bunbury, was well known in London for his comic scenes. His ability for 'reading character at sight' and his 'scrambling style', made him, according to Horace Walpole, 'the second Hogarth'.[17]

While serving in the West Suffolk Militia as lieutenant-colonel, Bunbury mixed in celebrity circles with David Garrick, Dr Johnson and Joshua Reynolds. But he also dabbled in comic sketches and printmaking. By the 1780s, there was a print shop on almost every corner of every London street, selling everything from expensive, high-quality engravings and prints of grand oil paintings, to cheap, crude reproductions. This meant that amateurs like Bunbury had ample opportunity to get a look-in.

Londoners were thirsty for caricatures, and print shops were popping up left, right and centre. But these caricatures hadn't just arrived from nowhere. The habit of contorting a face for comic value, or exaggerating facial expressions to hammer home the point, had been bubbling away for centuries.

## BISH BASH BOSCH

If you took a direct flight to Athens, and wound back the clock about 2,300 years, you might stumble across the Lenaia festival. If you were to enter the VIP area, you might bump into a chap called Menander, a prize-winning poet with 108 comedies under his belt. But the most striking part of Menander's comedies, which were performed in large open-air theatres, were the exaggerated, grotesque facial expressions of the actors.

Such contortions were not fashioned from their own flesh, but from masks made from stiffened and painted linen. These dramatic masks allowed actors to flit between roles, jumping between sex, age and social status with one swift motion. To play an old man, the costume department would sculpt a wide grin, furrowed brow and bald head, decorated with a wreath of ivy leaves and clusters of berries.

Now fast-forward 1,700 years to the workshop of a fifteenth-century Florentine stonemason, toiling away in the shadows of Brunelleschi's dome. You might see the same hellish faces emerging from the stone slabs, with contorted smiles, hollowed eye sockets and tumid lips.

Then, if you hopped over to Holland, in the same year, you might find these grimaces again in the elaborate drainpipes surmounting the churches, known as gargoyles. Such nightmarish visions may have sparked the imagination of the great Dutch painter Hieronymus Bosch. With oil paint and an oak board, Bosch created an entire vision of hell: fantastical and macabre. He played with the human form like putty. Human DNA was blended with animal, and emaciated and obese body parts were dislocated and melded with birds and fish.* Many of these victims of Bosch's lurid imagination had faces scrunched up in pain or so elongated that they were monstrous.

Detail from *The Garden of Earthly Delights*, Hieronymus Bosch, *c.* 1500.

* Much like Jeff Goldblum's bad day in the 1986 psychological thriller *The Fly*.

Leonardo da Vinci was more scientific in the way he played with the human form. 'When the lateral muscles pull,' he wrote in his notes in around 1507, 'so shortening themselves, then they pull behind them the lips of the mouth and so the mouth is extended...'[18] From this he worked out proportions: 'The ear is exactly as long as the nose ... The parting of the mouth seen in profile slopes to the angle of the jaw.'[19] With this knowledge, he could create the 'Vitruvian Man', a curly haired, naked Italian hunk, supposedly with the perfect proportions of a human being.

Leonardo had a blank slate, which he could manipulate. He had a theory for every expression. If, for example, you wanted to capture the moment your father erupts into fury when handed a parking ticket, Leonardo suggests, 'let him have his hair dishevelled, his eyebrows low and knit together, his teeth clenched, the two corners of his mouth arched'.[20] According to Giorgio Vasari, the bestselling biographer of the Renaissance artists, Leonardo was 'so delighted when he saw curious heads, whether bearded or hairy, that he would follow anyone who had thus attracted his attention for a whole day, acquiring such a clear idea of him that when he went home he would draw the head as well as if the man had been present'.[21]

Leonardo began to warp the human form, making it grotesque and gargoyle-like. Like Bosch before him, his deformed characters had animalistic features. Faces in which Kenneth Clark, the illustrious twentieth-century art historian, saw 'Caliban gruntings and groanings which are left in human nature when the divine has been poured away'.[22]

Leonardo might well have described these grotesques as *caricare*, an Italian word meaning 'to load or charge', for he was loading each characteristic to its full extent, and charging human features to maximum voltage. He might also have used the word *carattere*, meaning 'character'. The lexical origins are uncertain, but it was from the sketches of great artists like Leonardo that historians have sought to identify the origins of the word 'caricature'.

*Two grotesque profiles confronted*, Leonardo da Vinci, *c.* 1485–90.

The seeds of caricature found fertile ground in Italy towards the end of the sixteenth century. Once Renaissance artists had reached the pinnacle of art, or 'the shadow of the divine perfection',[23] as Michelangelo put it, they became creative. Artists began stretching the Renaissance rules – exaggerating proportions, pushing the standard to such extremes it became something new. This new trend was called Mannerism, taking the Renaissance ideal to extremes: figures so muscly they defied anatomy, architecture with stone cornicing so corpulent it bulged out of frame, colours and perspectives so displaced they warranted seasickness tablets.

Aboard this artistic flight riddled with graphic turbulence was Giuseppe Arcimboldo. Pushing the ideas behind caricature to the limit, he arranged fruits, vegetables, flowers, fish and books in such a way to appear as a portrait. These weren't just cheeks like rosy apples: these *were* rosy apples, positioned to appear as cheeks. You can hear the megaphone at the village fete: 'And for the prize for the face created out of produce from your own garden, the award goes to Giuseppe Arcimboldo for his portrait of Rudolf II, Holy Roman Emperor, created from cabbages, beans, peas, plums and all sorts. Well done, Giuseppe. Please come to the marquee to collect your rosette.'

*Vertumnus*, Giuseppe Arcimboldo, 1591.

Perhaps it was Annibale Carracci, the mighty Baroque painter, who was the first to dabble in caricature as we know it today. While the man paid the bills with impressive Adorations and Madonnas, his sketchbooks were filled with ink scribblings – quick portraits of long-nosed bishops, yawning husbands with absurdly large heads, and faces stretched and pressed and prodded to reveal real, living people. Pictures of people who are pondering their next meal, or bored in a meeting, or stuck in the dentist's chair.

The great sculptor Gian Lorenzo Bernini wasn't far off either. While he may have spent his days carving out the bodies of writhing, lustful hunks and heroes from gigantic slabs of marble, he still had time to capture his patron, Cardinal Scipione Borghese, in pen and ink. With the economy of Picasso's line, a powerful man was reduced to a bulbous, curvaceous, wallowing chinless wonder – perhaps the most succinct portrayal of a wine-fuelled, gout-ridden gammon in the canon of Western art. And Bernini's portrait of the captain of the Papal Guard of Pope Urban VIII, with a stretched tubular neck, wide smile and tiny eyes, looks more like a crazed earthworm.*

These private amusements of great artists soon blew up into a serious industry, with comic prints and caricatures produced with a single goal: to make money. One of the first of these entrepreneurial hacks was a Roman portrait painter called Pier Leone Ghezzi, probably introduced to caricature by Bernini. Ghezzi left his father's studio and began a prosperous five-decade career selling humorous illustrations and portrait caricatures, many based on stock characters from the *commedia dell'arte* tradition, a colourful style of theatre which emerged in northern Italy in the fifteenth century.

But in Venice, Ghezzi met his rival. Here lived the father–son team of Giovanni Battista Tiepolo and Giovanni Domenico Tiepolo.

* I do hope this *is* a caricature, rather than a portrait, otherwise the seventeenth century must have been a terrifying place.

From the heart of the lagoon, they churned out pen-and-ink drawings and caricature studies, pasting them into albums and catalogues, capturing the latest customs and dress of Venetian life. The Tiepolo Two started producing *types* rather than specific individuals : for example, creating an image of a typical well-spoken British actor rather than an image of Hugh Grant in particular.

By the mid-eighteenth century, these Italianate *caricaturas* had established themselves in England. They were brought back by artists and aristocrats returning from their Grand Tour, the trip around Europe taken by many to provide a grounding in the art and culture of classical antiquity and the Renaissance. Laden with artefacts, a weak grasp of Romance languages and a plethora of conversation topics for polite society, they probably had a few comic drawings from Ghezzi or Tiepolo, too.

So, was this 'The Arrival of Caricature in England'? It's as close as we get to such a thing. 'To trace the origin of caricature,' wrote Henry Angelo, 'would require much time and industrious research.'[24] But somewhere in this melting pot of Ancient Greek masks, Bosch oil-paint hellscapes and Italianate fruit salads, caricature really got going in Britain in the early years of the eighteenth century.

Let us take a moment to clarify exactly what a caricature is. Today, a caricature is defined as 'a funny drawing or picture of someone that exaggerates some of their features'.[25] If a big-headed man is portrayed with a head the size of a watermelon, the caricaturist isn't actually saying he walks around with a head this big in real life. But by distorting it to a ridiculous size, his big-headedness (either physically or in demeanour), is emphasised and mocked. Caricatures are a form of comic drawings, but there are plenty of comic drawings that depict the subject realistically, and these are not caricatures.

Comic drawings, including caricatures, are more often than not also satires. Satire can mean various things to different people: it derives from the Latin phrase *lanx satura*, meaning 'a mixed platter of fruits or nuts'.[26] The *Oxford English Dictionary* tells us that satire is defined as the use of 'humour, irony, exaggeration, or ridicule to expose and criticise prevailing immorality or foolishness'.[27]

Almost all forms of art can caricature or satirise a subject. Today, as in the late eighteenth century, 'caricature' and 'satire' are used almost interchangeably in common use, as verbs or nouns. One artist could be described as a caricaturist, a satirist, a printmaker, a commentator, a cartoonist and an illustrator, all in relation to one piece of art.

Of course, it wasn't always like that. In the early eighteenth century, there was a distinct difference between caricature and satire. Caricature was seen as part of an academic tradition, an exercise in anatomy and theory. Caricature was thus encompassed in the world of high art. Satire, on the other hand, was considered a form of low art, or popular culture: in 1704, it was deemed that 'anything sharp or severe is called a Satyr', and the word came to describe a variety of crudely cut, cheaply produced woodcut broadsheets, marked by folk imagery and scrolls or balloons of text, often produced as propaganda to be circulated around the streets.[28] Satire could describe books and plays too. For Samuel Johnson, satire was 'a poem in which wickedness or folly is censured', and Londoners were well accustomed to the poetry, prose and drama of satirical writers Alexander Pope and Jonathan Swift.[29]

Clear on all that? No? Don't worry. The first step for caricature to infiltrate British society came in 1736 and 1743, when an entrepreneurial English printmaker named Arthur Pond etched and printed 25 of the most popular Italian caricatures and bundled them into sellable packages. These charming, whimsical skits making a mockery of society 'caught on ... quickly with the London audience'.[30] This visual tittle-tattle captured the essence of a subject and conveyed the spirit of a character with such brevity, sometimes only using two or three strokes of the pen.

But it was not a smooth landing. Although caricature made it through customs, picked up its luggage and quickly recovered from its jet lag, it soon came up against a proud Englishman. It was met by the bulbous nose of a bigwig on the London art scene. William Hogarth was most displeased.

## THE HOGARTHIAN HARRUMPH

For Hogarth, these caricatures were the epitome of foreign frivolity: '*caricatura* is, or ought to be,' he wrote, 'totally divested of every stroke that hath a tendency to good drawing … Let it be observed, the more remote in their nature the greater is the excellence of these pieces; as a proof of this, I remember a famous *caricatura* of a certain Italian singer, that struck at first sight, which consisted only of a straight perpendicular stroke, with a dot over it.'[31]

Hogarth went to great lengths to warn against what he saw as a debased foreign art form by illustrating the difference between *Characters*, a likeness, or *Caricaturas*, the exaggerated form. In April 1743, he produced an engraving named *Characters and Caricaturas*. As hundreds of heads float around like bacteria in a microscope, some are categorised into 'characters' in the style of Raphael, and some are categorised as 'caricatures', in the style of Ghezzi, Carracci and Leonardo. The message? These caricatures were an affront to good taste and to be avoided at all costs.*

Henry Fielding, the author of the 1749 comic novel *Tom Jones*, was of the same opinion: 'Now what *Caricatura* is in Painting, Burlesque is in Writing and in the same manner the Comic Writer and Painter correlate to each other … He who should call the ingenious *Hogarth* a Burlesque Painter, would, in my Opinion, do him very little Honour: for sure it is much easier, much less the Subject of Admiration, to paint a Man with a Nose, or any other Feature of preposterous Size,

* Hogarth's dislike of caricature can perhaps be attributed to the fact it was in its very early stages. Compared to later years, early caricatures were generally flat, static and rarely executed with flair.

or to expose him in some absurd or monstrous Attitude, than to express the Affections of Men on Canvas.'[32]

Hogarth's attack was so vehement that Carracci himself penned a rebuttal for his art: 'Is not the caricaturist's task exactly the same as that of the classical artist? Both see the lasting truth beneath the surface of mere outward appearance. Both try to help nature accomplish its plan. The one may strive to visualise the perfect form and to realise it in his work, the other to grasp the perfect deformity, and thus reveal the very essence of a personality. A good caricature, like every work of art, is more true to life than reality itself.'[33]

The debate was never settled, and no doubt Carracci and Hogarth would have come to blows if they ever bumped into each other in a pub. Talking of making acquaintances, it is time we got to know the man who led the anti-caricature campaign. Hold on to your seats, everyone. There's a lot to get through.

William Hogarth was born to a lower-middle-class family in London. His father, Richard Hogarth, had been a classicist and writer of Latin and Greek textbooks. In 1704, Richard had the bright idea to set up a coffee house in Clerkenwell. But this caffeine fix came with more than an extra sprinkle of chocolate: any conversation in the coffee house had to be spoken in Latin. 'There will meet daily some learned gentlemen,' it was announced, 'who speak Latin readily, where any Gentleman that is either skilled in that Language, or desirous to perfect himself in speaking thereof will be welcome.'[34] Richard Hogarth volunteered himself as 'in the absence of others, being always ready to entertain Gentlemen in the Latin Tongue'.[35]

It seems Londoners weren't as eager to improve their classic declensions as Richard Hogarth had imagined. The coffee house folded in 1707, and he was imprisoned in lieu of outstanding debts. For four years his family lived alongside him in Fleet Prison.

It was an episode William Hogarth never spoke about, perhaps through embarrassment. But it may well have fired him up to never risk making the same mistake. At seventeen, he became apprenticed to a silver engraver. Then, as Gillray would do years later, he worked as an engraver making trade cards.

Like Gillray, Hogarth soon moved on from trade cards, attending St Martin's Lane Academy and Thornhill's drawing school in Covent Garden. Hogarth found little success with his family groups and portraits but developed a new genre of narrative etchings, often based on paintings. Instead of using his impressive skills for noble subjects, Hogarth dedicated paintings to STD-ridden aristos, gin-addicted mothers and the rife corruption of London life. By depicting these 'modern moral subjects' Hogarth used satire for what he considered to be its best purpose: to expose social ills and encourage reform.

*Gin Lane*, William Hogarth, 1751.

His visions of destitution have led to him being given the title of the 'Grandfather of Political Cartoon', or the 'Grandfather of Satire'.* Hogarth's great legacy was to cut through distinctions between high and low art and culture. He paved the way for highly trained artists to apply their skills to honest, 'low-life' subjects, to harness the powers of satire and make art that exposed modern depravity and called for change. It was said that 'with the death of Hogarth [in 1764], almost all the old school of humorous designers disappeared. He was the great luminary of this species of art, and when his light went out, all the lesser lights were extinguished'.[36]

For the next 50 years the race was on. Who would be Hogarth's worthy successor?

## PASTA PIN-UPS

There were several amateurs who tried their luck, and in the middle of the century there was success from the hand of an unlikely source. George Townshend was an army officer. While fighting as aide-de-camp to the Duke of Cumberland, at Culloden and in Flanders, he made hundreds of sketches of his travels. Then, in 1749, aged 25, he set off on his Grand Tour, discovered the caricatures of Ghezzi, and learnt to copy them. He soon harnessed the power of these *caricaturas*, unleashing them as razor-sharp tools to undermine political opponents. From 1756, Townshend produced political satire to such success that Horace Walpole reported that 'he adorns the shutters, walls, and napkins of every tavern in Pall Mall with caricatures of the Duke [of Cumberland] and Sir George Lyttelton, the Duke of Newcastle and Mr [Henry] Fox'.[37]

Despite a few distractions, which included receiving the surrender of Quebec after the death of General James Wolfe in 1759, he became a prominent amateur satirist with an acerbic temperament. He was

* Ten points to Gryffindor for anyone who can guess the 'Father'!

described as 'mercurial-humorous and witty, with a violent temper, disposed to ridicule, hasty judgements ... destitute of tact and decorum'.[38] His comic figures were laden with puns and jibes and were always on the verge of inciting claims of libel. Walpole delighted in his figures of prospective ministers: 'I laughed until I cried ... This print has so diverted the Town that today a Pamphlet against George Townshend was produced called "The Art of Political Lying". His genius for likeness is astonishing.'[39]

Townshend's success set the ball rolling for the role of caricature in political satire. One London couple, named Mary and Matthew Darly, watched on with interest. They noted that the British public, tired of moralising prints laden with classical fables, had an appetite for lighter humour. The Darlys started a bold new business, and from 1750 to 1781 they were at the heart of London's print trade.

They ran 'a shop opposite Hungerford market, in the Strand', the first to specialise exclusively in caricature and comic images.[40] Here, prints could be purchased and clients could take lessons in etching and drawing. Capitalising on the city's love affair with caricature, in 1762, the Darlys published a book, the *Principles of Caricatura*, which explained 'Ye Principles of Designing in that Droll & Pleasing Manner'.[41] No doubt it appeared on many a Christmas gift list that year.

Clients could even have their rough sketches engraved, printed and put on sale. 'Gentlemen and Ladies,' read a sign in the window, 'may have any Sketch of Fancy of their own, engraved, etched &c. with the utmost Dispatch and Secrecy ... by their humble Servant.'[42] George Townshend used this printing service regularly. As MP of Norfolk from 1747–64, and Lord Lieutenant of Ireland from 1767–72, he probably made better use of his time than polishing off political sketches. There were dinners, lunches and concerts to attend – and sometimes he even had to show his face at Westminster.

The Darly shop was attracting more and more trendy customers: young men with coats of pink silk, crimson velvet breeches, vast umbrellas, flowing ringlets of hair tied in ribbons and white satin waistcoats embroidered with gold. Who *were* these young fellows? They weren't French or Italian, but they didn't look anything like the typical English aristo popping in from the countryside.

For the Darlys' print shop was the latest destination for young English gentlemen, just back from the Grand Tour. Their dress and speech was continental, effeminate and – in the eyes of their parents – the epitome of inappropriate bourgeois excess. The 'travelled young men who wear long curls and spying-glasses', had developed, among other things, a taste for *macaroni* pasta.[43] 'There is indeed a kind of animal,' wrote the *Oxford Magazine* in 1770, 'neither male nor female, a thing of the neuter gender, lately started up among us. It is called a macaroni'.[44]

They were most famous for eccentric fashions. One trend was to wear such towering wigs that their *chapeau-bras** could only be removed with a sword.

With this new character on the London scene, the enterprising Darlys produced a set of mini-satires of the macaronis themselves. They were small, postable prints mounted on paste-card, and they were wildly popular. Oliver Goldsmith mentioned it in his comedy *She Stoops to Conquer*, when the young man Marlow cries out: 'I shall be laughed at over the whole town. I shall be stuck up in caricatura in all the print-shops, – The Dullissimo Maccaroni!'[45]

The macaronis were a hit. But they were also a phase. A fad. Like shoulder pads or flared jeans or ponchos, once non-fashionable society had *finally* warmed up to the idea, it was already on the way out. By 1776, macaronis were, as the great writer Frances Burney judged, 'no longer Bon Ton'.[46]

But while the rest of London shook off these ruffles with ease, the Darlys had become victims of their own success. They were so inextricably stuck in this cheesy pasta sauce that their shop at

* A three-cornered flat silk hat.

No. 39 the Strand would be known to society as the Macaroni Print Shop for ever more.

*The Macaroni Print Shop*, Edward Topham, 1772.

Despite this unintentional rebranding, in 1773, the Darlys curated the first ever exhibition of caricatures. The 'Darlys' Comic Exhibition' featured work by an anonymous array of '73 Ladies, 106 Gentlemen and 54 Artists'.[47]

Crowds were tickled by the simple, light-hearted prints of celebrities, London life and general *joie de vivre*. The most popular ones poked fun at the enormous, towering headdresses of fashionable young ladies, even influencing the fashions themselves. Soon, papers were writing of a woman with 'her head dressed agreeable to Darly's caricature'.[48] Another had 'her hair dressed in the extreme of the modern taste, the enormity of the size exactly resembling that which some of the print shops exhibits ... She was mobbed and had to flee the scene'.[49]

Everyone in London knew the name of Matthew and Mary Darly, and their 30 years of endeavour certainly did wonders for propelling the cause of satirical art. Never before had personal caricatures been given the full, serious attention of the London streets. It was in the Darlys' hub of amateur printmaking that George Townshend printed and sold his work, and where Henry Bunbury would fine-tune his skills to enter works to the Royal Academy Summer Exhibition. And now the print shop wasn't only reporting on society but influencing it too.

London's appetite for satire was insatiable. There were sell-out satirical plays and popular performances at the annual Bartholomew Fair in Smithfield. One man, George Alexander Stevens, made his career from live satire. From 1767 until his death in the 1780s he performed his wildly popular *A Lecture on Heads*. With a cast of 60 heads, made of wood and papier mâché, Stevens would dance around, acting out the caricature. 'He knew how to imitate the voice, their looks, and their manner with the most happy adroitness,' so that 'all ranks and classes in the nation' were 'caricatured before the public with the utmost humour and gaiety'.[50]

But caricatures were still made by amateurs. What if artists who had been taught by Joshua Reynolds and Johan Zoffany – who understood the metrics of a composition, or hatching techniques, or the mathematics behind perspective, or human anatomy – applied their skills to the 'low art' of caricature and satire? To put it another way: what would happen if the most sought-after interior designers applied their latest bespoke style to, say, Portaloos? Or if Jackson Pollock was booked to design your PowerPoint presentation for a team meeting? Or if Sebastian Coe and the London Olympics PR team were enlisted to sort out your village fete?

Soon enough, Rowlandson and Gillray became increasingly regular faces in the print shops of London. And it was from these print shops of enthusiasts, amateurs and anyone who enjoyed a good joke, where we might identify 'the rise of that extraordinary new phalanx of graphic satirists and humorous designers whose collective works form the burlesque, political, and domestic history of the reign of George the Third'.[51]

Henry Angelo later reminisced about this arrival of caricature in England:

> Satire, perhaps, is as old as society; but graphic satire is a modern invention. Yet, when we consider the wonderful aptitude of the pencil in pourtraying the ridiculous and *outré*, the never-ending invention of its capacities to expose and correct vice and folly, we are lost in wonder at the dulness of our predecessors in leaving it to so late a period as the last century, to '*find it out*'.[52]

With the technical skills of a Royal Academy education, Rowlandson's cheeky disposition and Gillray's Moravian cynicism, the pair were perfectly placed to 'find this out'. By the early 1780s, they had all the tools for success. All they needed was a cast of characters. Luckily, the stage was set: players from the greatest Shakespearean drama the country had ever seen were waiting in the wings.

# 3

# *A Kingdom Trusted to a School-Boy's Care*

## THREE JOLLY DOGS

It was a tumultuous start to the new decade. In the summer of 1780, tensions that had been building up since the Catholic Relief Act of 1778 finally erupted into the worst riots the city had ever seen. The anti-Catholic Gordon Riots tore through London, throwing the capital into unrest. While trying to keep the peace at home, Prime Minister Lord North was preoccupied with the final years of the American War of Independence, which had been raging for five long years. By October 1781, when British forces under Lord Cornwallis surrendered during the Siege of Yorktown, all hope was lost. 'Oh God!' the PM cried, 'it is all over!'[1]

But away from the world stage, Britons were busying themselves with progress. On New Year's Day 1781, a cast-iron bridge was opened near Coalbrookdale, crossing the River Severn. It was the first in the world, and a major milestone in the Industrial Revolution.

In London, the rambunctious 23-year-old Thomas Rowlandson was having a whale of a time. He lived happily and comfortably at 103 Wardour Street, where his affectionate Aunt Jane propped him up with pocket money and dollops of TLC. His prospects were bright:

he was still filled with 'all the freshness of his academic studies' and the 'youth of paramount promise'.[2]

Like Gillray, whose trade card read 'Gillray Portrait Painter', Rowlandson was still on his way to becoming a serious portrait painter, and his high-quality watercolours were shown at the Royal Academy Summer Exhibitions. But he also tried caricatures, illustrations, engravings and portrait miniatures on the side. And, to improve his drawing technique, Rowlandson embarked on sketching tours around the country and continent. He'd been back in France in 1778 and was probably in Rome in 1782.[3]

Outside the walls of Somerset House, Rowlandson was notorious for a quite different reason. He was a familiar face in the pubs of Piccadilly, drinking the house dry with his best pals Henry Angelo, the fencer, and Jack Bannister, the actor. Together they formed a tight-knit gang, fizzing with gossip and determined to enjoy life to the full. They called themselves the 'Jovial Trio', or the 'Three Jolly Dogs'.[4]

At this time, Londoners were drinking 84 million gallons of beer, 10 million gallons of wine and 14 million gallons of spirits per year.[5] No doubt the Three Jolly Dogs made a significant contribution to these figures. Rowlandson's tipple of choice was punch – a cocktail of brandy, water, lemon, sugar and nutmeg. But this wasn't served in a delicate martini glass. It wasn't ordered by the bottle, nor even by the carafe. These cocktails were ordered by the *bowl*, which was placed in the centre of the table, and the contents ladled out to each drinker's chosen vessel.

It was probably while swilling such sticky potations that the Three Jolly Dogs acquired another dear friend: a plump, respectable, rather conventional but wholly convivial young man, Henry Wigstead.

We've all met someone like Wigstead: the one who just *adores* interior design. The one who knows his *hygge* from his feng shui, who spends the party comparing Dulux *Wild Mushroom* to Farrow & Ball *Elephant's Breath*, who knows how to balance a ceramic side lamp with striking contemporary art. For Wigstead came from a family of interior designers who had made their fortune sprucing up London's grandest houses. With one eye on the wallpaper, and another on emerging talent, it was only a matter of time before Wigstead reached out to Rowlandson to commission bespoke prints for his wealthy clients.

But business meetings discussing commissions at the coffee house soon became raucous evenings over the punchbowl. Wigstead, a 'merry' chap 'who delighted in a little practical joke' was warmly welcomed into the Three Jolly Dogs drinking scene, often leading the pranks.[6] One joke was so terrific that Henry Angelo thought it worthy of including in his life memoirs, half a century later. During one drinking session, the Dogs were joined by the middle-aged satirical writer and doctor, Peter Pindar. Meanwhile Wigstead had come 'with some small, square pieces of alabaster'. After slipping one of these alabaster blocks into the sugar basin, he innocently handed the sugar tongs to Peter Pindar, who was in the middle of telling a story.

'Thank you, boy,' said Peter, putting in five or six pieces and, taking his teaspoon, began stirring, as he commenced his story. Unsuspicious of the trick, he proceeded: 'Well Sirs,– and so, the old parish priest. What I tell you (then his spoon was at work) happened when I was in that infernally hot place, Jamaica (then another stir). Sir, he was the fattest man on the island (then he pressed the alabaster); yes, damme, Sir ...'

The story continued, with Peter growing with frustration. 'By Sir, this sugar,' he exclaimed, 'it will never melt.' Bursting with frustration, he tossed the contents of the tumbler under the grate. 'We burst into laughter,' remembered Angelo, 'and our joke lost us the conclusion of the story. Wigstead skilfully slipped the mock sugar out of the way, and the doctor, taking another glass, never suspected the frolic.'[7]

Such japes and capers were soon spread far and wide. In 1782, Rowlandson and Wigstead consolidated their nascent friendship by setting out on a sketching trip into the English countryside. Rowlandson's sketchbooks tell a lively account of the expedition: bursting with life and laughter, they capture every unexpected thrill and hiccup of life on the road. And Wigstead, a regular draughtsman himself, was to fill his pages with architectural details – gildings, ornamental cornices and carvings.

Rowlandson had no time for architectural ornament. His first sketch shows his solo dinner in 103 Wardour Street the night before his journey, tended to by his red-faced, buxom housekeeper, Mary Chateauvert and the house cat. Another sketch depicts 4am the following morning, with the now somewhat flustered housekeeper bursting into Rowlandson's bedroom to wake him up. Next we have the moment he sets off from Wardour Street, showing Aunt Jane's tall, narrow four-storey Soho tenement, with sash windows and railings. On the steps, a loyal Mary Chateauvert waves goodbye, no doubt with a few cries of 'Take care of yourself, Master Rowlandson. Don't drink too much!'

*Chaise at the Door, Setting Out from Rowlandson's House in Wardour Street*, Thomas Rowlandson, 1784.

It must have been thrilling to escape the capital and experience the latest in travel technology. In recent decades, travelling to London had been 'no easy matter when a stage coach was four or five days creeping an hundred miles, and the fare and expenses ran high'.[8] But this was the 1780s. This was modern Britain. Now, wrote the agriculturalist and writer Arthur Young: 'A country fellow one hundred miles from London jumps on a coach box in the morning, and for eight or ten shillings gets to town by night.'[9]

Rowlandson and Wigstead set off in a post-chaise, a small yellow-and-black private carriage.* The carriage could sit two passengers, both facing forward. It was pulled by two horses, one of which had a rider on its back, steering the carriage with reins in his hand.

Soon, these young men of culture were whizzing out of London at high speeds of ten miles an hour. They headed west, staying at Hounslow, then Egham, then Bagshot – every moment captured by Rowlandson's sketches. First came a technical glitch: the wheel span off the post-chaise. Next, road rage: while traversing the South Downs between Stockbridge and Salisbury, they were overtaken by some reckless drivers (at which Rowlandson leant out the window to wave his fist). Then there was the bureaucracy of the booking office, where Wigstead leant on a desk watching paperwork being signed off with a feathered quill. Beside them porters huff and puff at the luggage to be loaded up – piles of trunks and bags and satchels and even a brace of game.

The travellers enjoyed their stay at Salisbury, visiting the coffee houses and admiring Earl Beauchamp's tomb in the cathedral. They crawled in and out of the fallen monoliths of Stonehenge. And once they hit the south coast, they battled high winds to sail across the Solent, exploring the Isle of Wight, visiting Cowes Harbour and sketching on the clifftops overlooking the Needles.

* Yellow was the cheapest pigment to buy in bulk for carriage paint.

On their return to the mainland – this time rowed by a group of sailors – they explored the hive of naval activity in Portsmouth Harbour. They climbed aboard the 74-gun Man-of-War, HMS *Hector*, where Rowlandson sketched the middle deck, teeming with sailors. They saw smuggling vessels cut in two. But the newest tourist attraction of the area were some ghostly masts emerging from the ocean.

This was evidence of one of the most tragic moments in British naval history, which had taken place two years earlier. Here were the remains of HMS *Royal George*, the largest warship in the world when she was launched in 1756. In August 1782, while anchored off Portsmouth in a shallow area called Spithead, she had been intentionally rolled to carry out maintenance on the hull. But the roll was misjudged, and the ship took on water and sank. With over 800 lives lost, it was one of the deadliest maritime disasters in British territorial waters.

As their sketchbooks filled up and their technique improved, Rowlandson and Wigstead found plenty of time to indulge in the amusements of the country towns. They took pains to record their encounters with the fairer sex. One sketch shows Rowlandson and Wigstead strolling through Lymington enjoying their *First Interview with Two Female Friends*. Rowlandson thought himself quite the charmer: another of his sketches shows him chatting up a beautiful woman as she leans out of her carriage, and then there's *The Pretty Hostess and Rowlandson With the Extravagant Bill* – the latter of which was left to Wigstead to deal with.

But the delights of the town took their toll – one sketch of the interior of a Portsmouth inn shows the two being 'all very much fatigued'. Wigstead, his belly bulging, has his legs up on the table, while Rowlandson sprawls across two chairs, no doubt missing the home cooking of Mary Chateauvert.

All in all, Rowlandson churned out 70 pen-and-ink sketches from the trip, which were compiled and published as *A Tour in a*

*Post Chaise*. It was a surprising collection. Here was a great artist – trained under the Royal Academy, taught by the nation's experts and equipped with the skills to create art to rival that of the ancient world – and yet, he was making sketches of the eighteenth-century equivalent of the luggage check-in at Luton Airport, or his own hung-over festering, or the staff on the ferry crossing at Dover. This was *not* what Reynolds had trained his students for.

However, the fresh air and fine company certainly improved Rowlandson's technique. By now, a couple of quick glances was all he needed to scribble down the scene before him – a valuable skill that was soon picked up by the printsellers of London. By April 1784, Rowlandson had his foot in the door of William Humphrey's print shop in St Martin's Lane. Humphrey wanted art that would sell, and fast. He needed quick-fire political squibs. Instant reactions to the debates in Westminster. Breaking news. Immediate comment. On location reporting. Bam. Bam. Bam.

Rowlandson's own political views were, of course, irrelevant. As he didn't own any freehold property, he wasn't even qualified to vote in the constituency of Westminster. But this was handy money on the side, and Humphrey had some important clients. Soon, Rowlandson was working up rough sketches, etching out William Humphrey's ideas, and adding his own amusing jokes where possible. He didn't know it yet, but this hack work would put him in good stead for the rest of his life.

## A GLANCE WITH THE EYEBROW

It's spring 1784. We're standing in the centre of London, outside 103 Wardour Street. Peer through the sash windows. You'll recognise that young man with the pile of wavy hair as young Tom Rowlandson. He's picking up a fruited spice bread put out by Mary Chateauvert, grabbing his overcoat, and setting out in the spring sunshine. He heads towards the Strand – keep up. He is on his way to a meeting at William Humphrey's print shop to discuss some new prints and, later on, heading to his usual watering hole with the Three Jolly Dogs.

As he paces along – a proud Dog about town – he has a pile of sketches under his arm of a recent trip to the Vauxhall Gardens. These pleasure gardens attracted crowds of Londoners with tight-rope walkers, hot-air balloon ascents, concerts and fireworks. For Rowlandson, this wonderland provided 'plenty of employment for his pencil',[10] and among his blotches and scribbles of brown ink are the whispering figures of the Prince Regent and his former lover, Perdita Robinson, or the dandy Edward Topham peering through a monocle at Georgiana, Duchess of Devonshire. The final composition would be a great success at the Academy's Summer Exhibition, later that year.

As Tom hastens his step on the approach to Covent Garden, there's shouting, then cheering, then laughing, then jeering. Crowds of people appear around the corner, surging towards a wooden platform in the main piazza where a man with enormous bushy eyebrows is standing. Dishevelled, unkempt and unclean, he seems to have come straight from a night of boozing. Yet, his presence commands the space. He talks like a Shakespearean hero. A booming voice throwing out classical references and daringly bold witticisms.

Rowlandson knew exactly who this was. Everyone had heard stories of the man's celebrity lovers, read reports of his £120,000 gambling debt or gossiped about his flamboyant French clothes. And yet, for some, this man was the greatest statesman of his generation. Others knew him simply as 'The Eyebrow'. He was dark, swarthy and so hairy that at his birth his father had likened him to a monkey.

His real name was Charles James Fox. As leader of the Whig Opposition, he was one of the country's most notorious politicians and the heart of European scandal and celebrity. And as, ladies and gentlemen, Fox is one of the lead roles of this great pantomime, let's take the time to become better acquainted with him.

*The Westminster Election, scene outside St Paul's*, Robert Dighton, 1796.

## FANTASTIC MR FOX

Charles James Fox was born with scandal in his DNA: his parents, Henry and Caroline, had eloped in 1744, leaving society buzzing with gossip. Henry was a Whig politician, considered by some as the greatest of his generation. Caroline, eighteen years his junior, was the eldest of the notorious 'Lennox sisters', whose scandalous lives provided much of London's gossip, and great-granddaughter of that 'Merrie Monarch', King Charles II.

In 1746, they leased a magnificent Jacobean country house in Kensington, set in a 64-acre plot of private grounds and working fields. It had been built in 1605 by the diplomat Sir Walter Cope and was known as Holland House, giving us the name of Holland Park today. But in 1749, when Henry and Caroline's third child was on its way, Holland House was being redecorated and the family based themselves in Conduit Street, now an artery of fashionable Mayfair, linking Regent Street to Savile Row. On 24 January 1749, little Charley Fox was born.

He was the apple of his father's eye, and this apple was spoilt rotten. The great statesman Henry Fox preferred to dine with his three-year-old toddler over anyone else, entranced by his being 'infinitely engaging & clever & pretty'.[11] On one occasion, young Charles demanded to witness the dynamite-powered demolition of a wall on his father's estate. The wall had already been demolished, but little Charley's word was law. The orders were sent through to rebuild the wall, and blow it up immediately. Hard to know what the builders thought.

Charles James Fox would never recover from this lack of discipline. His education at Mr Pampellone's school in Wandsworth was followed by a stint at Dame Milward's House at Eton College. After an exeat to France, he returned a full dandy, 'attired in red-heeled shoes and Paris cut-velvet, adorned with a pigeon-wing hair style tinted with blue powder, and a newly acquired French accent'.[12] Dr Barnard, the headmaster, was having none of it and took to flogging the boy himself. Charles was asked to leave in 1764, deemed 'too witty to live there – and a little too wicked'.[13] And after a taste of studying at Oxford University, he gave up on that too, leaving without a degree. It was, according to the young man, all 'nonsenses'.[14] The fact that Master Fox had completely botched his Eton–Oxford education didn't seem to be of any importance to him. Rather, he considered his regular trips to the continent – with wine and art and society and women – 'such a nurture in Education [as] was never seen'.[15] His indiscretions filled the gossip columns. During the 1770s, while Gillray and Rowlandson had been studying at the Royal Academy, the press was overflowing with Fox's misdemeanours, which were joyfully and relentlessly ridiculed by journalists and pamphleteers. As well as a string of high-profile mistresses, his gambling debts were unbelievable. Between 1772 and 1774 his ever-indulgent father was called in to pay a staggering £120,000 of debt – around £12.5 million in today's money.

Fox was a friend to the greatest artists and writers of London and Paris. He had travelled extensively across Europe and he was the wittiest man of London society. While also famed as a degenerate, he had been twice in government, and twice left it; and all before his 25th birthday. He was as much an enigma to his contemporaries as he is to historians.

Fox dived into the Westminster bubble, his famous charm directed towards eloquent political oratory. His arrival on the scene coincided with the struggle for independence of those thirteen colonies on the Atlantic seaboard of North America. It was, according to the *Evening Post*, a war which had been 'unnatural, unconstitutional, unnecessary, unjust, dangerous, hazardous and unprofitable'.[16]

All the colonists had wanted was no 'taxation without representation', and Fox was sympathetic to their cause from the outset. He called out the ministers as 'want of policy, of folly and madness',[17] and decried Prime Minister Lord North as the 'blundering pilot who had brought the nation into its present difficulties. Lord Chatham, the King of Prussia, nay, Alexander the Great, never gained more in one campaign than the noble Lord has lost – he has lost a whole continent'.[18] Powerful stuff. And probably taken with powerful snuff.

Despite embodying a lifestyle of his Restoration ancestor, Charles II, Fox made himself a sworn enemy of King George III. He was convinced that the King was a direct challenge to the authority of Parliament, and nothing short of a tyrant. When a motion passed the Commons by a vote of 233 to 215, named 'the influence of the Crown has increased, is increasing, and ought to be diminished',[19] Fox thought it glorious, and even took to wearing clothes of buff and blue – the colours of Washington's army.

In fact, the Crown was on the verge of collapse. Behind palace doors, George III was tormented by the never-ending upheaval in his own government and in the colonies. In 1782, he drafted an abdication letter, full of crossings-out and blotches and rewrites. 'His Majesty therefore with much sorrow,' the King wrote, 'finds He can be of no further Utility to His Native Country, which drives Him to the painful steps of quitting it for ever.'[20] The plan was to live a quiet life in Hanover, as his son, Prince George, took the reins.

But the letter was never sent, and King George stuck with it. On 2 April 1783, after fifteen years of grappling with the political game, criticising the King and questioning the war in America, Fox finally got to walk the real corridors of power. He led a coalition with a surprising partner, his bitter enemy, Lord North. Then, on 3 September 1783, the war was brought to a close as George III's representatives signed the Treaty of Paris.

But that autumn, Fox made a fatal move. He introduced an East India Bill, which, on closer inspection, seemed to put enormous wealth into the hands of his friends, giving them a platform to influence Westminster elections and augment their own power. It was known as the 'Magna Charta of Hindostan' and was perceived as an unwarranted power grab by Fox and his allies. The King would not stand for it. Those who supported Fox's bill, the king announced, would be regarded as a personal enemy. When the bill failed to pass the House of Lords, the King had an excuse to dismiss his hated Fox–North coalition, and after brazenly forcing Fox out of power, George's next action was equally shocking to the Whig members. 'The cloven foot of absolute monarchy begins to appear,' wrote the *Morning Herald*.[21]

On 19 December 1783, George III plucked out a lanky 24-year-old MP to be his new prime minister. He may have been the son of late prime minister William Pitt the Elder, the Earl of Chatham, but he had no real support in Parliament and only sneaked in through a pocket borough, a constituency where one wealthy patron could effectively dictate the votes and the actions of the MP. It was 'a sight to make surrounding nations stare; A kingdom trusted to a schoolboy's care'.[22]

As Pitt scrambled to gather a Cabinet, he was keenly aware that his time in office was unsteady. It was taunted as the 'Mince-Pie Administration': it'll be over by Christmas, they said. On 22 December 1783, Pitt admitted the ministry would survive 'for how many days or weeks remains to be seen'.[23] At 10.46 on the morning of 23 December 1783,[24] the King wrote to Pitt, saying: 'To one on the edge of a precipice every ray of hope must be pleasing.'[25]

As December frosts melted into the spring of 1784, a war of oratory played out in the House of Commons. Young Pitt, forced into the spotlight, impressed the House with speeches wise beyond his years, while Fox charmed his old friends, desperate to claw back his position as PM. After three months of verbal jostling, the matter was put to the people to decide.

It was this election that took Fox to the hustings of Covent Garden on that sunny spring morning of April 1784.

## FOXY FEMME FATALE

Elections of the eighteenth century were nothing like the ones we know today. There were only about 200,000 property-owning men in the country who could vote, and there was no secret ballot. However, they were much more fun, and far more dramatic, being marked by gluttony, bribery and violence. The voting period lasted several weeks, where the behaviour and mood of the crowds were seen as a legitimate gauge of public opinion. So, candidates would do everything in their power to schmooze voters, spending vast sums of money on wining and dining.*

One of the most hotly contested seats of the 1784 election was that of Westminster, the largest electorate in the country where three out

* Along with copious amounts of food and drink, voters would expect to be financially bribed. A low price would be around £5 a vote – over £400 in today's money.

of every four male householders could vote. It was also the seat that Fox was fighting for and, sure enough, swathes of loyal Foxites soon descended upon the coffee houses and taverns of Covent Garden. Polls opened on 1 April through to 5 May: this was a marathon, not a sprint.

The Westminster election was a spectacle to behold. Much like Edinburgh during the Festival Fringe, or the streets surrounding Wembley after an England vs Wales match, it was impossible not to get caught up in the chaos. One lady, a certain Hannah More, wrote about such an occasion. '*A propos* of elections,' she warned, 'I had like to have got into a fine scrape the other night. I was going to pass the evening at Mrs Cole's in Lincoln's Inn Fields. I went in a chair; they carried me through Covent Garden.' But her mode of transport caused the crowd to suspect her of being a Whig out campaigning, and she was surrounded by 'a hundred armed men'. 'A vast number of people followed me,' she continued, 'crying out, "It is Mrs Fox: none but Mr Fox's wife would dare to come into Covent Garden in a chair; she is going to canvass in the dark." Though not a little frightened, I laughed heartily at this, but shall stir no more in a chair for some time.'[26]

But Fox had a powerful tool. He had the most glamorous canvassing team in history. These canvassers arrived in a bustle of feathers, ribbons, silks and hearty cheers. Led by Georgiana Cavendish, Duchess of Devonshire, they included her sister, Harriet, Lady Duncannon; Anne Seymour Damer; the Duchess of Portland; Lady Jersey; Lady Carlisle; Mrs Bouverie; the three ladies Waldegrave, and Mary Robinson. Even the Prince of Wales gave his support.

While the Covent Garden crowds were enchanted by Fox and his celebrity team, Thomas Rowlandson was electrified. This political lothario was so suited to the pages of pen and ink. Rowlandson's hand jumped and danced across the pages of his sketchbook, trying to keep up with Fox's manic gestures, bushy eyebrows and wild head of hair.

Facing Fox's celebrity team, the campaign trail was more of an uphill struggle for the opposition candidate, Sir Cecil Wray. His only glamorous backer was a plump, elderly lady named Mrs Albinia Hobart. Rowlandson couldn't help but compare the two characters. One of his earliest prints for William Humphrey was a print called *The Poll*. In it, Mrs Hobart and the Duchess of Devonshire find themselves at either end of a seesaw. While the rotund Hobart is firmly stuck on the ground with no hope of lift off, the beautiful, slim, charming duchess flies high in the air – and high in the esteem of the Westminster voters.

*The Poll*, Thomas Rowlandson, 1784.
Metropolitan Museum of Art, The Elisha Whittelsey Collection, The Elisha Whittelsey Fund, 1959

It was unprecedented for someone like Georgiana Cavendish, a duchess, to take part in canvassing. She was so 'indefatigable in her canvass for Fox', that the suspicion of London society was aroused.[27] Was the Duchess more than merely a friend of The Eyebrow? Rumours of her impropriety were fuelled by accounts of her exchanging kisses for the guarantee of a Foxite vote:

> It was at this election that the beautiful Georgiana, Duchess of Devonshire, successfully wooed the electors for the great Whig leader by her smiles and her kisses. 'Your eyes are so bright, my lady, that I could light my pipe by them,' said an Irish labourer to her at Covent Garden.* She is said to have valued that compliment more highly than any she received during a long and brilliant career in social and political life. 'The Duchess having purchased the vote of an impracticable butcher by a kiss is said to be unquestionable,' says Earl Stanhope.[28]

It was the perfect material to produce some killer content. Thomas Rowlandson was off. He produced a flurry of election prints. On Monday 12 April 1784, the windows of William Humphrey's print shop displayed *The Devonshire, or Most Approved Method of Securing Votes*. Here was the Duchess dressed in the party colours of blue and buff, wearing a hat trimmed with feathers and ribbons. But instead of talking policy with a butcher and asking: 'Is there anything the Liberal Democrats can do for *you* in this election?' She's gone for a more direct canvassing technique: kissing. 'Huzzah!' her sister cries in the background. 'Fox for ever.'

The following Tuesday, William Humphrey pinned up another of Rowlandson's designs. Those strolling down the Strand might have done a double take at the vision in the shop window. It seemed to be a miniature version of Henry Fuseli's *The Nightmare*, a magnificent oil painting that had recently been exhibited at the Royal Academy.

Fuseli's masterpiece depicted a sleeping woman draped over the end of a bed, beautiful and sad. Yet the print shop window showed no such fair maiden. This was the naked, hirsute form of Charles Fox, the man running to be prime minister, stretching out across the bed sheets. It was appropriately titled *The Covent Garden Nightmare*.

* A great line for anyone currently navigating the dating scene.

*The Nightmare*, Henry Fuseli, 1781.
PD-US, Detroit Institute of Arts

*The Covent Garden Nightmare*, Thomas Rowlandson, 1784.

With the five-week voting window drawing to a close, this brigade of Foxites were still fighting on in the Westminster borough, their flirtations closely followed by Rowlandson's keen eye. He churned out another print on 30 April showing the *Procession to the Hustings after a Successful Canvass*. Here is the Duchess of Devonshire again, leading a gaggle of ladies with foxtails in their hair and wielding banners. Behind them follows a group of butchers, cheering on the procession with meat cleavers and marrow bones.

*Procession to the Hustings after a Successful Canvass*,
Thomas Rowlandson, 1784.
Metropolitan Museum of Art, The Elisha Whittelsey Collection, The Elisha Whittelsey Fund, 1959

Fox won the Westminster seat by a whisker: 6,233 votes to Sir Cecil Wray's 5,998.[29] On 17 May, the Prince of Wales put nine large marquees in the garden of Carlton House and threw a riotous party to celebrate. It was clearly a big night: Thomas Orde-Powlett MP saw the Prince vomiting in public in the early hours.[30]

Fox may have won Westminster, but the rest of the country were not persuaded by his charms. The Whigs lost a whopping 89 seats in the general election, and these MPs were dubbed 'Fox's Martyrs', a reference to the sixteenth-century *Foxe's Book of Martyrs*, a polemical account of the sufferings of Protestants under the Catholic Church, by John Foxe. Perhaps it was Fox's criticism of the Crown (which hinted at republicanism), his naked power-grab with the East India Bill, or the fact he had staunchly supported the nation's enemy in the American War of Independence.

The 1784 election was a landslide for Pitt. But it also put Rowlandson on the map as a brilliant graphic satirist and established Charles Fox, with all his eccentricities and foibles and follies, as the most bountiful gift to satirists ever created.

## A SPECIMEN OF ELEGANCE

The country now had a 24-year-old prime minister. But who, in heaven's name, was this boy? His father was William Pitt the Elder: the prime minister who led Britain to victory in the Seven Years' War (1756–63), trampling the French enemy and solidifying Britain's powerful position on the world stage. While battling enemies overseas, the Elder Pitt (let's call him Chatham, after his earldom) faced formidable opposition in the Commons in the form of Henry Fox, father of the star of *The Covent Garden Nightmare*. It goes down in the great family feuds of history: Montague vs Capulet, Pitt vs Fox, Potter vs Malfoy.

Chatham wasn't the only member of the family with political connections. His wife was Lady Hester Grenville, the sister of another former prime minister, George Grenville, who led the House from 1763–5. So, it was very much a *small world*. William and Hester had a 'delightful, promising little tribe'[31]: Hester, John, Harriet, William and James. They were indeed an impressive lot, educated at home by the family chaplain, Reverend Edward Wilson: they would write to their parents in Latin, offering their own comments on the London art scene. And although Chatham was known as the 'Great Commoner', the lives of his children were anything but. They received a rapturous reception when they popped into East Grinstead in 1767, with 'ringing of hand bells and strewing flours'. 'When we first entered the town,' wrote Hester, 'there were a great many young men drest in white with white wands who run by the coach.'[32]

The second son, William, may not have seemed the most promising character at first: he was a cheerful but sickly child with terrible handwriting. He later expressed regret for so many 'innumerable blots' and 'scribbl[ing] in such a manner that I am really ashamed'.[33] But it soon became clear that within this delicate body was a razor-sharp mind. According to Reverend Wilson he seemed 'never ... to learn, but merely to recollect'.[34] Such precocious intellect found its bearings in the world of debate. With monologues of Shakespeare and Milton bouncing around his cerebral cortex, and quotes from Greek and Latin translations darting around his frontal lobe, he was well equipped to instigate an intellectual argument about the most trivial issues. One imagines he might have made a most annoying sibling.

Alongside a propensity for spouting extracts of Shakespeare or pontificating in Ancient Greek, William was a lover of animals: 'William's little horse is a dark iron grey, and has a switch tail, they say it is about as handsome as Beauty.'[35] He seemed to take great responsibility for the pigeons that were kept on the estate at Burton Pynsent. In April 1772, he wrote to his mother regarding an attack by an 'audacious Hawk', reassuring her that the situation was quite under control: 'We have vow'd vengeance on him for this daring insult, and a gun is constantly kept loaded in the pantry for that purpose.'[36]

At seven years old, he took an interest in his father's career. 'I am very glad that you are well,' he wrote to his mother, 'I wish you and Papa joy at his being Earl Chatham and I am also very glad to hear he is Lord Privy Seal. I hope to hear by the next post that we are all to come to London.' And with such formalities over, he got on to more pressing matters: 'I shall desire to have the dog which you bought on the road.'[37]

On 26 April 1773, just shy of his fourteenth birthday, young William was admitted to one of the University of Cambridge's most prestigious colleges, Pembroke. He took up residence in October to study under George Pretyman, a clergyman who would become his life-long confidant. It seems unlikely that William Pitt immediately delved head-first into the social delights of Cambridge freshers' week. He was more likely to be found with his nose in a book: devouring the classics and English literature, deciphering Newton's laws of motion or getting to grips with history and political philosophy. And that's if he had ever been in Cambridge: his poor health kept him away from university until 1776, but from then he was a full-time student and seemed to warm up to the social scene.

And it was a social scene worth buttering up, for aristocrats were two a penny. Many would become political allies later in life, including Charles Long, John Pratt and Charles Manners.* He also became pals with the son of a wealthy merchant from Hull, a grammar schoolboy named William Wilberforce. Wilberforce, who had also been a sickly, delicate child with poor eyesight, approached his Cambridge days with less diligence than Pitt. After the deaths of a wealthy grandfather and uncle, Master Wilberforce's finances were gloriously healthy. They went straight towards funding long Cambridge evenings spent chatting over cards and punch. Later in his life, Wilberforce remembered Pitt the student as a jolly, generous fellow. 'No man,' Wilberforce wrote, 'ever indulged more freely or happily in that playful facetiousness which gratifies all without wounding any.'[38]

Pitt's happy student days were marred by continuing bad health, and he never completed his exams. No matter: as a nobleman, he enjoyed the privilege of graduating in 1776 anyway. But disaster struck the Pitt household in May 1778, when the great Earl of Chatham

* The future Lord Farnborough, second Earl of Camden and fourth Duke of Rutland, respectively.

passed away. His final moments were suitably noble. He listened to a reading of Homer's passage about the death of Hector. 'Leave your dying father,' he croaked to his son, John, 'and go to the defence of your country.'[39]

Pitt started his career as a barrister, but this wasn't enough to stimulate that enormous brain, and in 1780 he flirted with a career change. As the Royal Academy was opening up in Somerset House, and the anti-Catholic Gordon Riots erupted, Pitt's eyes were drawn to Westminster, his father's old stomping ground. In September 1780, on the dissolution of Parliament by Lord North, Pitt threw aside his law papers and jumped at the chance to join the Westminster rabble.

But this was a dog-eat-dog world, and the name of his famous father wasn't enough to get him in the door. He canvassed a university seat at Cambridge (in those days, universities had MPs of their own) but ended bottom of the poll. Pitt's saviour came in the form of the Duke of Rutland.

Although Pitt was born and bred in the south of England, the Duke offered him the Cumbrian borough of Appleby, under the boroughmonger Sir James Lowther. Lowther gave Pitt total freedom to do whatever he pleased in the constituency, as long as it was what Lowther wanted – unless 'our Lines of Conduct should become opposite'.[40] Without the financial means to support a contested election, Pitt accepted the offer. So, it was through these underhand means that William Pitt entered British politics, in the new Parliament of January 1781, at the tender age of 21.

Pitt made his first speech in Parliament on 26 February 1781. It was unplanned and unprepared, prompted cries of 'Mr. Pitt! Mr. Pitt!'[41] from the opposition bench who were impatient to hear from Chatham's son. Pitt opened his lips, and the house was spellbound. 'His voice,' it was recorded, 'is rich and striking, full of melody and force; his manner easy and elegant; his language beautiful and luxuriant. He gave in this first essay, a specimen of eloquence, not unworthy the son of his immortal parent.'[42] Lord North declared it 'the best *first* speech he ever heard',[43] with others claiming that Pitt 'was not merely a chip off the old "block", but the old block itself.'[44] Pitt himself admitted he had wielded 'the wand of the magician'.[45]

Those years of training had paid off. It was this oration *par excellence* that zoomed Pitt into prominence, gaining the respect of George III in 1783 and convincing the electorate in 1784. The Mince-Pie Administration would keep Pitt in office for the next seventeen years. Fox had ballsed up his one chance, and his mistake had cost him dearly: he would spend the ensuing years desperately trying to claw his way back to power.

The battle lines were drawn. And taking front row for this epic drama were Thomas Rowlandson and James Gillray, watching each scene unfold with forensic examination. This Pitt vs Fox drama, they discovered, was more than worthy of the satirist's pen.

# 4

# *A Stillness the Most Uncommon*

## PARALYSED BY A LOADED PISTOL

As the results of Pitt's landslide victory came through, George III breathed a sigh of relief. It was a weight off his shoulders to know that, at least for now, the reins of power were far from the reach of Fox and his gang. And, what's more, the summer held much to look forward to. For London was about to host a lavish celebration: 'The most important single event in the history of England music.'[1] A series of five concerts were held in Westminster Abbey between 26 May and 5 June 1784, to mark 25 years since the death of George Frederick Handel.

The abbey was decked with wooden galleries to seat 4,500 attendees, where 525 musicians would perform Handel's masterpiece, *Messiah*.[2] George III was a big Handel fan, having once told Charles Burney, the most important music historian of the day, he was 'very fond of old music ... I don't like the present compositions. They are too quick and hurrying.'[3] And before Handel died in 1759, he sensed the future king was a fan boy: 'While that boy lives,' Handel had told Burney, 'my music will never want a protector.'[4] It was in the Handel celebrations of 1784, at the end of the fifth concert, that the King stood up during the 'Hallelujah Chorus', and it's been tradition to do so ever since.

As the 1780s pressed on, Pitt proved himself to be a worthy candidate for prime minister, despite facing formidable scrutiny from Fox, Richard Brinsley Sheridan and Burke on the opposition benches. The King and Pitt had similar minds. They both provided logical, mathematical solutions to practical problems. The King disapproved of Pitt's Whiggish support of Catholic emancipation and parliamentary reform, but in general, they saw eye to eye on foreign policy, economic measures, and a determination to keep Fox firmly out of office. Pitt and the King were not friends. But they respected and needed each other, and that was enough.

As Pitt grappled with the reins of power, Gillray and Rowlandson faced their own crisis: they were fast approaching the big 3–0. Both were still on a mission to make it big: Gillray as a serious engraver and Rowlandson as a master watercolourist. Since 1783, Gillray had been determined to find success with stipple engraving, taking a break from caricature, hence his notable absence from the 1784 election commentary. His trade card, presented in an elaborate hand with rich, Baroque swirls, read: 'Gillray, Portrait Painter, No. 7 Little Newport Street, Leicester Fields'.[5] While he still lived with his parents in Milman's Row in Chelsea, Gillray worked from a rented studio in Little Newport Street, on the edge of today's Chinatown, which was bustling with artists and craftsman.

There was no doubt that he was as talented as the high-flyers earning vast sums of money from engraving. Once a painter such as Reynolds had finished their canvas, they would look for a good engraver (say, Gillray) to make the engraving. These spin-off engravings would often be more profitable than the original painting, so skilled engravers were in high demand. Gillray spent three years earnestly trying to orchestrate a commission. He wrote to Benjamin West in 1786, confessing: 'I fear I am too late to have the happiness to engrave the Picture which has lately occupied my whole thoughts.'

The picture in question was West's *Last Supper*, and Gillray wrote that he 'should embrace it as the highest honor of my life' to be commissioned with engraving the masterpiece.[6]

He didn't get it. In fact, apart from a few bits of work here and there, Gillray never received a major commission, in either engraving or painting. Perhaps it was his association with popular caricature that put patrons off. Perhaps it was his tendency to put his own stamp on the work when all that was required was to produce an exact copy. And he was unlucky, too, that he worked at a time when Gainsborough, Reynolds and George Romney were his direct competition.

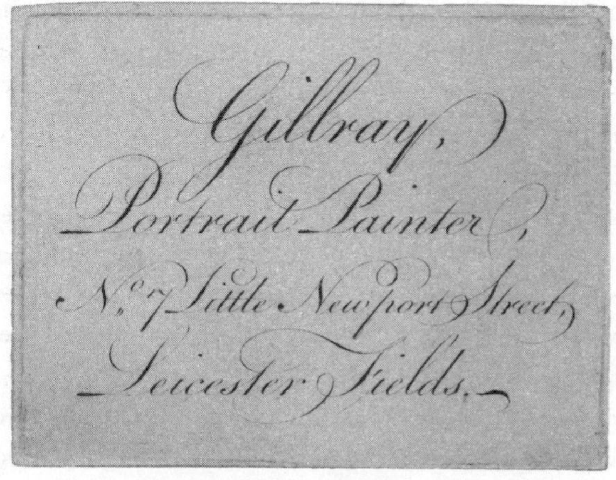


Trade card of James Gillray (undated).
© Trustees of the British Museum

By 1786, thank goodness, Gillray was back on the caricatures. As he and Rowlandson realised they might not make the cut as the Royal Academy's next great names, their satirical work was growing in demand. They were familiar names in London's print shop windows and had gathered a reliable bevy of customers among the publishers, tradesmen lawyers, office holders and small-scale collectors who hoovered up this kind of affordable art. Sure, they might only be big fish in the small pond of caricature, but this pond was growing fast and close to flooding the banks.

In 1786, as Rowlandson mulled over his possible career prospects, he bade goodbye to the sash-windows of Wardour Street. After ten happy years, it was time to move on. Rowlandson, Aunt Jane, Mary Chateauvert and a young servant named Mary Barridell boxed up their belongings and found a new base five minutes north at 50 Poland Street.[7*]

The view at the back of the house was a depressing one: the forbidding workhouse of St James's Westminster, built in 1725 to house over 700 impoverished men and women. As these poor souls shuffled along the alley beside 49 Poland Street to enter the complex, many knew they might never leave. The mortality rates were high: an infant under the age of four had a life expectancy of only one month in a London workhouse.[8] Many were buried in the Parish burial ground, conveniently located just behind the workhouse.[9]

It was a rougher part of town, and Rowlandson had a nasty welcome to his new lodgings. One mid-December evening in 1786, Rowlandson and Angelo enjoyed an evening out. By midnight, Rowlandson had returned to Poland Street, parting with his friend at a nearby corner. As he knocked on his own front door, waiting for Mary Chateauvert to bring him in from the freezing December cold, a lurking ruffian attacked him. Rowlandson was pushed to the ground, paralysed with fear by the loaded pistol pointed in his face. The man extracted Rowlandson's watch and about three guineas and scarpered into the black night.[10]

Seconds later, the door opened and a horrified Mary Chateauvert helped her shocked master into the warmth of the house. The following day, Rowlandson, furious at the violation, hired a professional

* Incidentally, at No. 28 lived another young man trying to make his way in the art world: the young William Blake. More on him later …

'thief-taker' and, along with Angelo, the three men scoured the dens, warrens and brothels of St Giles and Seven Dials. No success.

But a couple of days later, Rowlandson was called to identify potential suspects for a similar crime that had been just committed. After one suspect began chatting back, Rowlandson (seemingly out of spite) played a part in dobbing him in, despite him bearing little resemblance to the Poland Street attacker. The man was hanged. Rowlandson was delighted. 'Though I get knocked down,' he recalled, 'and lost my watch and my money, and did not find the thief, I have been the means of hanging *one* man. Come, that's doing something.'[11]

This was a city where violence and death were a familiar and expected part of life. Where punching a man in the face could be considered a mild misdemeanour.[12] Where a man was allowed to beat his wife, children and servants and get away with it, as most acts of domestic violence were within the law.[13] Where, by the close of the eighteenth century, over 200 crimes were punishable by death.[14]

Those condemned would be transported to the gallows along a three-mile route by cart; in some areas of the country, they were even forced to make the journey sitting on their own coffins. They were often heckled by a jeering crowd of several thousands. Until 1783, there were executions at Tyburn eight times a year, some of which saw twenty separate hangings.[15] When pirates or sailors were hanged at Execution Dock in the east of the city, their bodies were left to rot in gibbets as a ghastly warning.

So, while our Georgian ancestors might have chuckled at a Gillray print, or enjoyed a Handel opera, they may have also booked a front-row seat to see the latest victim hanged by the neck until they were dead. Or, after an evening at a Covent Garden opera, they might have enjoyed some cock fighting, with birds specially reared and fitted with sharpened spurs tearing each other to pieces to the bloody end. Although Rowlandson's delight at putting a man to death seems quite shocking to modern sensibilities, he was a product of his age. Such satisfaction was akin to overcoming a planning controversy with the local council. London may have appeared as a city of fluffy meringue, where elegant ladies enjoyed polite conversation and good taste, but the real, beating heart of the city was a dangerous world, where Hogarthian macabre was very much part of everyday life.

As Rowlandson recovered from the trauma of the robbery, he had more bad news from the north: his father was back in town. William Rowlandson had returned to the capital in disgrace. His textile business in Richmond had gone bankrupt, and he had taken up cheap accommodation at 49 Broad Street in Bloomsbury, near the top of Drury Lane. It was a tense time. As he oversaw the bankruptcy proceedings and waited for the documentation to be processed, all he could do was twiddle his thumbs. And he was totally reliant on the generosity of his London contacts: the savings of Aunt Jane, the profits of his son's art or the charity of his son-in-law, the printmaker and painter, Samuel Howitt.

Thomas Rowlandson's relationship with his father was hardly a close one, having not lived together for two decades. They were awkward, impatient and embarrassed by one another. Thomas was a metropolitan man, successful and popular. It made his father's failure to support his family – both in London and Yorkshire – all too apparent. Yet, as a dutiful son, Thomas probably helped out where he could: in his new studio at Poland Street, he probably put his disgraced father to work with the day-to-day admin, completing jobs usually reserved for the intern: distributing prints across the city, photocopying, and making rounds of tea. Finally, on 27 November 1788, a certificate of conformity was issued. Two days later, a pair of Rowlandson prints appeared in the print shop windows, published not under Thomas' name, but under William's. It was a decent thing to do, a public announcement that his father was in the clear, and able to trade once again.

William Rowlandson wasn't the only disrupter arriving in London from the north. During these years, a certain Scotsman made his way to the city as another fresh-faced, ambitious artist on the scene. He was a man who would become an old friend and long-term conspirator of Rowlandson and Gillray. His name was Isaac Cruikshank.

## A SCOTSMAN IN LONDON

If you were a poor trader in Edinburgh's port of Leith in the 1740s and you failed to pay your taxes, there's a good chance you would be paid a visit Andrew Crookshanks, the customs inspector. In the usual way of things, Crookshanks was likely to give you a good grilling, but if you'd failed to cough up in 1745, you might have got away with it. For this particular inspector was a Jacobite, who supported the restoration of King James II's descendants (at that point Bonnie Prince Charlie) to the British throne. And in 1745, he took a self-appointed sabbatical and pinned his colours to the mast of the Jacobite rising.

It was the wrong call: Crookshanks was wounded at the Battle of Culloden and fired from his inspector job. Luckily, Andrew and his wife, Elizabeth, were befriended by a family of master printers and publishers, the Ruddimans, who helped the family get back on their feet. They moved first to the New North Kirk parish in Edinburgh and then to the Canongate, the lower part of what is now known as the Royal Mile, where Isaac was born on 5 October 1764, becoming the fifth child and third son of the Crookshanks. His baptism was recorded in the Canongate parish register on 14 October 1764, as the son of Andrew Crookshanks, 'indweller at Canongate',[16] and Elizabeth Davidson. The boy would prove himself to be suitably athletic and a keen flautist.

Isaac Cruikshank grew up in a city that was on the cusp of monumental change. Just two years after his birth, the young architect James Craig won a competition to design the New Town, an ambitious reimagining of urban landscape. Had the Crookshanks children glanced across the Nor'Loch* as they played in the wynds

* The city's cesspit, which is now Waverley Station.

and closes of the Royal Mile, they might have glimpsed blocks of stone being delivered from Craigleith Quarry; blocks that would become rows of elegant Georgian streets. And when Isaac was ten, he might have spied the great Scottish architect Robert Adam pacing out lengths to design Register House. The New Town made Edinburgh a fitting capital for a city bursting with the ideas of the Scottish Enlightenment.

One visitor, Edward Topham, visited what became known as the Athens of the North in the 1770s. For him, the trip was defined by battling the natural elements:

> As Edinburgh is situated on the borders of the sea, and surrounded by hills of an immense height, currents of air are carried down between them with a rapidity and a violence which nothing can resist ... In walking over it this morning I had the pleasure of adjusting a lady's petticoats which had blown almost entirely over her head ... one poor gentleman, who was rather too much engaged with the novelty of the objects before him, unfortunately forgot his own hat and wig, which were listed up by an unpremeditated puff, and carried entirely away.[17]

In 1783, when Isaac was around the age of twenty, his father died, possibly as the result of an old Culloden wound playing up. Not long afterwards, Isaac came out of the closet as a painter. He studied with a local artist, possibly the caricaturist John Kay, who showed him the ropes of drawing and engraving. Later the same year, Isaac was off. He travelled with his master to London, just in time to catch George III's dismissal of the Fox–North coalition and controversial appointment of the schoolboy PM, William Pitt.

Isaac settled in the heart of the print scene on Stanhope Street, between the Strand and Drury Lane. Like Rowlandson and Gillray, he made a concerted effort to sell paintings and exhibit his watercolours, but the demand wasn't there, and the bills were piling up. He turned his hand to any work that could produce cash fast, and soon he was churning out lottery tickets, song sheets, illustrations for cheap books and chapbooks, prints and caricatures of all descriptions.

By 1788, this young man, now spelling his name 'Cruikshank', found comfort from another Scot in London, a young lady from Perth named Mary McNaughton. Mary was the daughter of a Highland naval officer, who had been killed at sea. She had moved to London to live with an uncle and aunt in Finchley and soon caught the eye of young Isaac Cruikshank; they tied the knot in Soho on 14 August 1788. The Cruikshank summer wedding was strong evidence that opposites attract: Mary was from the Highlands, strong-willed, frugal, hot-tempered, devout and industrious, while her new Lowland husband had a boisterous, bibulous, impish energy. Mary, it seems, wore the trews in the Cruikshank household.

With a young wife by his side, Cruikshank settled down in St Martin's Court, a back alley that runs behind today's Leicester Square Tube Station, now the home of West-End stage doors. In these blissful early years of marriage, Cruikshank's artistic career picked up. In the summer of 1789, Isaac and Mary – now six months pregnant – wandered over to Somerset House in their finest attire to visit the Royal Academy's Summer Exhibition and see a watercolour of Isaac's, *Return to Lochaber*, which had made the cut.

Mary gave birth on 27 September 1789 to a bouncing baby boy named Robert, who was to be 'cradled in caricature'.[18] And the success continued: the following year Isaac's *Visit to the Cottage* was accepted for the Summer Exhibition, with *The Distress and Triumphs of Virtue* being exhibited a couple of years later.

However, any attempt to make a living by selling paintings was far less successful than churning out engravings, the tittle-tattle of the print world, which provided a reliable income for a growing family. Isaac etched the copper from his pencil sketches and watercolour designs, while Mary added the hand colouring and lettering, sometimes even etching simple shapes herself. As the 1790s approached,

Isaac and Mary Cruikshank's finances were in decent health, and they could enjoy the rewards of hard work and the delights of London life.

It was hard to say the same for Cruikshank's contemporaries. James Gillray was darting all over the place: in 1788, he moved to Temple Bar in the Strand, and then, in 1790, he spent a three-year spell in his old hunting ground, talking lodgings on the King's Road in Chelsea. And Tom Rowlandson was dealt a great personal blow. His dear Aunt Jane – his mother in all but name, and his closest companion for some quarter-century – died, aged 61. Aunt Jane was buried beside her husband James in the churchyard of St Botolph's Bishopsgate. But this cloud had a silver lining as Tom suddenly found himself in possession of a large fortune: his inheritance from Aunt Jane is estimated to have been more than £2,000, over £210,000 in today's money. For the first time in his life, he was financially independent.

These unsettling events paled in comparison to those in anotherLondon household. As Rowlandson's father regained some stability, and Cruikshank settled down with his troop of bairns, the father of the nation, King George III, hurled the country into a monumental crisis.

## HOW NERVOUS I AM!

The crisis stemmed not from foreign invasions, riotous uproar, plague or famine. The disaster stemmed from the royal palace, from inside the King's body itself. In the autumn of 1788, the King was tormented by stomach pain, his urine turned blue, and he began hallucinating. Reports from royal physicians at Kew Palace described the King speaking in nonsense at high speed.

By November, the severity of the situation was taking its toll. Queen Charlotte was 'almost overpowered with some secret terror', regularly bursting into tears, crying: 'How nervous I am!'[19] 'A stillness the most uncommon reigned' over the royal household. 'Nobody stirred; not a voice was heard; not a step, not a motion.'[20]

At a family dinner on 5 November, the King 'had broken forth into positive delirium, which long had been menacing those who saw him most closely, and the Queen was so overpowered as to fall into violent hysterics'.[21] The King's eyes were like 'nothing but blackcurrant jelly, the veins in his face were swelled, the sound in his voice was dreadful; he often spoke until he was exhausted, and the moment he could recover his breath began again, while the foam ran out of his mouth'.[22]

On 19 November, the King talked virtually non-stop for nineteen hours, darting between sense and nonsense.[23] 'He fancies London is drowned and orders his yacht to go there,' Lord Sheffield reported, 'he took Sir George Baker's wig, flung it in his face ... and told him he might star gaze.'[24]

On one occasion, as the princesses walked out on the lawn, they were startled to see their father 'struggling at the windows, making efforts to open them, gesticulating at his daughters and banging in frustration on the pane. But how could this be their father, this pale and haggard man wearing a nightgown and nightcap in the middle of the day?'[25]

Doctor after doctor came to treat the King. Their treatments were based on balancing the four humours within the body – black bile, yellow bile, phlegm and blood – and their understanding of mental illness was pretty much medieval. Some suggested the King should drink 'the blood of a jackass ... after passing a clear napkin through it two or three times'.[26] They tried pushing his body to extremes to literally 'shock' the illness out. As well as being denied food, he was dosed to the brim with powerful emetics and laxatives and administered freezing baths and leeching.* Doctors tried to draw the illness out by strapping the unfortunate patient into a straitjacket (his 'hated waistcoat')[27] and covering him with arsenic-based powders, causing his royal skin to erupt into bubbling blisters.

* Leeching was a gruesome treatment whereby a living leech was placed on the skin and encouraged to suck out the patient's blood and – the theory went – provoke a blood flow.

All the while, George's true condition went undiagnosed. Most terrible was the fact that, in moments of relative sanity, the King was well aware of his own decline. 'The King is very sensible of the great change there is in himself and [the Queen's] disturbance at it,' wrote a member of the household.[28]

He occasionally showed flashes of his old quick-witted self. When the new doctor, Francis Willis, arrived, the King asked if he was a clergyman or doctor. Willis replied: 'Sir, Our Saviour himself went about healing the sick,' to which the King responded: 'Yes, but he had not seven hundred pounds a year for it.'[29] On another occasion, while walking in the gardens with Dr Willis, the gardener offered him a basket of exotic fruit, to which the King replied, 'Get another basket, Eaton, and pack up the Doctor in it and send him off at the same time.'[30]

It wasn't the first time a king had gone loopy: the royal households of eighteenth-century Europe were no stranger to madness. Queen Marian I of Portugal was declared insane in 1792. George's brother-in-law, King Christian VII of Denmark, suffered from paranoia and hallucinations. There were serious questions about the mental health of both Tsar Peter III (assassinated in 1762) and Tsar Paul (assassinated 1801).[31]

Nevertheless, while the King was zapped and probed and pinched and prodded in the lonely rooms of Kew Palace, he left a power vacuum at the heart of Westminster: the country was paralysed. Without the security of his royal backer, Pitt was on shaky ground. His position as PM relied on the King's support – and hasty recovery. Fox and his Whig followers saw an opportunity to seize power. With the King out of action, his son Prince George was poised to become Prince Regent, taking the reins of power until his father recovered. It was a waiting game: the country could only last in a state of political paralysis for so long.

Over the past five years, Pitt and Fox had rooted themselves firmly in opposing political positions. Pitt, who owed his position to George III's patronage, had spent his career defending the royal prerogative – a set of powers, privileges and rights that had been enjoyed by the monarchy for centuries. On the opposite bench, Fox had been vindictive in his attacks on the monarchy and was famed for his libertarian, even revolutionary, beliefs. He wrote to Edmund Burke, the philosopher and statesmen, in 1779: 'There is no man who hates the power of the crown more, or who has a worse opinion of the Person to whom it belongs than I.'[32]

And in 1785, he had riled the Commons to push their own authority: 'the people of England have a right to control the executive power, by the interference of their representatives in this House of parliament.'[33] It was, therefore, a great surprise to listen to Fox's speech on 10 December 1788, instructing MPs 'to waste not a moment unnecessarily but to proceed with all becoming speed and all becoming diligence to restore the sovereign power and the exercise of royal authority'.[34]

It was a volte-face of impressive proportions. For Fox, the King's illness was a natural and perfect demise. If the Prince of Wales, his great ally and friend, were on the throne, it would be a green light for a Foxite *coup d'état*.

His case for the Prince of Wales becoming Prince Regent was compelling: 'There was then a person in the kingdom different from any other person that any existing precedents could refer to – an heir apparent of full age and capacity to exercise the royal power.'[35] But Pitt was waiting in the wings, plotting the counter-attack. To counter Fox's scheme, and keep his own job, Pitt also changed his position. Suddenly, the loyal monarchist was making speeches hammering home the sanctity of parliamentary power.

The nation held its breath and grabbed the popcorn, for this was a political spectacle like no other. While Pitt sweated and plotted to keep his parliamentary seat, Fox schemed and seduced in a bid to slink through the doors of power. And where had Prince George been in all of this? He was taking a more relaxed approach, reported to be 'drinking and singing'. Any concern for his tormented father was 'not of that deep and rooted sort'.[36]

It was another crisis that was perfect for satirical comment, and with the situation changing day by day, printmakers were churning out content in a frenzy before the story changed again. On 25 November 1788, the behaviour of Prince George was featured in the window of Samuel Fores' print shop at No. 3 Piccadilly. Through the panes of glass, pedestrians peered, via the imagination of Tom Rowlandson, straight into the King's bedchamber.

These passers-by were confronted with a scene entitled *Filial Piety!* With such a title, you'd expect to see a demonstration of dutiful obedience and devotion towards a parental figure. But it's hard to see much filial affection in Rowlandson's print. The King, traumatised by three months of treatment from his doctors, has been seeking some R&R in the form of Holy Communion, delivered by a bishop reading from *A Prayer Restoration of Health*. Behind the bishop is a painting named *The Prodigal Son*.

But this is no Prodigal Prince. Right on cue, in comes Prince George and two of his pals – a failed army officer and a playwright – bursting into the royal bedchamber, dancing, drinking, waving their hats and knocking over tables and communion wine. The Prince blurts out in a drunken slur: 'Damme, come along, I'll see if the Old Fellow's — or not.' The dash here could be replaced with 'dead', or 'mad', or perhaps a hiccup. Either way, the bishop's mouth drops open in horror at such impropriety. The King turns away in misery, his expression reminiscent of any parent whose toddler has screamed for attention at 6am on a Sunday morning. And here's the takeaway message – perhaps this Prince George chap is not such a suitable candidate to run the country in the King's absence, after all.

Fox was only too aware of the Prince's recklessness. He admitted on 15 December: 'I am rather afraid they will get some cry against the Prince for grasping as they call it at too much power.'[37] The rhetoric wrestle was still in full fight, but Fox was determined: 'We shall have

*Filial Piety!*, Thomas Rowlandson, 1788.
© The Trustees of the British Museum

several hard fights in the H. of Cs. This week and next, in some of which I fear we shall be beat … but at any rate the Prince must be Regent and of consequence the Ministry must be changed.'[38]

The Prince of Wales was aware that he was a walking PR disaster. He didn't have a spin doctor, but he managed to acquire the next best thing: his 'House painter'[39] was none other than Henry Wigstead, the former travelling companion of Thomas Rowlandson.

Wigstead was a familiar face in the Prince's household. He had spent the previous summer redesigning the interiors of the Prince's Brighton Pavilion, which included painting 40 garden tubs verdigris green and black. Brighton* was a holiday resort for the very best of London society. Here one could 'have the view of a large piece of water, commonly called the English Channel'.[40] They could 'indulge in a peep of the ladies dipping into the water, or bobbing at a wave in rough weather'[41] – but only a *peep*, for the Master of the Ceremonies

* Or Brighthelmstone as it was then known.

'sent the gentlemen, for decencies sake, two hundred yards further to the westward'.[42]

Wigstead was quick to capitalise on the Prince's reckless spending habits, and soon made himself his personal print dealer. He filled the royal walls in Brighton with London's comic art – some was Wigstead's own, some was Rowlandson's. It was no surprise that when the Prince needed to make a compelling case for his regency, Wigstead was his go-to man. If this were a Bond film, the Prince would swivel in a desk chair and pick up the phone: 'Get Wigstead in. I need prints. Fast. Before father recovers.' Phone slams down. Cut to London cityscape.

Wigstead was summoned to Carlton House. The orders were given to come up with the most cutting, acerbic caricatures to support the Prince's cause; they needed to persuade the people he was responsible enough to be Prince Regent, and paint Pitt's gang as the true power-grabbers.

A royal commission! No doubt Wigstead and Rowlandson scribbled and etched into the early hours, to push and pull and zap creative sparks. Once a few drafts were ready, Wigstead would don his finest attire and speed back to Carlton House. When he received the royal thumbs-up, he would scurry back to Rowlandson's studio on Poland Street with the good news, taking the staircase two at a time …

'Tom! Tom! I'm back!'

The unshaven young Rowlandson jumped up from his bed. His floor was strewn with paper, his hands covered in ink: 'What did he say?! He likes them?'

'We're on: he likes the idea of King Egbert, and the one of the Queen's dresser. But not the one in Hyde Park – apparently, it's too louche.'

'Too louche? That's rich coming from him! But bravo, bravo, sir!'

'Yes, yes! But time is of the essence, Tom. I need them ready to go – drafted, etched and printed by Monday. I don't want to hear you've been in the Lamb and Flag all weekend, all right? This is a big deal. I overheard in Piccadilly that the King's condition is getting worse and worse. We might be able to spin out a few commissions from this.'

'All right, all right, I'm on it.'

'Good man. I'll run over and let Fores know at once.'

'Godspeed!'

Wigstead's commission involved not only 'designing the different political subjects', but also 'sending the prints per Mail coaches to every town throughout the Kingdom'. This was a serious marketing drive, and only came to light when the Prince's unpaid bills were examined by auditors two decades later. They discovered an entry relating to Wigstead's 'sundry attendances at Carleton House', which read: 'Money expended / during the time of his Majestys Malady / by order of … Mr Henry Wigstead.' The expenses were 'For Copper', 'Paid Mr Rowlandson for etching' and 'Paid a Printer and for Paper'.[43]

On 20 December 1788, the Saturday before Christmas, the result of Rowlandson's efforts was a last-minute addition to Samuel Fores' Christmas window at No. 3 Piccadilly. But it was signed by a certain Tom Brown, from Spa Fields, Chelsea. This no doubt bamboozled the Christmas shoppers of Piccadilly: 'Spa Fields, Chelsea? Where's that? You ever hear of that?'

Rowlandson would have foreseen such confusion. Tom Brown was a pseudonym, and Spa Fields, Chelsea was a fictional address. For this print was commissioned by none other than the Prince of Wales himself, delivered under a cloak of anonymity.

The print in question brought Pitt and Queen Charlotte to the heart of the fracas, loaded with the accusation that they were both after King George's power.* The print shows them happily parading

* This was highly unfair, considering the Queen was on the verge of a mental breakdown herself.

along, the crown hovering above their heads, split equally down the middle. Pitt has become so pally with the Queen that he holds up her scarf: 'You are such a *gent*, Mr Pitt,' she might have gushed. But the star of the picture is a rotund lady, bouncing along at the front of the party. This is Mrs Schwellenberg, the dresser of Queen Charlotte, who has really got into the spirit of the power grab. Instead of necklaces and pins, she carries the Lord Chancellor's purse and mace and proclaims her imminent promotion: 'Take care to secure the Jewels – I have hitherto been confin'd to the wardrobe but now mean to preside at the council and with Billy's* assistance the name of Schwellenbig shall be trumpeted to the remotest corner of Rag Fair!'

The Queen, who tramples upon the Prince of Wales's feathers and coronet, which are inscribed: 'My Sons Right', appears to play the innocent pawn: 'I know nothing of the matter, I follow Billy's advice.' And Pitt, who had been dubbed King William IV by the opposition, is given his own dose of slander: 'I think myself as much entitled to be Regent as the Prince of Wales,' he announces.

*The Prospect Before Us*, Thomas Rowlandson, 1788.
Metropolitan Museum of Art, The Elisha Whittelsey Collection, The Elisha Whittelsey Fund, 1959

* William Pitt's.

But don't imagine Thomas Rowlandson would slink back to his lodgings at Poland Street to relax for Christmas with his out-of-office firmly on. And don't suppose he had grown an inch of loyalty to the cause of the Foxite–Prince of Wales allegiance. For the windows of No. 3 Piccadilly were treated to a Boxing Day gift: Rowlandson's attack on Charles James Fox himself.

## OF REASON HE CAN MAKE TREASON

This time, Rowlandson gave London the six heads of Fox, lined up like a museum display. Each head has a label: 'Out of Place in Character'; 'In Place out of Character'; 'As he might have been', with Fox wearing the cap of liberty; 'As he would have been', with Fox wearing a crown; 'As he should have been', with a decapitated head; and 'As he will be', wearing the Prince of Wales's coronet. The message? This man is a political hydra. He will drop his principles for any chance at power and is never to be trusted. Punchy stuff.

*The Political Hydra*, Thomas Rowlandson, 1788.
Metropolitan Museum of Art, The Elisha Whittelsey Collection,
The Elisha Whittelsey Fund, 1959

Three days later, on 29 December, the windows of London's print shops were ablaze with new material. Another hot-off-the-press Rowlandson vision graced the panes of No. 3 Piccadilly. Named *A Touch on the Times*, Prince George appears to be ascending the throne, though the steps that support the throne, engraved with 'Publick safety' and 'The voice of the people', are disastrously cracked. Instead of representing Liberty and Justice, Fox holds a dice box and a short, blunt weapon known as a cudgel. Pitt busies himself by trying to extinguish flames labelled 'Puppet Shew' and 'Rebellion', as a British lion cowers at his feet. And while they dance around the British constitution, the haggard figure of Commerce succumbs to the influence of gin.

*A Touch on the Times*, Thomas Rowlandson, 1788.
Yale Center for British Art

If you were to wander the ten minutes up the road to 51 New Bond Street, you might have caught the printseller Hannah Humphrey pinning up Gillray's latest piece. *Prince Pitt* showed the prime minister reaching up to snatch the crown from a high shelf. Gillray casts him as Shakespeare's Claudius, who, by murdering Hamlet's father and marrying Hamlet's mother, usurped the crown and prevented the young Hamlet from becoming king. 'A cut purse of the Empire,' the print notes, 'and the rule that from a shelf the precious diadem stole, and put it in his pocket.'

But just five minutes around the corner, on 308 Oxford Street, a work by another London printmaker, William Dent, as displayed at the shop of William Moore, named *The Wonderful Word Eater, Lately arrived from abroad*. Fox, sporting an enormous Fox tail, tramples on the cap and staff of Liberty, the sword of Justice, and on papers

*The Wonderful Word Eater*, William Dent, 1788.
© The Trustees of the British Museum

*The Word Eater*, Thomas Rowlandson, 1788.
Metropolitan Museum of Art, The Elisha Whittelsey Collection,
The Elisha Whittelsey Fund, 1959

inscribed 'Rights of Parliament', 'Bill of Rights' and 'Magna Charta'. Taking the concept of eating one's words to a literal level, Fox is seen munching through a long scroll of his past speeches: 'The Influence of the Crown has increased, is increasing and ought to be diminished …' Chomp, chomp, chomp. A description is added below, to introduce us to Fox: 'Who wonderfully outdoes all the wonderous Fire Eaters, Stone Eaters, Toad Eaters, &c &c that ever exhibited, engaging to crack, scronch, swallow and digest as many of the largest and hardest Words in the English language as will reach round Westminster, with as much facility as Demosthenes swallo'd pebbles.'

It seems likely that Rowlandson peered through the glass to inspect William Dent's work, for a day later, Londoners were treated to his next work when *The Word Eater* appeared in the window of Samuel Fores' shop.

Rowlandson had obviously heard the Picasso misquote, that 'Good artists borrow, great artists steal', for his latest print was a pretty blatant copy – and improvement – of William Dent's work. It shows Fox making his case to the Commons. As he unscrupulously uses the texts and principles of the 'Rights of the People' and 'Magna Charta' to his own advantage, the argument is that he'll use any principles to land in power. The border below describes this 'Advertisement Extraordinary':

> This is to inform the Publick that this extraordinary phenomenon is just arrived from the Continent and exhibits every day during the sittings of the House of Commons before a select Company … He eats single words and evacuates them so as to have a contrary meaning – for Example, of the Word Treason he can make Reason and of Reason he can make Treason, he can also eat whole sentences and will again produce them either with a Double Different or Contradictory meaning.

On 3 January, James Gillray offered a rebuttal. He presented Pitt as *The Vulture of the Constitution*, an enormous bird of prey, perched on the crown of King George. With mighty talons and monstrous strength, the avine Pitt bends and warps the Prince of Wales' coronet, tearing out its ostrich feathers with his teeth.

Five days later, Rowlandson produced a print which was equally damning to Pitt's reputation. Wigstead and Rowlandson must have had a flick through *The Anglo-Saxon Chronicle*, for they gave Pitt the role of Egbert, the ninth-century King of Wessex. The scene is the River Thames, and Pitt and his accomplices, the Lord Chancellor, Baron Thurlow and his cousin Henry Dundas, are on a boat trip. They've commandeered the Treasury Barge, added a new flag bearing Pitt's crest (a stork and anchor), and they are propelling themselves with whatever they can find, a spoon, a club, a mace and a cannon. They make sail for St Stephen's, the seat of the House of Commons, and behind them a chained-up Prince of Wales is being towed, futile to resist such authority.

*The Modern Egbert, or The King of Kings*, James Gillray, 1789.

With all this to-ing and fro-ing and hurling and whirling of satirical prints based firmly on hearsay and rumour, by 5 February 1789, Pitt was no longer able to put off taking action: he introduced the Regency Bill to the Commons, and by mid-February, it was ready to go to the Lords. It ruled that in the case that King George III's illness did not resolve, which seemed increasingly likely, he would need a replacement. Prince George would assume the position as Regent, ruling in his father's name.

But, in a masterstroke of Pitt's doing, the Prince's hands were pretty much tied, and his position rendered useless. He would have no powers to create new peers, nor grant pensions, nor manage the King's estates, nor meddle in the royal household. Most importantly – and crushingly – he was obliged to keep the King's present government. So, even if the Prince *did* become Regent, there was no way he could plant the Foxites in the seat of power. It was, according to Burke, 'verging on treason, for which the justice of their country would, he trust, one day overtake them and bring them to trial.'[44]

Unsurprisingly, the Prince was fuming. He wrote a letter addressed to the Cabinet and his mother, Queen Charlotte, giving his take on the fiasco. Pitt's proposed regency, he claimed, would be a 'project for producing weakness, disorder and insecurity in every branch of the administration of affairs, a project for dividing the royal family from each other, from separating the court from the state and thereby disjoining government from its natural and accustom'd support'.[45]

The Prince's powerless position was duly noted by the print-makers. They dressed him up in children's clothes, ridiculed him with an enormous headdress of feathers, and positioned a child's walking frame next to him. In one Rowlandson attack, titled *Suitable Restrictions*, as the childlike Prince reaches forward for his crown, he is restrained by Pitt, who pulls on a leash, crying: 'Hold, not so fast Georgy.' Meanwhile, the rest of the Foxites gamble for power, crying out: 'My game for a Crown.'

Pitt may have restrained the powers of Prince George, but he hadn't blocked the way for regency altogether. The country held its breath as the Prince, one of the most irresponsible, immoral and frivolous men of the day, prepared to take the helm. But change was afoot at Kew. The King's 'usual singular expression' of 'What! What! What!' had returned for the first time since his illness began.[46] Soon, the bulletins were announcing an 'advance in recovery' for the King.[47] The country burst into ecstatic celebration. Prisoners were given beer and roast beef, oxes were roasted on spits and the parties lasted three days. In the village of Brassington, Derbyshire, the locals drank through 200 gallons of ale.[48]

London was bright with illuminations: Josiah Wedgwood displayed an illumination of Hygeia, the goddess of health, in Greek Street; Sir Joseph Banks produced one of the King healed 'by the genius of Physic'[49]; and the Bank of England displayed a transparency of a 17-foot-tall Britannia. The King and Prime Minister Pitt enjoyed rapturous cheering from the public, but the people hadn't forgotten the blatant attempted coup from the opposition in a time of national crisis: Charles Fox was hissed and the Prince of Wales' coach mobbed and pelted.

By spring 1789, the King was fully recovered. The Regency Crisis was over. Yet again, Fox had missed his chance and Pitt had hung on to his position by the skin of his teeth.

As the curtains closed on this constitutional catastrophe, it was obvious that London had changed. The barrage of satire that had powered the Regency Crisis was a powerful new force that now commanded the streets of Piccadilly. How the great and powerful 'tremble at the thoughts of seeing their vices and follies attacked by the keen shafts of ridicule'.[50] Never before had graphic satire played such a formidable role in the nation's politics. Nor had such comic drollery so effectively shaped the opinions and events of a city in plight. Never again, for one moment, would Rowlandson, Gillray or Cruikshank question their destiny: these three would be the leaders of the Golden Age of British Satire.

# 5

# *Now That's What I Call Satire!: 1789*

## A FORMIDABLE FORTRESS OF FREEDOM

As these satirists settled into their flirty thirties, they were riding the wave of a booming London print trade. With vast fortunes and political reputations on the line, much like the advertising worlds of today, it was fast-paced, cut-throat and driven by money. London was replacing Paris as the throbbing heart of the print world. London's artists and publishers were becoming household names across the continent.

Everything from scientific illustrations to satire to garden design to architectural plans were flying back and forth across the Channel – some fine and expensive, some crude and cheap. A stroll through the city would provide a decent panorama of the range available: 'What is high Humour at *Wapping*, is rejected as nauseous in *the City*: What is delicate Raillery in *the City*, grows *coarse* and *intolerable* as you approach *St James's*'.[1] And at the centre of this money-making whirlpool, with printing presses turning night and day, were the sparks of Rowlandson, Gillray and Cruikshank's artistic genius.

These Bright Young Things were in a cradle of creative freedom. London was a place where you could say what you bloody well liked.

Since the Licensing Act had expired in 1695, censorship had effectively ended, and what had been considered 'heretical, seditious, schismatical, or offensive books' could now be freely published.[2] 'I know not why,' argued the Enlightenment philosopher John Locke, who lobbied for the bill, 'a man should not have liberty to print whatever he would speak; and to be answerable for the one, just as he is for the other, if he transgresses the law in either.'[3]

The final years of the seventeenth century saw the first flickers of modern Britain taking shape: the Bill of Rights in 1689, the Bank of England in 1694 and foundations for the first modern Cabinet government in 1701. The proportion of the general public who could read was growing, making publishing a profitable venture: books, newspapers, periodicals and pamphlets were sold on every street corner of London. Now, well-informed, literate citizens filled the coffee houses and salons with debate. It was a public sphere saturated with polemic. Even the theatres joined in the discussion: John Gay's *The Beggar's Opera* may have appeared to be a farce about criminality and prostitution, but it was widely understood as Tory propaganda, attacking the Whig minister Robert Walpole.

By the late eighteenth century, Britain was a bastion for freedom of speech. While French printmakers risked prosecution for slander or seditious libel, the British equivalents didn't hold back. They satirised and ridiculed the royal family with vindictive determination. Foreign visitors often noted this with amazement: 'The English do not spare themselves,' one French-born American wrote, 'their princes, their statesmen, and their churchmen, thus exhibited and hung up to ridicule, often with cleverness and humour, and of course a sort of wit.'[4]

Visitors could hardly believe that within yards of the King's palace 'a manufactory was working the press night and day, in throwing off libels against himself – his family and ministers', who 'saw themselves publicly pilloried in the window of a satirist on the spot which they frequently passed twenty times in their morning walk ... and every copper-scratcher, does the likes with impunity'.[5] One 'old general of the German Legion', was supposed to have exclaimed: 'Ah! I dell you vot – England is altogeder von libel!'[6]

Such attacks were nothing new for King George III, who took the flack from writers, satirists and poets throughout his life. Political thinkers and statesmen, such as Horace Walpole, Benjamin Franklin, Richard Brinsley Sheridan, Paul Revere, Edmund Burke and Thomas Paine, were all free and willing to spew out satiric abuses. The poets were no less determined: William Blake, Tobias Smollett and Lord Byron turned from their romantic ponderings to ridicule the King's weaknesses. It all served to confirm the notion that Britain really was a 'formidable fortress of freedom'.[7]

The late eighteenth century was also a period that saw a softening of taste and a relaxation of manners. In the 1740s, the world had been a delicate place: it was actually considered indecent to laugh. The Earl of Chesterfield, Philip Dormer Stanhope, the great statesman, diplomat and man of letters, felt it necessary to warn his son against such a mistake: 'Frequent loud laughter is the characteristic of folly and ill manners; it is the manner in which the mob express their silly joy at silly things; and they call it being merry. In my mind there is nothing so illiberal, and so ill-bred, as audible laughter.'[8] The following year, he expanded on the theory: 'Horse-play, romping, frequent loud fits of laughter, jokes, waggery, and indiscriminate familiarity, will sink both merit and knowledge into a degree of contempt. They compose a most merry fellow; and a merry fellow was never yet a respectable man.'[9]

But, now, with restricting standards somewhat relaxed, and working in a city with lax censorship regulations, artists were freer than ever before to let their imagination run wild. So, with the sky the limit, where did the ideas for these prints come from?

As Rowlandson stumbled through the streets of Covent Garden after a night of gambling, or Henry Wigstead gave stirring speeches to friends at Old Slaughter's Coffee House, or James Gillray and his printseller Hannah Humphrey spent the night playing whist over a punchbowl, somewhere in this swirling haze of life and laughter, this manic hub of drunken creativity, sparks began to whizz and zip.

More often than not, ideas for the prints were a collaborative effort. Gillray's letters are packed with him pushing new concepts to publishers, and most caricatures were discussed extensively and given the go-ahead before the final design was signed off. Once the idea was mapped out, the publisher would then commission the print from a suitable artist – just as newspaper editors might sense the mood of the nation and commission journalists to follow a certain editorial line.

The print shops were fashionable meeting places in their own right, swarming with eccentrics from the political, theatrical and literary spheres, overlapping with rival artists dropping in to deliver the latest commission and discuss the next. It was such a fluid process that one German journalist didn't bother to distinguish between the role of printmakers and printsellers, lumping 'Gillray, Fores, Holland, Rowlandson' into 'various artists', all one and the same.[10] The owners of these print shops generally acted as a publisher, too: they owned the premises and presses and employed artists and printers; it was rare that the artist would self-publish. The publishers were the real money-makers, for it was the publisher, not the artist, who owned the rights to reproduction and reprints.

The London caricaturists' 'season' was mainly winter and spring. They produced less in the summer and autumn months, as Parliament was not in session and any celebrity worth caricaturing was enjoying the sea air at Weymouth or Brighton.

London's print trade had traditionally flourished in the shadows of St Paul's Cathedral. But as the likes of Royal Academy-educated Gillray began raising the quality of output, print shops started to attract a wealthier clientele. During the 1780s, shops were opening up in the smartest areas of London: Mayfair and St James's.

The pioneering leaders of the publishing scene were three remarkable individuals: Samuel Fores, William Holland and Hannah

Humphrey. Each owned their own print shop, spitting distance from one another. From these mighty fortresses, they could lure the most fashionable and politically active customers, perusing the streets with cash ready to splash.

Samuel Fores was a bookseller's son. In 1783, he founded a print business at No. 3 Piccadilly near the Haymarket – which today looks out at the iconic Piccadilly Circus advertising screen – called the Caricature Warehouse, specialising in hand-coloured, singly issued satirical prints or caricatures. Fores was full of brilliant ideas, fiercely competitive and a man of strong passion – he fathered fourteen children.[11]

Fores' great rival came in the form of William Holland. Holland was a 'man of genius' and a passionate thesp who adored Shakespeare.[12] The image on his shop's street sign was a picture of David Garrick performing Richard III, probably a copy of Hogarth's original painting. When not selling prints and pamphlets, he 'wrote many popular songs, and a volume of poetry, besides being the author of the pointed and epigrammatic words which accompanied most of his caricatures'.[13] He was in business in July 1783 at 66 Drury Lane, and by the end of 1786, he had moved to 50 Oxford Street.

According to a large watercolour by Richard Newton, the walls of Holland's Oxford Street establishment were covered from floor to ceiling in prints, watercolours and drawings – just like the Exhibition Room of the Royal Academy. And admiring this display of japes and jocularity were society ladies, City tradesmen, young bucks, clergymen, officers and children – some gossiping, some laughing, some examining prints through a glass and some examining each other through a glass.

There was a third horse in this race: the formidable printseller Hannah Humphrey, who ran a 'successful business selling her own publications alone'.[14] Perhaps business was in her blood, for her three siblings, William, George and Elizabeth, were also successful in the trade of luxury 'curiosities'.

William Humphrey started out as a publisher, giving Gillray his first few commissions, but soon found more success dealing prints. William 'carried on this trade for many years with great success' but changed tack slightly 'and imported more curious English Portraits than any other individual'.[15] While Hannah and William paved the way in the art world, their sister Elizabeth ran a shop on behalf of her husband, the mineralogist Adolarius Jacob Forster. Adolarius had clients across the most glittering palaces in Europe.* And George Humphrey was an expert international dealer in – wait for it – *shells*.

Hannah Humphrey began her career as a printseller on St Martin's Lane, moving to 18 Old Bond Street in 1779. It was from here that she began to commission and publish some of Gillray's greatest works.

These three print shop owners were mighty rivals who competed directly and forced each other into bigger and better marketing campaigns. William Holland boldly claimed that 'In Holland's Caricature Exhibition Rooms may be seen, the largest Collection of humorous Prints and Drawings in Europe'.[16] While Fores claimed that his 'Grand Caricatura Exhibition' was 'the most complete Collection … Ever exposed to public View in this Kingdom'.[17] Fores even brought in a few lurid attractions to get the punters through the door: he exhibited the 'head and hand of the unfortunate Count Struenzee, who was beheaded at Denmark'.[18†]

Selling prints could be a lucrative business: publishers would jostle for position, sharp elbows out. Copyright law did not exist as we know it today. Hogarth had tried to combat the market of fakes, pushing through the Engraving Copyright Act of 1734, but there was nothing to stop printsellers adapting concepts and pinching

* He died suddenly while negotiating an enormous deal with Tsar Alexander I, worth 50,000 roubles.

† This was probably a plaster cast.

elements from one another's work, as with Rowlandson's blatant copy of William Dent's *Wonderful Word Eater*.

On several occasions, the leading printsellers (I'm looking at you, Samuel Fores), published pretty similar versions of recent Gillray prints that Hannah Humphrey had produced. Fores went unpunished, most likely because Gillray's prints were such high quality that none of Hannah Humphrey's fashionable customers would be seen dead with a *fake* Gillray. 'Because a caricature is not the kind of thing one would care to go to law about,' one foreign visitor observed, 'Gillray puts up with this piracy, without attempting to protect his property.'[19]

## BACK TO THE COPPER PLATE

So, with the concept approved and the commission signed off, how were these designs made?

The artists needed to be able to capture a likeness of every big name in politics and society. This meant making sketches of them from life, on location. The best place to find politicians was the House of Commons itself, where they were sitting ducks for satirists to get a close-up view of their victims. At this time, the House of Commons was in what had once been St Stephen's Chapel, a richly decorated medieval chapel built by King Henry III to compete with the Sainte-Chapelle in Paris. After Henry VIII moved the royal family out of the Palace of Westminster, his son Edward transformed it into a meeting place for the Commons and the chapel had been used by Parliament since 1547.

By the late eighteenth century, it didn't betray much of its ecclesiastical past, having been extensively remodelled by the likes of Christopher Wren and James Wyatt. The walls were whitewashed or covered by oak panelling, original furnishings were cleared away, and the stained-glass medieval windows were either replaced with plain glass or walled up with smaller windows cut into the new stonework.

The Speaker's Chair was placed on the altar steps* and the debating chamber was about fifteen by ten metres in floor space, two storeys high, with galleries fixed to three of its walls. A false ceiling was installed to help to improve acoustics and a ventilation lantern added in the ceiling to cool the place down. The walls were reduced in thickness to accommodate extra seating required since the 1707 Acts of Union.

A Strangers' Gallery provided a space for up to 120 male visitors to watch debates. Access was granted by the payment of a fee to the doorkeeper or a written 'order' from an MP. About a third of these seats were filled by the press, whose proprietors paid a fee each session. And later on, ladies could also watch the debates by poking their head through one of the gaps in the ventilation lantern in the ceiling, high above the chandelier in the middle of the chamber. The Anglo-Irish novelist Maria Edgeworth recorded the experience:

> What seemed like a sentry box of deal boards and old chairs placed around it: on these we got and stood and peeped over the top of the boards. Saw the large chandelier with lights blazing, immediately below: a grating of iron across veiled the light so that we could look down and beyond it: we saw half the table with the mace lying on it and papers, and by peeping hard two figures of clerks at the further end, but no eye could see the Speaker or his chair – only his feet; his voice and terrible 'ORDER' was soon heard. We could see part of the treasury bench and opposition in their places – the tops of their heads, profiles and gestures perfectly.[20]

It was worth a view, even from the ventilation lantern. For parliamentary debates were far more theatrical than today. Arms flailed with grandiose gestures, mighty statesmen welled up with tears,

* This could be the origin of today's tradition of bowing to the Speaker.

objects were thrown across the floor. MPs were even known to make a point of eating oranges or cracking nuts as diversionary tactics.[21]

Perhaps such exploits come as no surprise, considering that the speakers, who debated well into the small hours, were powered through the pontifications by vast amounts of wine. This was an age when wealthy men might expect to sink six bottles of claret in one evening, totalling about 40 units of alcohol.[22] And Pitt and Sheridan, preferring port, drank about 60 units of alcohol each on a daily basis.[23]

Luckily for the likes of Gillray, Rowlandson and Cruikshank, the male-only Strangers' Gallery provided a clear view to sketch their hiccupping politicians and capture a rough portrait. They would then head home, work up the sketches and begin copying them onto a metal plate for the etching to begin.

## ETCHING AND ENGRAVING

There are stories of Gillray working like a mad professor – furiously scraping directly onto copper plate in a frenzy, his hands bloodied from cuts and copper shavings flying everywhere. Sadly, these claims have been disproved by the survival of piles of preparatory drawings and sketches, many of which are gathering dust in the great archives of the British Museum, the Frick Gallery, the New York Public Library and the Fitzwilliam Museum in Cambridge.

These sketches, however, do betray a manic exuberance. Enormous zigzags, frantic whirls, blotches, scribbles and crossings-out fill the pages, putting the pen through its paces with every conceivable type of line. Sometimes a grid adds order to the chaos, sometimes brown ink gives depth to the black. Sometimes notes give extra details; the Earl of Sandwich was annotated with 'White Hair', 'Black Pallor', 'Short and thick'.[24]

It's likely that grid lines would be added to scale up or scale down a sketch, especially with prints of more complex figures. Once the design was finalised, there were two ways to make a print, both using a metal plate. These were variations of the intaglio process, that is, when the ink sinks into sections that are cut away from the plate. It's the opposite of relief printing, where the sections that are cut away don't pick up the ink. The design would be transferred onto a copper plate and carved out using a sharp metal tool, making marks and notches and nicks. The plate was inked to fill the pits and furrows of the artist's design and then wiped, so that the rest of the surface was clean. This ink-filled copper plate would be placed face-up on the bed of a printing press and covered with a damp piece of paper. When pressure was applied to the paper by a roller, the damp paper took up the ink and a print was created. This could be repeated until the metal plate clogged up.

This was the basic process, but there were all sorts of ways to make these marks on the copper plate. One of the most common techniques was using a burin, an engraver's principal tool. A burin has a very sharp V-shaped end. Heavy pressure creates a wide and deep furrow, while lighter pressure produces a thinner, lighter line. And these more delicate lines might be used to add finer spidery touches, add emphasis or build up wispy hairs.

Another option was to use a drypoint needle. This tool looks just like a modern pencil, with a metal point replacing the soft graphite. The artists used it just like a pencil too. The furrow it created was shallower than the engraved line of a burin, so less ink would be held, and the printed line would be lighter.

The drypoint needle was generally secondary to the burin, as it was used for shading or emphasis. The ink is held not so much by the furrow itself as by the raised edge – the sides of the furrow – and this could be controlled by the angle at which the needle was held against the plate.

Now we have a line drawing, but what about areas of tone? These could be created by cross-hatching or even random squiggly lines. Dots or stipples of various patterns and density could create all sorts of textures. Gillray referred to stippling as his 'common dotting manner'.[25] Purpose-created tools would speed up the process, many of which look like nightmarish Victorian dental equipment. They were held like a pen, with different attachments on the pointy end. You could attach a rolling tool, which had a little wheel with dots on. As you rolled your way across the plate it would leave behind a trail of regular dots and lines.

This type of intaglio is engraving. It's a physical process, where sharp tools cut lines directly into the metal plate. The second type of intaglio is etching, a chemical process, where lines are burnt into the surface of the metal plate using acid. A copper plate was also used for this process but, unlike engraving, the plate was covered with a darkened, acid-resistant wax 'ground'. When the design was complete, the copper plate was given a bath – in acid!

The acid would 'bite' into the plate where the copper had been exposed by the etching needle, leaving a groove. The areas that were still covered in wax remained untouched. The thickness of the resulting etched lines would depend on the width of the needle used and the length of acid-dunking – so it was important to not fall asleep with your plate in the bath. Five minutes would do the trick. Once the wax was washed off and the plate was inked up, practice prints might reveal gaps in the design. Perhaps the lines were too thin here, or the acid hadn't bitten in there. A drypoint needle could pick these up until the artist was satisfied.

The result of these engraving and etching processes was a monochrome print. But more shading could be added with a further process, aquatint. The artist would apply a resin to the copper plate as either a powder or liquid. It was heated to bond with the plate, creating a grainy, textured surface. When the plate was dipped in acid, the acid penetrated between the grains, resulting in a large area of shading. The resin would need to be applied either right at the start or just after the basic design had been etched, and multiple layers could be used to build up different shades. So, there was lots of room for error: it took a decent amount of experience to predict how the colour would land. Sometimes, artists might work over or 'ground' the copper plates using a semi-circular fine-toothed tool, called a 'rocker'. This would create a half-tone image, known as a mezzotint.

Now we have a pretty complex monochrome print, with all kinds of lines and shading. But what about a pop of colour? Not all prints were coloured, as it was an expensive process. Once the paper, typically ten by fourteen inches* had been engraved or etched and then dried, they might be glitzed up with shades of Venetian red, ultramarine or Egyptian blue. Prints were hand-painted in inks and watercolours, often by apprentices with instruction from the artist.

The method was constantly improving. The colouring stage became less time-consuming once ready-prepared cakes of watercolour pigment were available to buy in the 1780s, and by 1790, newly invented woven paper was preferred for its smoother surface, which took a watercolour wash better than the ridged laid paper. That's not to say they ended up all the same; sometimes prints were coloured later on. George Humphrey was producing collections of Gillray's work for nearly five years after his death, presumably with whatever zany colour scheme he desired. So, while multiple copies of one print might survive today, the different versions have different colour schemes, depending on who coloured it.

One way for publishers and artists to keep rights of publication was to engrave the publication date, the publisher's print shop, the location of the print shop and who came up with the design. Of course, they used this as another opportunity to mock the Royal Academy, signing off with Latin terms of academic convention. Here is a handy guide:

* About the size of an A3 piece of paper.

A.P. Artist's proof
B.A.T., Bon à tirer: Proof print approved by artist and ready to be handed over to the master printer
Cael., caelavit: Engraved by
Cum privilegio: Privilege to publish from some authority
Del., delt., delin., delineavit: Drawn by
Disig., designavit: Designed by
Divulg., divulgavit: Published by
Eng., engd.: Engraved by
Exc., excud., excudit: Printed by or published by
F., fac., fec., fect., fecit, faciebat: Made by
H.C., Hors commerce: Not for commercial sale
Imp., impressit: Printed by
Inc,. incidit, incidebat: Incised or engraved by
Inv., invenit, inventor: Designed by or originally drawn by
Lith., litho., lithog.: Lithographed by
Pins., pinxit: Painted by
Scrip., scripsit: Text engraved by
Sc., sculp., sculpt., sculpsit: Image engraved by.[26]

The art of engraving and etching and colouring was complex, and often each stage was completed by a different expert: the artist providing the original design, then the plate printer, engraver and colourer. Fast-forward to December 2021, and I decided to try my hand as an etcher after booking on to a Covent Garden etching course. It took a day to create a postcard-sized print and I was reprimanded several times along the way: 'No, Alice, only a tiny bit of Brasso, that's far too much,' or 'Is there a reason you're using a drypoint needle already?' or 'Please wear protective eyewear if operating the acid bath.'

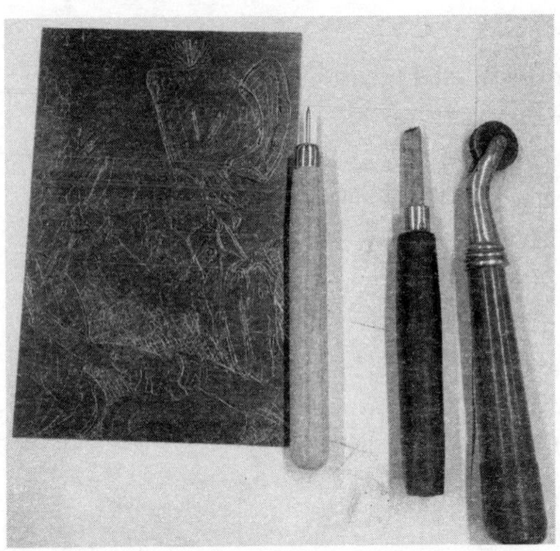

Here are the tools I used to mark up the metal plate.

Here is my original design (traced from Gillray), the metal plate and the final prints. The first print was quite faint, so I carved into the plate again to darken some lines. Unfortunately, one careless slip left Mr Pitt with a moustache.

It was incredibly tricky, complex and frustrating, and I realised that any etching lessons taught at the Academy Schools would have come in pretty handy. Henry Angelo, the fencing friend of Thomas Rowlandson, thought Gillray was a dab hand at the whole thing:

> The facility with which [Gillray] composed his subjects, and the rapidity with which he etched them, astonished those who were eye-witnesses of his powers. This faculty was early developed – he seemed to perform all his operations without an effort.[27]

And Angelo couldn't help but mention one behind-the-scenes anecdote about Gillray's work:

> Many years ago, [Gillray] had an apartment in a court in Holborn. A commercial agent had a commission to get a satirical design etched, but he had repeatedly called in the absence of the artist. He lived westward, and on his way to the city called again, and found Gillray at home.
>
> 'You have lost a patron,' said he; 'you are always out.'
>
> 'How – what – what is your object?' said the artist.
>
> 'I want this subject, drawn and etched,' said the commercialist; 'but now it is too late.'
>
> 'When is it wanted?'
>
> 'Why, to-morrow?'
>
> 'It shall be done.'
>
> 'Impossible, Gillray!'
>
> 'Where are you going?'
>
> 'Onward to the Bank.'
>
> 'When do you return?'
>
> 'At four o'clock.' (It was now eleven.)
>
> 'I'll bet you a bowl of punch it shall be completed, etched, and bitten in, before that time.'
>
> 'Done!'

> The plate was finished, it contained many figures, the parties were mutually pleased, and the affair ended in a drunken bout at a tavern, at the employer's expense.[28]

The finished copper plates were put through a press. Many print shops had a rolling press in-house, which would print trial proofs of finished and semi-finished plates, and sometimes print on demand for customers. Printsellers aimed at around 500 prints for a first edition.

Completed prints would be displayed in the multi-paned bow windows of printseller shops, listed in their catalogue, and adverts put in the papers. As soon as a print went up, uproar broke out in the streets, as everyone wanted a look in at the latest hot take. Soon the wealthier punters came trotting over the threshold. As the customer perused, the printseller schmoozed: 'An excellent choice, sir, you have the most exquisite taste.' In 1790, the typical prices for a folio mezzotint (ten by fourteen inches) were one shilling for a plain print and two shillings for coloured.[29] These could be bought in the shop or delivered via mail order.

Prints were bundled together in a collection, and in the same year these bound folios might be five guineas for plain and seven guineas for coloured.[30]* The publishers bundled together their bestsellers, just as records labels do today: *Now That's What I Call Satire!: 1789*, or *James Gillray: The Best of the 1780s*. These were often lent out for the evening for guests to flick through at balls or parties; Samuel Fores charged a fee of two shillings and sixpence. A deposit of a pound was required, no doubt as a ballast against red-wine stains.[31]

The shops relied on a steady stream of wealthy regulars popping in to browse through the latest prints. From 1803, Hannah Humphrey formally supplied the Prince of Wales with satiric delights.[32] Despite being a regular victim of Gillray's sharp wit, the Prince could appreciate the man's japes. In a single year, he bought 121 Gillray prints,[33]

* Between £300 to £600 in today's money.

*Very Slippy Weather*, James Gillray, 1808.
PD-US, Library of Congress

and on his death in 1830, there were 2,750 caricatures recorded in the royal library.[34] King George was also a fan: 'The King was frequently incensed, sometimes gratified, and generally inclined to be amused by the sallies of Gillray … His caricatures are said to have been regularly conveyed to the court circle at Buckingham House, Windsor, and Weymouth.'[35]

Once the prints were safely home, they might be kept in cabinets, shallow drawers in tables, or sometimes leather-bound portfolios to be brought out when guests came over. Many were bought to be displayed on walls: 'When framed and glazed they make a handsome appearance and Fashionable Furniture.'[36] Soon the walls of dressing rooms, bedrooms, closets, small dining rooms, billiard rooms, corridors and even staircases were adorned in satire.

From cornice to skirting board were rows of prints, pasted to sheets of pasteboard, varnished and made into wall hangings and screens. And the gaps between the prints were filled with all sorts of ornamental frills: floral swags, bows, ribbons, chains, urns and festoons. Sometimes the paper frames themselves provided the illusion of the prints being hung from the walls, in a triumph of *trompe l'œil*. For expensive collections, curtains were drawn across the walls to protect the prints from light damage.

It started a crafting boom, becoming a hobby enjoyed by young ladies, who might enjoy pasting their collections of prints to the walls of a small sitting or dressing room. They could purchase paper frames, ribbon swags and other decorative paper embellishments from the print shops, too.

Print shops also sold to commercial clients. It was common for shops to swap stock, sell prints from other shops, and give discounts to merchants, provincial shopkeepers and foreign dealers, who would disperse the London prints far and wide, or paste them on the walls of taverns, coffee houses and barbershops.

After the first print run, the etched plates tended to get clogged up and needed cleaning or touching up with a burin. If there was still demand, the plates could be reworked or even another plate recreated. These plates were probably stacked up in backrooms in great piles, and if the print shop ever went out of business, competitors lunged in to get their hands on them. They might buy up the plates and start a new print run or print the occasional impression if a customer particularly requested it.

This was the never-ending cycle that propelled the careers of Rowlandson, Gillray and Cruikshank. These artists brought the genius, certainly, but they were only one cog in the print shop machine. Behind every pop star is a determined agent: behind every satirist was a savvy printseller, who could sense the shifts in public opinion and commission accordingly. It was the printsellers who got the pieces printed on time, and shared them with the public – without which, the art was rendered powerless. William Holland, Samuel Fores and Hannah Humphrey were, in short, the ones who made it all happen. By the end of the 1780s, they each commanded a tightly run ship, with a well-oiled engine, spinning quicker and slicker as each year passed. They pressed on, full steam ahead, ready to take on the most tempestuous of seas.

# *Act II*

# 6

# *The Foulest and Most Atrocious Deed*

## A LIGHT STRUCK OUT

On 14 March 1790, a British naval captain returned to England after a three-year expedition. The trip had been an unequivocal disaster, and the captain should have been long dead. But, against the odds, he had survived, and when he stepped foot on home turf, he brought with him a thrilling, dramatic story of endurance.

In the autumn of 1787, the captain and his crew had set off in a sloop named *Bounty*. Their destination was the South Seas, and they were tasked with transferring breadfruit from Tahiti to the Caribbean, to supply food for the enslaved people working on British plantations there. The captain, William Bligh, reported that one night, his men 'came into my Cabin while I was a Sleep, and seizing me, holding naked Bayonets at my Breast, tied my Hands behind my back, and threatened instant destruction if I uttered a word'.[1] Bligh and eighteen loyal crewmen were set adrift in a small boat, at the mercy of the vast ocean. They successfully navigated almost 4,000 miles to the nearest settlement, and eventually Captain Bligh made it back to England in one piece. History would know it as the Mutiny on the *Bounty*.

When Captain Bligh finally returned to London in 1790, he may well have found a few things had changed. As he prepared himself for an audience with the King, he might have noticed young ladies avoiding him in the streets. Was it his haggard appearance? Or the smell of a salty sea dog? Actually, it wasn't personal. For over the previous two years, there had been a string of terrible attacks. Over 50 women, many of them wealthy, had reported being followed by a large man, who would stab them with a knife or spike, which was attached to his knees.

Sometimes, women would be asked to smell a bunch of flowers and then be suddenly, horrifically, spiked in the face. The crimes of the London Monster, as he came to be known, sent paranoia through every warren and alleyway of the metropolis. Women began to wear copper pans over their petticoats and the No Monster Club was founded (members would attach club pins to their lapels to reassure ladies of their innocence). By June 1790, a man was finally arrested and sentenced to six years in Newgate Prison.

Had Bligh nestled down into a coffee house and scanned the papers, he might have been drawn to a new hot topic of conversation: a book entitled *The Interesting Narrative of the Life of Olaudah Equiano, or Gustavus Vassa, the African*, which had been published the year before. Written by Olaudah Equiano, a man who had once been enslaved, it was fast becoming a bestseller, marked out for the quality of its imagery, description and literary style.*

Perhaps the papers would have picked up on Josiah Wedgwood, who had spent four years painstakingly trying to duplicate one of the treasures of antiquity, the Portland Vase. Finally, in the summer of 1790, his jasperware triumph was displayed to the public on Greek Street, Soho – an exhibition so popular that ticket numbers were capped at a whopping 1,900. There were also reports of the new Forth

* It went through nine editions in Equiano's lifetime, and it was published as far and wide as Russia, Holland and the United States.

and Clyde Canal and of James Wyatt's engineering triumph: Syon Park now boasted the first cast-iron footbridge in Britain.

The summer also saw another election hustings. This time it was Pitt leading a coalition against a faction of Whigs led by Charles James Fox and the Duke of Portland (the namesake of Wedgwood's Portland Vase). Yet again, Pitt would be the victor. But the veterans of Old Slaughter's Coffee House had bigger debates to mull over than what was happening in Westminster.

In 1789, Londoners had received dramatic news from across the Channel. *The Times* reported: 'The disputes which have for some time past convulsed this neighbouring kingdom, have at length been brought to a crisis, which no man could have foreseen or supposed. The relation of what Paris has been during last week, fills the mind with horror ...'[2]

Paris' Bastille prison had been attacked by a mob. 'No personal safety,' the papers declared, 'no protection of property, and the lives of the first men in the State in such momentary danger, as to oblige them to fly their country, and seek an asylum in this land of liberty. Such is the picture of Paris at this instant; and rebellion has so widely spread, that no one can judge where it will have an end.'[3]

The events in France provided much to ruminate over. Was this the French version of Britain's Glorious Revolution of 1688 or of America's upheaval in the previous decade? Were those who stormed the Bastille acting in the same vein as Oliver Cromwell all those years before, throwing aside the feudal order? Were their cries of '*Liberté, égalité, fraternité*' part of the inevitable rise of freedom and enlightenment?

Charles James Fox seemed to think so. In response to the Storming of the Bastille on 14 July, he declared: 'How much the greatest event it is that ever happened in the world! and how much the best!'[4] He told the Commons that the new French constitution, which had been drawn up with the help of Thomas Jefferson, was 'the most stupendous and glorious edifice of liberty, which had been erected on the foundation of human integrity in any time or country'.[5]

Fox wasn't the only one to welcome the early stages of this French experiment: a wave of optimism swept through the country. For William Wordsworth and Samuel Taylor Coleridge, these were the first steps towards a more democratic society, the realisation of Romantic ideals of individualism and human potential. Committees and societies popped up all over the place to argue for constitutional reform. Let's get rid of rotten boroughs, they petitioned. And let's call time on this corrupt, corpulent government, they argued.

Sensing this growing momentum, the printsellers supplied a good deal of sympathetic material. William Holland responded to the fall of the Bastille with a print labelling the events in Paris as *The Downfall of Despotism.* Gillray made an etching of a painting, titled *The Triumph of Liberty in the Freeing of the Bastille, dedicated to the French Nation by their respectful admirers James Gillray and Robert Wilkinson.*

In November 1789, a Welshman named Richard Price weighed in on the debate. He saw the events in France as the glorious dawn of a new era. His published sermon revealed a penchant for the dramatic:

> Behold all ye friends of freedom ... behold the light you have struck out, after setting America free, reflected to France and there kindled into a blaze that lays despotism in ashes and warms and illuminates Europe. I see the ardour for liberty catching and spreading; ... the dominion of kings changed for the dominion of laws, and the dominion of priests giving way to the dominion of reason and conscience.[6]

But not everyone shared Fox's enthusiasm for Price's vision. Least of all, one of Fox's erstwhile most loyal allies, Edmund Burke. Burke had a niggling dread that couldn't be put to bed that disaster lay ahead. His *Reflections on the Revolution in France*, published in

November 1790, tore apart Price's sermon and predicted the collapse of civilisation in France and the outbreak of European war.

It was another vicious public spat, and Gillray turned to the copper plate to make his mischief. His take on the events came in the form of an enormous nose emerging from a billowing cloud. A nose with spectacles and googly eyes invading a miniature room to 'smell out a rat'. The nasal intrusion belonged to Edmund Burke, the rat being Richard Price. From Gillray's print, we can presume Price was a man of incredible stoicism for he seems relatively unfazed by this nightmarish nasal intrusion.

But Burke's nose is accompanied by two hands brandishing the symbols of his belief: the British crown and a Christian cross. 'Have you forgotten these? Where is your conscience, man?' Burke seems to be saying. For Price is surrounded by his latest works, their titles altered by Gillray. On his desk is a tract defending the 'Benefits of Anarchy, Regicide, Atheism'. At his feet lies an open book: 'Treatise on the ill

*Smelling out a Rat*, James Gillray, 1790.
PD-US, Library of Congress

effects of Order & Government in Society, and on the absurdity of serving God, & honoring the King'. And framed above Price's head is a scene entitled the 'Death of Charles I or, the Glory of Great Britain'.

As Gillray takes us on this psychedelic dive into Richard Price's nightmares, Burke himself would soon be tormented, for a new best-seller was in the works. It was the brainchild of Thomas Paine, an English-born American, famous for causing trouble with his political writing. His pamphlets in America (*Common Sense*, published in 1776 and *The American Crisis*, published in 1776–83) had sent shockwaves through patriots, inspiring the original move to declare independence.

And now Paine was applying his power of persuasion to the readers of Great Britain. As an 'Answer to Mr Burke's Attack on the French Revolution', Paine published *The Rights of Man* in two parts; the first in March 1791; the second in February 1792. It would become one of the most important political books ever written.

Paine put forward the idea that a government that was truly based on justice should support both the natural rights of mankind, including life, liberty, free speech and freedom of conscience, and also civil rights relating to security and protection. He pointed out practical injustices, such as the fact that only a fraction of the people who paid taxes were entitled to vote. With a vision ahead of his time, and using complex calculations, he showed how taxes could be reimagined to provide social welfare, 'not as a matter of grace and favour, but of right'[7]; taxes that would provide education, child benefit, pensions for the elderly and relief for the poor.

Most dangerously, Paine called for radical revolution, defaming the state of British government: 'A banditti of ruffians overrun a country, and lay it under contributions. Their power being thus established, the chief of the band contrived to lose the name of robber in that of Monarch; and hence the origin of Monarchy and Kings.'[8]

Paine renounced any profits from the book; he was on a serious mission to circulate it as widely and as cheaply as possible, to reach a larger, less wealthy readership. This was not an exercise in political theory and philosophy. This was a clarion call to British radicals to seize the day. Copies were read aloud in inns and coffee houses. The second part, published in February 1792, sold 200,000 copies, and by the time of Paine's death in 1809, the number had reached 1.5 million.*

Paine's success presented a serious threat to Pitt's government. While Paine was away, visiting his aunt in Kent, his publisher, J.S. Jordan of 166 Fleet Street, was prosecuted for seditious libel. Most likely fearing for his life, Jordan pleaded guilty. On 21 May 1792, the same writ was issued against Paine himself, and two days later, Gillray unleashed his attack.

This great political writer was reduced to nothing but 'Tommy Paine, the little American taylor'. Gillray made him ragged and grotesque, belittled by a large pair of shears attached to his waist and a cocked French hat labelled 'Vive la Liberty'. He is measuring up a gargantuan crown with a tape measure 'for a new Pair of Revolution-Breeches', reeling off an entire soliloquy of his own. 'Fathom & a half! Fathom & a half!' puny Paine cries out, 'Poor Tom! ah! mercy upon me! that's more by half than my poor Measure will ever be able to reach!'

But there was a surge of support for 'Tommy Paine', materialising in organised action. Thomas Hardy, a shoemaker, and John Thelwall, a silk merchant, took matters into their own hands. They set up the London Corresponding Society, a radical political reform movement championing Paine's ideas. Soon enough, momentum was growing, with societies being set up all across the country, especially popular in industrial towns that had little representation in Parliament.

When the news came from across the Channel that, in the heat of August 1792, Parisians had stormed the Tuileries Palace and brought an end to Louis XVI's power, the British radicals must have been exhilarated. Finally, it seemed France was on its way to a constitutional monarchy. What would be next? Would it be voting rights?

* I look forward to similar sales figures for this book.

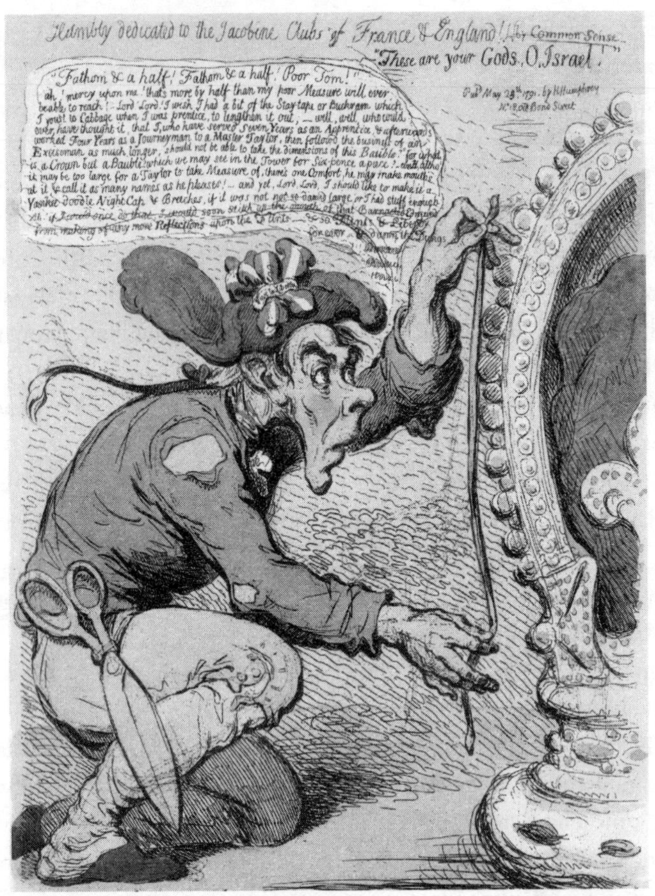


*The Rights of Man; –or– Tommy Paine, the little American taylor, taking the measure of the Crown, for a new Pair of Revolution-Breeches*, James Gillray, 1791.



Or a reform of the justice system? Such hopes were soon dimmed by further developments in the French capital. Gripped with fear that foreign and royalist armies were about to attack Paris, and fearful that the imprisoned Swiss mercenaries would break free and join them, France's governing body, the Legislative Assembly, called for volunteers to gather on the Champ de Mars.

On 2 September 1792, at 1pm, the Minister of Justice, Georges Danton, fired up the braying crowd. He asked for their help: 'We ask that any one refusing to give personal service or to furnish arms shall be punished with death ... The [bell] we are about to ring ... sounds the charge on the enemies of our country.'[9]

At 2.30pm, the crowd dispersed with an extraordinary power. The French government had given them permission to finish the life of anyone who wasn't deemed to have toed the line. The Parisian streets, which Rowlandson and Angelo had frolicked through not many years before, became the scene of four days of bloodshed. The city was convulsed with a wild, devilish madness befitting Bosch's visions of hell. It was known to history as the September Massacres.

## WAKE ME UP WHEN SEPTEMBER 1792 ENDS

Back in London, the papers covered the events with grim detail. On Monday 10 September 1792, *The Times* reported:

> The streets of Paris, strewed with the carcases of the mangled victims, are become so familiar to the sight, that they are passed by and trod on without any particular notice. The mob think no more of killing a fellow-creature, who is not even an object of suspicion, than wanton boys would of killing a cat or a dog ... In the massacre last week, every person who had the appearance of a gentleman, whether stranger or not, was run through the body with a pike.[10]

Londoners were also told about the Princess de Lamballe, one of the close friends of the queen, Marie Antoinette:

> When the mob went to the prison *de la Force*, where the Royal attendants were chiefly confined, the Princess De Lamballe went down on her knees to implore a suspension of her fate for 24 hours.

> This was at first granted, until a second mob more ferocious than the first, forced her apartments, and decapitated her. The circumstances which attended her death were such as makes humanity shudder, and which decency forbids us to repeat: – Previous to her death, the mob offered her every insult. Her thighs were cut across, and her bowels and heart torn from her, and for two days her mangled body was dragged through the streets.[11]

The following day, on Tuesday 11 September 1792, the *St James's Chronicle* reported:

> A gentleman who left Paris yesterday week assures us that the terrible accounts detailed in the London Papers of the dreadful cruelties transacted in that unfortunate capital, so far from being exaggerated, come very short of the truth. That 6,000 people were absolutely murdered by one Jury of Twelve, sitting in one of the prisons. That three large wagons were employed without intermission for six and thirty hours, in carrying the dead bodies out of Paris, and throwing them promiscuously into a pit dug for the purpose.[12]

On Wednesday 12 September 1792:

> At the Place Dauphin, the mob had made a fire, and before it several men, women, and children were roasted alive. The countess PERIGNAN with her two daughters, the daughters first, and the mother after, were stripped of their cloaths, washed with oil, and roasted alive, while the mob were singing and dancing round the fire, and amusing themselves with their cries and sufferings.[13]

And it seemed the Parisians were even turning to cannibalism: 'The mob brought six priests to the same fire and then cutting some flesh from the body, ordered the Priests to eat it.'[14]

Londoners were, as I'm sure you are, in disbelief: sickened and horrified by the harrowing descent of a neighbouring European capital. It seemed that this was not a revolution which championed Enlightenment principles and rational thought after all. Surely the early supporters would backtrack? Thomas Paine had no intention of doing so. As an elected member of the French National Convention, he was tasked with the monumental job of writing a new constitution. On 13 September 1792, Paine crossed the Channel. He never set foot on English soil again.

With rumours of French atrocities spreading like wildfire through the streets of London, there wasn't much need for the satirists to exaggerate. The following week, on 20 September 1792, Hannah Humphrey may have grimaced as she pinned up *Un petit Soupér, a la Parisiènne: – Or – A Family of Sans-Culottes refreshing, after the fatigues of the day*.

If Gillray had admired the French revolutionaries in 1790, after the bloodshed, this was no longer the case. Perhaps it was the chilling

*Un petit Soupér, a la Parisiènne*, James Gillray, 1792.

newspaper reports, the growing power of Jacobin extremists, or his Moravian cynicism that turned him. Either way, he invited his viewers to be a *une mouche sur le mur* in the ramshackle lodgings of a French revolutionary family. These *sans-culottes** (whose identity is betrayed by an actual lack of breeches altogether) are feasting. Not on raw horse mince, but on the legs and arms and heart and lungs of an aristocrat. It's a scene from a horror film: demonic adults with sharpened teeth stuff themselves with the limbs, organs, eyes and ears of their victims. Three small children madly devour a bucket of intestines, and behind an old hag roasts a child's body on a spit, her eyes popping with mad desire. Body parts are stored in the rafters, ready to be consumed, and outside are the latest victims of the Paris massacres, and the next meal for these monsters. The head of this gruesome family, wearing a *bonnet rouge* and *cocarde tricolore*, sits on a sack inscribed '*Propriété de la Nation*'. The crown, sceptre and mitre of French royalty spill out onto the floor, which is splattered with the blood of the French people.

As Londoners reeled in shock at Gillray's gruesome print, the revolution in France was galloping on. The following day, 21 September 1792, the *Proclamation de l'abolition de la royauté* was announced. The Bourbon dynasty, which had ruled since 1589, was abolished, giving birth to the first French Republic, with the National Convention, a single-chamber assembly, taking the wheel.

In the autumn of 1792, Britons held their breath. Not only was the French Revolution spiralling wildly out of control, the new

* The term '*sans-culottes*' literally means 'without breeches' in French. It was first used in the 1790s as a term for members of the radical, militant French lower classes who supported the revolution. During the Reign of Terror it was also a term adopted by educated classes to demonstrate their patriotism. The costume of a typical sans-culotte was made up of long trousers (*pantalons*) instead of the silk breeches (*culottes*) of the upper classes. They also had a short jacket and the red cape of liberty. It was imagery that would be used with gusto by the British satirists.

Republican government had ambitions to spread its mantra, infecting Europe with its ideas of liberty. 'Grant fraternity and assistance to all people who wish to recover their liberty,'[15] the generals were instructed. Was this really fraternity? Was this really assistance? Or did the Republican government just give permission to invade any nation that didn't play to their tune? Across the Channel, it appeared more like a blatant declaration of war.

As Pitt sent the militia to Sheffield, Yarmouth and Shields to pre-empt any potential uprisings, Paine continued to antagonise the government by publishing works to fire up the Corresponding Societies. In turn, the government set a date for Paine's trial: he would be tried *in absentia* on Tuesday 18 December 1792. In the countdown to the date, Paine and his lawyer were targeted by vicious personal attacks: an effigy was burnt in Exeter, his books were banned for sale in Chester, and hundreds of loyal addresses to King George III were declared in defiance.

As Britain seemed to be on the cusp of falling apart, there was one question that raced through William Pitt's mind, tormenting his sleep and jolting him awake at night, his heart pounding in his chest. How similar, Pitt must have questioned, was this to the behaviour in France two years before? Was this the start of the British Revolution? And if so, was Jacobin fervour in England soon to overthrow the British constitution itself?

## A SWIM IN MILK AND HONEY

Pitt wasn't the only one having nightmares. John Reeves, an admin-loving lawyer, was jittery too. In November 1792, Reeves calmed his nerves by heading to the pub. At the Crown and Anchor tavern on the Strand, he started a new movement to fight back against the Corresponding Societies. He established the Association for Preserving Liberty and Property against Republicans and Levellers. It was known on the streets as the John Reeves Association.

The mission was to stir up a spirit of feverish patriotism, commission pamphlets and be on super-high alert for any whisper of Jacobin support. ('What did you say? It's time the Queen is gone?' 'What? No, no! I just said it's time to put the *BAKED BEANS* on!'). Reeves gathered a vast number of followers and the John Reeves Association soon became the largest political organisation in the country.

As a propaganda war waged on the streets of London, the caricaturists were the port of call for the London branch of the Reeves Association. It was considered that not only were satires 'the organ though which the feeling and the general mood of the people is expressed freely', they were also considered a powerful force to initiate change: 'In all revolutions caricatures have been employed to animate the people ... those who know how to master its variety also know how to master public opinion.'[16]

The Reeves Association was fully prepared to harness the power of a cutting Gillrayic monologue or a Cruikshankian bulge of the bottom. As such, the society became the driving force behind some of the best political satires of the early 1790s, demonstrating the mad reality of Jacobin ideals and contrasting political anarchy in France with pleasant, peaceful British life.

But Mr Reeves didn't have to call up a PR agency to get the satirists on board. Instead, the idea fell into his hands. He was the recipient of a letter sent by a Mr Nixon, who wrote that he felt obliged to topple 'the Recent Discontents that has been so industriously spread over every part of this Kingdom'.[17] The letter contained an idea for a print 'intended for the beer houses & other Places of Resort of the People in Trade'.[18]

John Reeves seemed happy enough to commission the print, but who should etch the design? Mr Nixon happened to be well acquainted with Rowlandson and hurried to recommend his friend: 'Mr Rowlandson I best leave to Recommend to your attentions he will do it More Justice than any one I know, & if I meet you approbations will set about it Immediately, he lived at No. 52 Strand – seeing him this morning – he will call at the Crown & Anchor.'[19]

The choice was approved, and on the morning of 19 December 1792, Nixon paid a visit to the esteemed artist. Rowlandson had moved out of Poland Street the previous year and now took rooms at No. 52 the Strand, beside an alley called George Court, which dropped steeply down towards the river.

Nixon's visit must have been a success. That very afternoon, Rowlandson wandered back along the Strand and headed for the Crown and Anchor. This famous watering hole, once the regular haunt of Johnson and James Boswell, no longer exists, but it was located opposite the Wren church of St Clement Danes, just up from what is now Temple Tube Station. The vast function rooms, which could host hundreds, had held Handel debuts, dinners for the Royal Society and every kind of political rally.

Terms were agreed with the Reeves Association, and the artist set off to transform a new set of copper plates. It was a busy Christmas for Rowlandson: before the month was up, he had moved house. After just a year at his Strand address, in December 1792, he took a lease with 83 years left to run, for a consideration of £189 and at a rent of five shillings.[20] His new lodgings were at 2 Robert Street, just behind what is now Charing Cross Station.

It was good fortune that Rowlandson was commissioned by the Reeves Association, for around that time one of his publishers, William Holland, found himself in hot water. Alongside satirical prints, Holland published books and pamphlets, many of which expressed radical sympathies. He'd even published Thomas Paine's *Address to the Republic of France* as a six-penny pamphlet. But Holland pushed his luck with the sale another of Paine's provocative works, *Letter Addressed to the Addressers*. On 17 December 1792, he was prosecuted.

As Holland awaited his fate, the wait for Thomas Paine's delayed trial was finally over. With the accused hiding in exile, a brilliant lawyer named Thomas Erskine set out to vindicate him, defending the freedom of the press and arguing that 'opinion is free and ... conduct alone is amenable to the law'.[21] Although he failed to turn the jury, Erskine's defence was met with rapturous applause. Outside, a mob cheered: 'Erskine for ever!'[22] They unhitched the horses from his carriage and pulled it themselves, personally delivering the hero to his Fleet Street lodgings.

Paine may have been found guilty and sentenced to be hanged, but his public support was very much alive. Despite the recent prosecution of William Holland, over 30 reports of Erskine's stirring speech were printed and spread far and wide. It gave Pitt's administration the green light to lay down the law and ramp up prosecutions for sedition.

The rest of the Piccadilly printmakers trod carefully. Gillray kept his head down, furiously carving out wiry limbs and pointed teeth into copper plates, the horrible visions of ragged *sans-culottes* emerging from trays of acid.

On 21 December 1792, those passing by No. 18 Old Bond Street were given the chance to peek into the private, personal life of two very different figures. The first, entitled French Liberty, is a lean and ragged *sans-culotte* – again, literally without trousers – who is deluded and nearing starvation. His room is a picture of poverty, with broken windows and peeling walls. With only raw onions and live snails to eat, he warms his talon-like toes on a tiny, whimpering fire. Despite his suffering from the food shortages ravaging Paris, he glories in France's new status as a republic and the imprisonment of King Louis XVI. In Gillray's best stab at a French accent, he cries out: '*O! Sacre Dieu*! – vat blessing be de *Liberte Vive le Assemblè Nationale*! – no more Tax! no more Slavery! – all Free Citizen! ha hah! by Gar, how ve live! – ve svim in de Milk & Honey!'

This man with insect-like limbs is compared with the misery of British Slavery. This is a grossly fat Englishman suffering from the excesses of indulgence: his bloated face is blotched with drink and his shoes are slashed to accommodate his gout-ridden feet. He tucks into a large joint of beef, a foaming tankard and a decanter of Hock. But still the Englishman complains: 'Ah! this cursed Ministry! they'll ruin us, with their damn'd Taxes! why, Zounds! – they're making Slaves of us all, & Starving us to Death!'

*French Liberty, British Slavery*, James Gillray, 1792.
Metropolitan Museum of Art, Gift of Adele S. Gollin, 1976

In the final week of that tumultuous December, MPs in Westminster were desperately scrambling around to halt the spread of French revolutionary spirit. They debated whether to bring in the Aliens Act, which would put a stop to any French Republican stepping foot on English soil. Tensions were high and voices were raised. For not only was the future of peace in Britain on the line, but, if events unfolded as they had in France, the life of every nobleman was in danger.

Edmund Burke, the mighty orator and author of *Reflections on the Revolution in France*, felt that words could not express the enormity of the potential challenge ahead. While speaking in the Commons on 28 December 1792, he thrust a shining dagger into the air. This was, he declared, everything that Britain could expect from France, and it was of utmost importance 'to keep the French infection from this country; their principles from our minds and their daggers from our hearts'.[23]

As was becoming custom, the moment was immortalised in print by Cruikshank within the week. On New Year's Day 1793, it was the latest addition for Samuel Fores' window display at No. 3 Piccadilly. And next to it was more fruit from Rowlandson's

*Reflections on the French Revolution*, Isaac Cruikshank, 1793.

partnership with the Reeves Association. In a similar vein to Gillray's print of the Frenchman made of Twiglets and the you-are-what-you-eat-Englishman, Rowlandson gave us a direct French–English comparison in a print entitled *The Contrast*.

This time it appears as if you are looking through a pair of binoculars, albeit with a different view for each eye. The left lens shows British Liberty and, guess what, it's paradise! Utopia at last! Britannia seems to be having a picnic. She sits in the shade of an olde English oak tree, holding the scales of justice and Magna Carta. The British lion purrs at her feet and an enormous ship with full sails drifts into the distance. A long list of Britain's merits accompanies the scene, which seem too good to be true: 'Religion, Morality, Loyalty, Obedience to the Laws, Independence, Personal Security, Justice, Inheritance, Protection, Property, Industry, National Prosperity, Happiness.' In the right lens of this bizarre set of binoculars, we're given a day in the life of French Liberty. She's a terrifying Medusa,

*The Contrast*, Thomas Rowlandson, 1792.
Metropolitan Museum of Art, Gift of Adele S. Gollin, 1976

standing triumphant over a decapitated body. And these satirists weren't holding back: on the spikes of her trident are two human hearts and a head. A hanged man is swinging in the distance. The values for this nation? 'Atheism, Perjury, Rebellion, Treason, Anarchy, Murder, Equality, Madness, Cruelty, Injustice, Treachery, Ingratitude, Idleness, Famine, National & Private Ruin, Misery.' And as if the message hadn't been hammered home already, in huge capital letters, Rowlandson asks: 'WHICH IS BEST?'

The print was simple and hard-hitting. Like Lord Kitchener's call to arms in the First World War, this was to be distributed as far and wide as possible, dispatched with specific orders to place it in pubs and barbershops and transfer-print onto beer mugs. The lesson was clear. Stick with those ancient British liberties deriving from the Magna Carta and you'll get 'justice', 'prosperity' and 'happiness'. Choose the path of revolution, and you'll live in a society of 'misery', 'injustice' and 'ruin'.

That same day, Cruikshank had a stab at the French = bad, English = brilliant motif. He was finishing up a print entitled *French Happiness*, *English Misery*, with a few extra sparkles of his own. In Cruikshank's poverty-stricken French room, there are now *four* ragged and famished French *sans-culottes*. They tug frantically at the limbs of a frog, saying: 'Aha by Gar So we serve all the Enemies to Liberty and Equality.'

And what is in the English half? Scenes of the British everyday: juicy sirloins and frothing pitchers aplenty. 'Here goes, the King & Constitution for ever,' they cheer. The fire blazes bright. The room is decorated with favourite songs: 'O the Roast Beef of old England', 'God save the King' and 'Rule Britannia'. Through the window we can see a pastoral idyll: branches laden with rosy apples and men sowing and driving oxen. Jolly old England indeed.

In the shadow of William Holland's arrest and the trial of Thomas Paine, just a fortnight before, Humphrey and Gillray may well have felt it worth toeing Pitt's line. On 2 January 1793, the fruits of Gillray's

*French Happiness, English Misery*, Isaac Cruikshank, 1793.
Royal Academy of Arts, London; Oxford, Bodleian Library Curzon b.08(132)

labours were presented to the pedestrians of Old Bond Street. In this number, Gillray lashed out at the official public enemy number one: Thomas Paine.

Here, Tommy Paine appears as a tailor again, a jab at his father's humble origins. Dressed in the French revolutionary uniform of a *bonnet rouge* and *cocarde tricolore*, his tailor's measuring tape dangles from his pocket with the label 'Rights of Man'. His client today is Britannia, a buxom young woman. But while she is being fitted with a new Parisian corset, it Doesn't. (Sharp intake of breath.) Seem. ('Breathe in please, madame!') To be. Going. (Another gasp.) On.

Paine might be trying to force Britannia into the French way of doing things, but it's just not going to fit: he pulls at the laces of her corset, his foot on her derrière for support and his face turning red with the strain. Playing on political and physical meanings of 'constitution' and 'form', the print was entitled *Fashion Before Ease; – or – A Good Constitution sacrificed for a Fantastick Form.*

*Fashion before Ease*, James Gillray, 1793.

## THE UTTERMOST DIABOLICAL STRETCH OF SAVAGE CRUELTY

But the events in France were about to take a dramatic turn. On 21 January 1793, 1,000 years of continuous French monarchy came to a shattering end in one slice of the guillotine. King Louis XVI was executed. The revolutionaries named him Citizen Louis Capet, tearing apart the sanctity of monarchy by plucking out a surname from the tenth-century founder of the Capetian dynasty, Hugh Capet.

Most Britons were horrified. The London papers were wild with fury. On 25 January 1793, *The Times* reported: 'The REPUBLICAN TYRANTS OF FRANCE have now carried their bloody purposes to the uttermost diabolical stretch of savage cruelty. They have murdered their King without even the shadow of justice, and of course they cannot expect friendship nor intercourse with any civilised part of the world.[24]

'The name of Frenchman,' it vowed, 'will be considered as the appellation of savage, and their presence shunned as a poison, deadly destructive to the peace and happiness of Mankind.' And the government of France was deemed rotten to the core, too: 'The majority of the National Convention, and the Executive Government of that truly despotic country, are comprised of the most execrable villains upon the face of the earth.'[25]

William Pitt was stunned: 'On every principle by which men of justice and honour are actuated, it is the foulest and most atrocious deed which the history of the world has yet had occasion to attest.'[26]

Jack Bannister thought it a whole new league of savagery, even when compared to a country that had committed regicide less than two centuries before. 'Charles the First,' Bannister explained, 'was treated with a gentleness, consideration, and humanity, which left the iniquitous public proceedings against him entirely a distinct atrocity ... the puritans of England were not, in any respect, reduced to so low a level as the atheists of France.'[27]*

But the same sentiment was expressed by the print shop windows of Piccadilly. On 1 February 1793, as France declared war on Britain and the Netherlands, Samuel Fores was busy updating his windows with the latest from Cruikshank.

After weeks of bashing out images of bloodthirsty *sans-culottes*, Cruikshank seemed to have been stunned into a moment of sombreness. Here was Louis XVI in his final moments. He stands alone

* Charles I would, no doubt, have objected to Bannister's historical analysis.

on the scaffold, looking up to the sky and feeling the warmth of the winter sun on his face for the final time. Behind him, the guillotine, and beyond are faint suggestions of bayonets, flags and bugles. But the braying crowds are not part of this image. It's peaceful, calm and still. A glance into Louis' final moments. As if he were still struggling to process the event itself, Cruikshank made no attempt to satire or ridicule. Entitled, *The Martyrdom of Louis XVI*, *King of France*, the King's final words are quoted: 'I forgive my Enemies, I die Innocent!!!'

*The Martyrdom of Louis XVI*, *King of France*, Isaac Cruikshank, 1793.

But eleven days later, having processed the news, read the reports and begun to sense the public mood, Cruikshank gave us the brutal aftermath of the guillotine's work. We're still on the scaffold, but the deed is done. This is no longer a moment of solemn silence. The head of Louis is held up, pouring with streams of blood. His decapitated body lies motionless behind. And the biting satiric comment is back, too, for the man who holds the head is Louis Philippe Joseph d'Orléans: the dead King's cousin, who had voted for the execution. Louis Philippe, as he was known, had been one of the wealthiest men in France; he saw the King's death as a bid to achieve constitutional monarchy. But Cruikshank had no time for that, scorning him with a speech bubble: 'Behold the Progress of our System.'*

But this was all too subtle for the Humphrey–Gillray team. And, what's more, Gillray knew he could do something similar, but ramp it up to really shock Hannah's customers – wasn't that what such a dreadful scene deserved? On 16 February 1793, in the window of 18 Old Bond Street, Gillray gave us a vision of spine-chilling, harrowing terror.

Portrayed with total realism, Gillray depicted the moment immediately after the execution (which he named 'assassination'). The silver blade is wet, and lying on the scaffold is the decapitated head of the King, eyes pressed into a pool of sticky, hot blood. But out of the King's head billows an enormous crimson swirl. It's already filling the image, suffocating it, overpowering it. Within this flume are the desperate, warning words of Louis. A monologue despairing at the fate of France: 'Ah! ruined, desolated Country! dearest object of my heart!' He laments the situation of his family: 'My Brothers are driven into exile; – my unhappy Wife & innocent Infants are shut up in the horrors of a Dungeon.'

* This was the last spring Louis Philippe would see: he was guillotined himself, ten months later.

He begs Britain to realise the terrible outcome of Jacobin rule: 'O Britons! vice-gerents of eternal-Justice! arbiters of the world! – look down from that height of power to which you are raised, & behold me here! – deprived of Life & of Kingdom, see where I lie; full low, festering in my own Blood!' He compels them to act: 'Revenge the blood of a Monarch most undeservedly butchered, – and rescue the Kingdom of France, from being the prey of Violence, Usurpation & Cruelty.'

*The Blood of the Murdered crying for Vengeance*, James Gillray, 1793.
Royal Academy of Arts, London; New College, Oxford University, Oxford

On 1 March 1793, remembering Fox's sympathies with the French radicals, Gillray dressed Fox up in the clothes of a *sans-culottes*, singing the revolutionary song *Ça Ira!* with blood-stained hands. 'The blood of the French king is on your hands,' Gillray is saying. 'I haven't forgotten that this was the work of *your* people, and Hannah Humphrey and I will make damn sure that no one else forgets it too.'

Fox was horrified at the execution of the King, but the damage was already done. He had championed the French revolutionaries for several years and taken a radical stance throughout his life. Fox was, for some Britons, a repulsive public enemy. Cruikshank felt he was politically destroyed with no way out.

On 25 March 1793, Fox appeared in a Cruikshank print, in what must have been one of the most lonely, unhappy moments of his career. With no one to turn to, the great statesman considers the tools of suicide: will it be poison or the dagger? And in great flashes of lightning zigzags, the thoughts which torment him reveal a mind wracked with fear. 'Thy Country Expatriate thee,' says one inner demon, 'Thy Crony's Impeach thee,' taunts another.

*Which way Shall I turn me How shall I Decide*, Isaac Cruikshank, 1793.
© Trustees of the British Museum

The attack is relentless: 'The Wigs forsake thee. The Prince discards thee. Thy Friends Abjure thee. The People despise thee. All true friends to their King & Constitution Abhor thee.' And while two sunbeams provide a glimmer of hope, they offer little consolation: 'The Sans Culottes admire thee.'

It was a bleak moment for Charles James Fox.

# 7

# *A Bullet Whizzes to Catch the Phizzes*

## GOOD RHENISH WHITE WINE AND EXCELLENT OLD HOCK

The start of the French Revolution was one great, big *ZAP!*

It changed Europe for ever. France's centuries-old framework – the absolute monarchy, the feudal system and the prominence of the Catholic Church – was abruptly eradicated in the most brutal and bloody way. The political landscape was turned on its head, with no precedent. The world would never consider the notions of authority or political power in the same light.

With this surge of high-voltage power bursting through a dusty network, sparks soon snapped elsewhere. For the next 22 years – yes, 22 years – Europe was dragged through fighting worthy of Greek mythology. It was an epic saga that would only be resolved when almost 200,000 troops came head-to-head at Waterloo in 1815.

Britain teamed up with Spain, Holland, Austria, Prussia and Sardinia: the First Coalition. Britons put on their best bonnet of patriotism and rallied with gusto. The man to lead the charge was George III's second son, the 29-year-old 'grand old Duke of York' of nursery rhyme fame. He set sail across the Channel to help defend

Holland and Belgium from France's aggressive expansion. By the end of March 1794, it seemed the tables had turned. The French began retreating in confusion and the First Coalition pounced. They crushed resistance in the north, town by town, croissant by croissant. Hannah Humphrey's diary – had such a brilliant source existed and survived – might have read something along these lines:

> 30 June 1793: News from that dastardly, devilish country! We are on our way to trampling down those *sans-culottes*. Those foul Frenchmen full of frog-legged folly. As I was preparing the latest print orders for Horace Walpole this morning, James burst in with news from the Crown and Anchor. The Duke of York's siege of Valenciennes, the French town next to the Belgian border that has been putting up a fight for the past six weeks, has come to an end. The enemy surrendered. Not only that, they've hailed their conquerors as 'King of France' – can you believe it! The road to Paris is open. Mark my words – that revolutionary government will be gone by summer's end. Who'd have thought that debt-ridden drunk, the Duke of York, would have done his country such a service! Bravo, sir!
>
> 20 July 1793: This morning I was visited by Rupert Green, a young man of 25. 'M-Miss Humphrey, is it?' he enquired, hopping on the doorstep. 'I've been sent on behalf of my father, the publisher Valentine Green, you might know him!'
>
> Of course I knew him! Mezzotint engraver to the King no less. It turns out Valentine Green is running a collab with Christian von Mechel, a printseller from Basel. Since the public are still obsessed by the Siege of Valenciennes, they've decided to commission a full-scale history painting. 'We've managed to get Philip James de Loutherbourg to paint it!' young Rupert piped at me, 'and – and he is heading out to sketch the battlefield and camps imminently, touring the battle area, preparatory sketches of the

various commanders and soldiers, and he'd like Mr Gillray to accompany him.'

30 July 1793: Today, James set off, his first trip abroad! He's going to keep a holiday diary, he tells me. He was gone by seven in the morning with the post-chaise full of inks and papers. Off he sped down Bond Street, first to pick up young Rupert Green (who I imagine is over the moon at joining the trip) and Big Phil, and then the three of them set off to the south coast.

I confess I miss him a little already – dear Gilly! How shall I manage without you? The papers have already made their jokes, of course. The *Morning Post* were wondering how the artists will make sketches of this event when it's already happened. This tickled me greatly. Will the siege be performed again 'for the amusement and instruction of the artists?' it asked. Gilly needs no such thing; his imagination is already as wild as unkempt as a rogue's. Good luck, Gilly! God speed!

Gillray did indeed keep a holiday diary, although unfortunately it wasn't exactly gripping stuff. 'Slept in Bond Street,' it began.[1] Then, 'at seven on Friday morn – went to Miss Greens', to pick up Rupert, and 'set off at Eight in Post Chaise'.[2] After collecting Loutherbourg, they headed for the south coast, arriving at Dover at 10.30pm.

Perhaps we would consider twelve hours to cover such a distance as positively medieval; today the same journey takes an hour by train. But this speed was considered the peak of modern travel, as confessed by one junior army officer at the time, who was completely confident in the state of the nation's roads. 'If my journals should ... be perused at the end of two hundred years,' he mused, 'there will, even then, be little curious in them, relative to travel, because our island is now so explored, the roads are, in general, so fine, and our speed has reached its summit.'[3]

James Gillray, Philip de Loutherbourg and Rupert Green spent another night in Dover, then set sail. The crossing was far from smooth, as Gillray's holiday diary will testify: 'Set off from ye Port about 8 at night—brisk gale—about 50 Passengers—began to be sick—about 1/2 an hour—went to bed—better, slept &c till about 5 in the Morning—Cabin full of drunk Passengers—the floor full.—some very sick—up about 6—fine Morning—came into ostend, about 7 o Clock ...'[4]

As they rattled through the countryside towards Valenciennes, Gillray thought it the 'finest county for fertility I ever saw', with a good 'deal of Tobacco planted along ye way'.[5] He made note of the 'good Rhenish white wine' and 'excellent Old Hock' he had enjoyed. Working hard, Mr Gillray, or hardly working? As they totted up the miles, the pages of their sketchbooks began to fill. There were jottings of imperial ammunition wagons, scrawls of English drummers and scribbles of kilted Highlanders. And as they dived deeper into war-ravaged Europe, Gillray noted there started to appear 'numbers of Crucifixes on ye sides of ye Way'.[6]

The sketching party reached the Valenciennes area by 4 September 1793. Loutherbourg set out to piece together the site of the battlefield, studying the shattered windmills and broken steeples that soared out of the landscape like jagged pieces of broken glass. Gillray tracked down the soldiers and generals who fought in the battle. Once he had found them in the camp, he made a portrait sketch for Loutherbourg to work from for the final painting. According to Henry Angelo, it was 'a task which none but [Gillray], perhaps, could accomplish', for he had only moments to capture an exact likeness.[7] Or, as Gillray described his own work: 'As the bullet *whizzes*, so I caught their phizzes.'[8]* With all the whizzing and phizzing it's no surprise Gillray's enthusiasm for keeping a holiday diary soon waned and the entries dried up. All we know is that the sketching team were back in London by October.

* 'Phiz' being a slang term for 'face'.

Their return was seized upon by London society, desperate to hear the latest from the continent. Today, they might have been accosted by hundreds of reporters at the arrivals gate of Heathrow. 'What did you see, Mr Gillray?' the journalists would have yelled, pushing forward with microphones and cameras. 'What was Valenciennes like?' 'Did you meet any *sans-culottes*?' 'Did you *eat* any *sans-culottes*?!'

King George was 'no less eager than his loyal subjects, to take a peep into the portfolio' of the artist's work – perhaps to see what his wayward second son, the Duke of York, was really up to.[9] Loutherbourg and Gillray were summoned to St James's Palace. King George took a careful look at Loutherbourg's sketches of battered walls and ruined steeples and showered the artist with royal compliments. But on turning to Gillray's work, his praise was less forthcoming. King George gave Gillray 'a look which seemed to express, – Mr. Gillray, you might as well have remained at home'.[10] The King 'freely confessed that he could not read the likenesses, as he did not understand the *stenography* of the painter's art'.

But this was Gillray's USP! This was his God-given ability! This was the very reason he had been taken on the sketching trip! To capture the *exact likeness of the subject*, the essence of character, the pinpoint of a personality. 'I was a fool for going abroad,' Gillray is said to have thought, 'and a greater fool for going so far out of my way – at home.'[11] But he wasn't finished with the King. For, quick as a flash, he sketched out a royal portrait and presented it to His Majesty. Could mighty King George really not 'read the likenesses' or understand the '*stenography*' – the shorthand – of Gillray's work, when it was his own portrait? The gamble paid off: 'so far from offending', it 'exceedingly amused the King'.[12] Yet again, Gillray's wit had made its mark on high society, whether high society liked it or not.

But the real work was yet to begin. Loutherbourg had 4.5 square metres of blank canvas to fill. He set off piecing together the sketches, arranging figures in the space, laying out the landscape, working through proportions, the figures, then portraits, taking in the

Prince of York's waistband an inch, a dash of airbrushing here, a dash of classicism there. And, *voilà*! These were no longer overweight, gout-ridden officers, who owed their place to nepotism. These were *heroes*.

Adverts were soon filling the London papers. 'In this Picture,' the *St James's Chronicle* announced, one could see 'portraits of twenty-six of the principal Officers of the combined Armies' at the very scene of the siege of Valenciennes.[13] Punters paid a shilling to gawp at it in person at the Exhibition Room on Pall Mall. And wealthy souvenir hunters could pick up an engraving from the shop of 'Messrs. V. and R. Green', a lucrative result for Gillray.[14] It went down a storm. Loutherbourg received '£500 and Mr Gillray's expenses'.[15] The collab had produced a hit.

## CARRY ON CRUISING

But while the government was happy enough to allow artists to scamper around the continent to make heroes of their generals, they were seriously worried about the pamphlets, prints and publications that were being produced on the streets of London. The French Revolution had opened a Pandora's box of radical ideas, which were now swirling around the British Isles and threatening to incite revolution on home turf.

These were not calm waters for Pitt and his government. These were perilous seas, choppy and changing and full of lurking perils, and they would inspire one of Gillray's greatest works, itself inspired by the tale of Scylla and Charybdis from Greek mythology, meaning 'to choose the lesser of two evils'. In Gillray's scene is a dramatic seascape with a small boat in the centre, sitting dangerously low in the water. The vessel in question? *The Constitution*, carrying a lanky captain, William Pitt, and a particularly buxom damsel in distress, Britannia herself. It's a scene worthy of a *Carry On* casting: Kenneth Williams playing aloof, sensible Pitt, complete with flared nostrils,

*Britannia between Scylla and Charybdis*, James Gillray, 1793.
PD-US, Library of Congress

pinched lips and sideways glances, trying to avoid eye contact with Barbara Windsor opposite, playing his blushing, giggling heroine.

Their destination is a distant island, the 'Haven of Public Happiness'. Fat chance of ever reaching that, though. For, despite the *Carry On* cast, the rest of the scene is pure Spielberg: sharks, natural disasters, mythical monsters. On Pitt's portside is a towering rock with crashing waves: the lair of Scylla. If she emerges from the waters, this six-headed sea monster will engulf the ship in one fell swoop. But Gillray's metaphor is far more terrifying than being ripped to pieces by a watery brutess. For, surmounting the rocks is a *bonnet rouge* with a *cocarde tricolore*: the uniform of the French revolutionaries. This is the 'Rock of Democracy'. And emerging from this libertarian lair are the 'Dogs of Scylla', silently tracking the boat with shark-like menace. These sharks are a most unusual breed, for they bear the heads of Fox and his allies, Joseph Priestley and Richard Brinsley Sheridan. In their dogged loyalty to France's revolutionary principles, will they snap up the constitution and throw Britannia to the depths with it?

While Captain Pitt plots a course to avoid the perils of Scylla's radicalism, another hazard lies to starboard. Here is Charybdis, known in Greek mythology as a great, twisting whirlpool off the coast of Sicily. In Gillray's re-telling, this is the 'Whirlpool of Arbitrary Power' and, just visible in the murky waters, a royal crown is submerged and upturned. It's a danger Pitt must avoid – the nepotism and old corruption of monarchical government, where decision making lies with those elected through rotten and pocket boroughs – a government that opposes egalitarian liberty in every way.

The constitutional vessel is *currently* on course for a 'middle way'. But, as Gillray demonstrates, there was every chance it could be blown off course. Place your bets now! Will Mr Pitt be sucked up by the whirlpool and spat out in a sewage pipe? Will Britannia make it to the Haven of Public Happiness? The odds are high! And stakes are higher! 5–1 for *The Constitution* overturned! 2–1 Charles James Fox requires a life jacket! Roll up! Roll up! Put your bets in now, madam! Cash only!

Gillray's print was a brilliant visualisation of Pitt's dilemma. Drift too far towards the arbitrary power of the Crown and the Foxites would kick up a stink. But give too much slack to those who sympathised with revolutionary France and revolution might find its footing on the streets of London. For Pitt, the only option was to lay down the law, even at the expense of civil liberties. It wasn't worth risking September Massacres 2.0 on this side of the Channel.

And so, carrying the precious cargo of Britannia, it was no surprise that Pitt's government were prepared to come down hard on ideas, writings and pamphlets that could steer the constitutional vessel towards the hazards of Scylla's lair. Thus began Pitt's very own 'Reign of Terror'.

## A NEIGHBOURHOOD OF VOLUNTARY SPIES

Pitt's new rules came thick and fast. Habeas corpus was suspended in 1794, meaning that anyone could be arrested on a whim and thrown behind bars without trial. In 1795, it became illegal to hold political gatherings of over 50 people or even for an individual to 'imagine, invent, devise or intend death or destruction, or any bodily harm tending to death or destruction, maim or wounding, imprisonment or restraint, of the person of ... the King'.[16]

As well as these 'Gagging Acts', as they came to be known, Pitt had £10,000* to spend on government propaganda, without having to account for it.[17] Gillray was to be on the receiving end of this: between 1797 and 1801 he was secretly paid £200 per year to whip up support. Pitt also employed a network of spies, informers and agents provocateurs for good measure. These were mostly everyday citizens, sent out to report on any whiff of radicalism from conversations overheard in a coffee house between neighbours expressing sympathy for the impoverished Frenchman in a desperate position, for example. And foreigners were kept under close watch by the Alien Office, which extended surveillance operations all over Europe. It operated 'without bustle, noise or anything that can attract Public Attention', providing the government with 'the most powerful means of Observation and Information'.[18]

Watching on from the sidelines, this secret service was to 'depress the cause of freedom'.[19] Even Jane Austen, hidden away in the depths of Hampshire, hinted at it in her writings. In *Northanger Abbey*, which was conceived and written in the late 1790s, she described England as a country 'where every man is surrounded by a neighbourhood of voluntary spies'.[20]

With the enactment of Gagging Acts in the mid-1790s, the country also faced harvest failures and economic depression. The mood was tense. Pitt was keenly aware of the tightrope on which he walked: 'My head would be off in six months were I to resign,' he admitted.[21] The King, too, believed his days could be numbered. According to the Lord Chancellor, the Earl of Eldon, George was assured 'he should

* Almost £1.5 million in today's currency.

be the last King of England'.[22] He was already the King who lost America. Was he to oversee the collapse of the British monarchy, too?

Publishers and printmakers had to tread especially carefully. A Rowlandson jest or a Cruikshank quip would provide the sparks to ignite a bone-dry haystack. The prescient warning of the antiquary and draughtsman Francis Grose that caricaturing was a 'dangerous acquisition, tending rather to make the possessor feared than esteemed', seemed to be proving itself.[23] Radical books and pamphlets put some printsellers at risk, as the government set out to prosecute 'not only the authors and printers' of these radical books, but 'those who keep them in shops, or hawk them in the streets for sale; or, what is much worse, are employed in circulating them from house to house'.[24]

On 1 December 1795, Samuel Fores stuck his neck above the parapet. He published Cruikshank's brazen commentary on the clampdown. Playing on the story of *Gulliver's Travels*, first published in 1726, he gave London a crowd of gesticulating Lilliputians. But this angry group of both Foxites and radicals have been rounded up and tied together. They face the gigantic figure of Pitt, dressed in the royal uniform of Windsor. 'He'll put us out to a Certainty,' the tiny people squeal. As Pitt lunges down to look closer at the outspoken victims, he prepares to catch them with a handy tool, perfect for the job: a giant cone inscribed 'For Preventing Seditious Meetings'. 'Aye! Aye!' cries Pitt, as he prepares to silence the radicals, 'My Seditious Lads / I'm down upon You / I'll darken your day lights / I'll stop your throats.'

Cruikshank's vision was not far off the truth, for troublesome printsellers were indeed locked away. Those who stocked Thomas Paine's *Rights of Man*, or whose prints encouraged radical or revolutionary fervour, were thrown behind bars in the most notorious prison in London.

Slimy, dark and rife with disease, Newgate Prison had struck fear into Londoners since the days of Henry II. Stories abounded of plagues driving people to cannibalism and the spectre of a coal-black dog taunting the condemned, turning them mad with fear. This

*The Royal Extinguisher or Gulliver Putting out the Patriots of Lilliput!!!*, Isaac Cruikshank, 1795.


was the prison whose formidable walls were known to Sir Thomas Malory, Titus Oates, Oscar Wilde, Ben Johnson, Giacamo Casanova and Daniel Defoe. Defoe described his experience, through the voice of Moll Flanders:

> 'Tis impossible to describe the terror of my mind, when I was first brought in, and when I looked around upon all the horrors of that dismal place … the hellish noise, the roaring, swearing, and clamour, the stench and nastiness … joined together to make the place seem an emblem of hell itself, and a kind of entrance to it.[25]

When London's radical printsellers were whisked away to Newgate, they had every reason to be fearful. Along with centuries of terrifying tales, since 1783, it had been the main site for London's executions. Between 1783 and 1799, 559 poor souls were hanged in front of a jeering crowd.[26] On one grisly day, the crowd were treated to twenty executions.

But the 1780s also saw the prison rules loosen up. Family and friends could visit freely and radical prisoners began coordinating political campaigns behind bars. One of those was Henry Delahay Symonds, 'many years an active and considerable bookseller in Paternoster-row', who had fallen foul of Pitt's heavy hand.[27] 'In the commencement of the crusade against the French Revolution, he suffered four years imprisonment in Newgate, and paid a heavy fine for vending some political pamphlets.'[28] He was soon joined by another bookseller, James Ridgway. The pair immediately joined forces and continued their support of the radical cause. William Holland was finally thrown behind bars in February 1793 (perhaps to the relief of his great rivals, Hannah Humphrey and Samuel Fores). Holland was sentenced to a year's imprisonment, leaving his Oxford Street shop in the capable hands of a young talent, Richard Newton, who regularly visited his master behind bars.[29] He found that the prison was now overflowing with radicals, and it had become a lively hub for debate and discussion. When Newton popped over to visit Newgate, to check in with the boss and keep the Holland printing empire ticking over, the young artist recorded what he saw, described genteelly as a *Promenade in the State Side of Newgate*.

*Promenade in the State Side of Newgate*, Richard Newton, 1793.

## BEYOND THE LATITUDE OF SOBER SPECULATION

Seeing their rivals being carted off to prison must have given pause to fellow printmakers and printsellers. Was publishing a print really worth spending up to four years in prison? Joseph Ritson didn't seem to think so. He was an antiquary, publisher and staunch supporter of the French Revolution – but not staunch enough to spend time in slimy, cold Newgate Prison. 'I find it prudent to say as little as possible upon political subjects', he wrote, 'in order to keep myself out of Newgate.'[30] Instead he busied himself by compiling the Robin Hood ballads, rewriting the rules of spelling and making waves as a vegetarian activist.

The war with France was providing its own challenges for the London print scene. The established continental trade was scuppered, forcing printsellers to refocus on the home market or look for more underhand routes abroad, even using smugglers to get through the blockades of territories under French control. Some took more creative measures to get the punters in. Samuel Fores advertised a topical, albeit morbid, attraction at No. 3 Piccadilly: a six-foot working model of the guillotine.

Gillray was keen to keep his head above water. He had no intention of spending Christmas behind bars – it wasn't worth the risk of missing out on the convivial festivities in those Piccadilly pubs. He made a volte-face, slotting into Pitt's strict regime and joining the defence of the status quo. He 'suddenly switched sides, and began to fire all his arrows at Fox in particular, and the old Opposition in general'.[31]

It was a no-brainer for the artist, for Fox had become, effectively, a political outcast: despite the regicide, despite the war, despite the radicalism, Fox *still* leant sympathy to the French cause. In light of this, many of his loyalist supporters, including the Prince of Wales, deserted him. The Foxite party had withered down to a handful of dogged supporters. Now that 'the Opposition are poor', as Gillray admitted, 'they do not buy my prints and I must draw on the purses of the larger parties'.[32] Of course, Gillray was still actively pulling apart the government within the realms of the rules. But it does beg the question, did any of these artists have a sense of political loyalty? Did they throw party allegiances up in the air, for the sake of a good print?

In general, printsellers commissioned whatever would sell. They worked for the market, giving the people what they wanted. It was up to the printsellers to judge the national frame of mind and commission accordingly. Although William Holland had radical sympathies, he still described himself as 'Mr Anyside'.[33]

Throughout the 1780s, Rowlandson, Gillray and Cruikshank took whatever work they could get. They regularly switched between political sides, sometimes arguing for polar opposites within the same week. In 1784, the year Pitt won his first election, Rowlandson was paid for at least 50 political satires, and according to the wishes of the print shop, roughly half of these were pro-Fox and half pro-Pitt. And while Rowlandson had worked for the *British Mercury*, a liberal paper run by radicals, a few years later he was strolling down to the Crown and Anchor to file his work for the anti-Jacobin Reeves Association. It would be like today's journalists working freelance for both the *Guardian* and the *Daily Telegraph* and switching between them week on week.

Gillray was said to have 'worked to order, or upon impulse, irrespective of any settled political opinions'.[34] Henry Angelo was convinced Gillray did whatever was needed to put bread on the table, writing: 'He probably never inquired further into motives … if he could supply the wants of his mouth by the industry of his hand, he was fulfilling all the moral and physical obligations of his nature.'[35]

Gillray's non-commitment certainly kept his contemporaries guessing. When rumours spread of him having received a secret state pension, he remained an enigma. Writing in 1831, John Landseer, a fellow painter, engraver and father of Sir Edwin Landseer (another artist, most notable for designing Trafalgar Square's lions) was still trying to figure it out, concluding that despite the commissions, Gillray's 'heart was always on the side of whiggism and liberty'.[36]

Even Gillray's general demeanour was confusing to his contemporaries. In 1824, the *Somerset Gazette* remembered him as 'a careless sort of cynic who neither loved nor hated society'.[37] Tom Rowlandson's great friend, Henry Angelo, couldn't make head nor tail of what was going on inside Gillray's mind:

> How the phrenologists would have christened the little mountains on the chart of such a cranium as that of Gillray's; or what discoveries the physiognomists might have made in the map of such a face as his, lies beyond the latitude of sober speculation to make out ... The mental course of such eccentric characters elude philosophical inquiry; such individuals can only be compared to themselves.[38]

It might be easy to scorn these artists as lily-livered, boneless invertebrates, devoid of principles. But, don't forget, it was tough making a living from printmaking and printselling – especially when a large chunk of one's earnings went on propping up pubs on the Strand. Martin Rowson, one of the great cartoonists of our own time, has been keen to jump to the defence of his predecessors: 'I'm compelled as an act of professional solidarity to say give [Gillray] a break. Cartoonists aren't romantic heroes. For the most part we're just hacks trying to make a living by giving our readers an opportunity for a bit of a giggle.'[39]

And printsellers maintained convivial relationships with the victims of their prints. Despite much of Hannah Humphrey's income coming from Gillray's vicious attacks on Fox, Humphrey was happy to sing his praises, according to Henry Angelo's memoirs. He recalls an occasion when Fox visited Humphrey's shop, not long after she had published a particularly damning print of The Eyebrow:

> Mr Fox met the affair with a bolder front; for, hearing that the said political print was exhibited in the window of the old caricature shop in St James's Street, he bent his way thither, and, opening the shop door, good humouredly addressed Mrs Humphreys with, 'Well, my goodlady, I perceive you have something new in your window;' and, pointing to the very print, paid his eighteen pence for it, received his change out of half a crown, rolled it carefully up, and, putting it in his pocket also, smiled a 'good morning to you,' and gently shut the shop door on his departure.[40]

Hannah was totally charmed and 'overcome with the gentle manner of Mr Fox, the tear glistening in her eye'. Watching him walk away along St James's Street, she swooned to her assistant: 'Ah, Betty, there goes the pattern for all gentlemen! Everybody loved Mr Fox.'[41]

It was no surprise that Betty and Hannah were swooning over charming Mr Fox. He was one of the stars of this serial blockbuster mega-hit saga playing out in the windows of Piccadilly. But if season 1 recounted the great rivalry of Pitt and Fox, another killer dynamic pairing, rippling with juicy gossip, was needed to launch us into season 2. A family betrayal. A stoic, dutiful and sober father, constantly foiled by his louche, licentious, frivolous disgrace of a son. The father living life in moderation, devoted to his wife. The son indulging in every possible excess, drinking and gambling and wasting money on this and that, on everything and nothing.

By the late eighteenth century, it seemed that the stars were perfectly aligned for such an epic saga. For these exact characters were to be found at the centre of British society. And the satirists were sat in the front row, watching their every move with pens poised.

# 8

# *Frugal Meals and Horrors of Digestion*

## A STATE APPROACHING TO NUDITY

Had James Gillray tuned his radio to 104.1 FM on a summer afternoon in 1794, he might well have heard a report that piqued his interest:

> Reporting live for BBC Radio Berkshire. In the early hours of the morning, a round, red-faced gentleman sporting riding-dress and a broad-brimmed hat was reported to be quizzing local villagers about turnips. He was determined to make conversation, which alarmed some villagers: 'Well, Friend,' he was reported to have said, to one yokel, 'where a' you going, hey? – what's your Name, hey? – where d'ye Live, hey? – hey?' He was accompanied by a bony woman with a German accent. We'll keep you updated with this story as soon as it breaks. Back to the studio.

This Wanderer of Windsor was no raging madman (at least not yet). The man in question was King George III, who had been sitting on the throne for the past 34 years. The King was fascinated by farming and agriculture and developed a habit of dropping in to see the local bumpkins unexpectedly, to quiz them about the latest yields. It earned him the nickname of 'Farmer George'.*

George's interest in the land couldn't have come at a better time. For he lived through the British Agricultural Revolution: a period from around 1750, during which British farming really took off. With an increasing population and improvements to land productivity, wheat yields increased by about a quarter over the century.[1] The driving force came from country gentlemen, keen to improve the efficiency of their own land. They began writing up their findings, debating theories about turnip productivity and arguing the case for 'improvement'. By the 1770s, so many books had been published on farming that the Scottish writer and judge, Lord Kames, opened his 1776 treatise, *The Gentleman Farmer*, with: 'Behold another volume on husbandry!'[2]

King George delighted in the debate. He was an eager writer himself, sometimes publishing under the pseudonym Ralph Robinson. How could agriculture improve the wealth of the nation, the King asked? How profitable are these shiny new methods? How much higher are the yields for wheat and barley, against rye?

It wasn't what you'd expect from the most powerful man in the land. But King George enjoyed a sober, simple life, guided by straightforward common sense and duty. 'I only prefer eating plain and little,' the King once admitted, 'to growing diseased and infirm.'[3] Had he lived long enough to watch *The Good Life* on TV, George would have been on the side of Tom and Barbara, not Margo and Jerry. His rustic interests were reflected in his simple habits and mannerisms; his conversation was punctuated with verbal tics of 'What? What?' or 'Hey? Hey?' often used at the end of a joke or question to mean 'What say you?'[4]

Despite his German ancestry, George III was a true Englishman. He was born in St James's Square, London, and never visited

* This worked well, as the Ancient Greek word for farmer is *georgós*.

the family seat of Hanover. He was happily married to his wife, Queen Charlotte (née Mecklenburg-Strelitz), and, unlike many other men at the time, never kept a mistress. He enjoyed fresh air, often hunting, riding, discussing barley yields or bathing in the chilly waters at Weymouth. His most precious times were intimate family dinners with the favourite of his fifteen children.

In the summer of 1792, Hannah Humphrey decided this farmer–king deserved a visual monologue of his own. With her finger always on the pulse of the nation, Humphrey commissioned a Gillrayic portrait of the King. The result was a triumph: it was beautifully etched and exquisitely coloured. The subject matter, however, was far from noble.

Gillray's etching took his fans behind closed palace doors: the most private quarters of the royal family. Here, they found a man of habit, carrying out his regular morning routine: after waking at 7am, the King would wash, dress and take a walk. At Windsor, he might pop in to see the horses. At Kew, he would do the rounds with the workmen, checking progress and suggesting improvements. By 9am, he would gather with Queen Charlotte and the princesses in the breakfast parlour. And *this* was the moment that Gillray chose to share with the nation.

The room doesn't appear to be a breakfast parlour of kings. If you were hoping to be blinded with the glimmer of silver platters and polished palace floors, you'll be sorely disappointed. This isn't minimal, or even bare. This is *shabby*. And *shabbiness* was totally inappropriate. Just look at the King's breeches: an enormous patch on his bottom!

George has taken every measure to prevent wear and tear: he's tucked the end of the tablecloth into his collar to protect his clothing. He sits on a grand chair, but it's covered in sheets to protect it from spillages. The room is decorated with a beautiful carpet, but a mat is placed under the King's feet to protect the fibres. Even the bell pull is covered in a bag to protect it from greasy fingers.

*Temperance enjoying a Frugal Meal*, James Gillray, 1792.


If you invited King George to a drinks party, he would spend it putting glasses on drinks mats. He'd also be the one on the non-alcoholic beers, for King George wasn't big on booze. In the foreground of Gillray's print is a grand silver flagon, decorated with the royal arms and labelled '*Aqua Regis*': royal water.

But most frugal of all, the King's breakfast is a boiled egg and some salad leaves. While some might consider a boiled egg the mark of a breakfast connoisseur, cooked to a five-minute runny-yolked perfection, the Bond Street promenaders would have taken issue with this rustic meal. For this was a mighty king; a man who once controlled the American colonies, who commanded the greatest navy in the world, a man who had the globe at his feet. He was expected to act and eat and drink according to His Majesty.

Hannah Humphrey's clients would have adored Gillray's trail of clues, laughing and shrieking as their eyes darted across the page: 'They haven't even lit a fire! In deepest winter! And look at the figure in the fireplace!' Instead of a roaring fire, the grate is filled with foliage of the season: snowdrops, holly and mistletoe. It's so chilly that the carved figure in the fireplace has sprung to life, warming his hands in a muff. In the foreground are a collection of books, including *Dr Cheyne on the Benefits of a Spare Diet* and *Essay on the Dearness of Provisions*.

Wasn't this good news? A king diligently sticking to a budget, taking care not to waste taxpayers' money? The public didn't see it that way. It seemed *suspicious*. The rumours that ran through London's streets were that George and Charlotte were only scrimping and saving to hoard public money; that they locked away great piles of gold like a pair of pantomime baddies.

Gillray was only too happy to play up to these miserly rumours. Have a close look at the fireplace surround: a small pair of scales are ready to weigh out the guineas. And look at the candelabra beside it. To save money, only one of the candlesticks is lit, the other being covered by an extinguisher in the shape of a crown. The base of the candelabra is decorated by a figure of Munificence, but she holds two barren cornucopias: her generosity is empty. Now, move your eyes to the left, and look at the wall behind the Queen. Here is a heavily bolted door of a strong-room – presumably where the supposed hoards are kept. Pinned to it is a list of colossal, impossible sums of money: 'Table of Interest, 5 pr Cent. 5 Million … 250,000.'

Gillray really comes into his own with the wall decor. Above the chimneypiece is a spoof of the biblical story, *The Fall of Manna*, where round cakes descend from heaven and are caught in sacks by gentlemen wearing Georgian dress, who presumably intend to selfishly store them away rather than share them. Then there are frames labelled *The Triumph of Benevolence* and the *Parting of the Loaves & Fishes*. But both are empty! No sharing is to be expected here, it seems. And to make a further mockery of the King's rumoured miserliness, there is a portrait of *The Man of Ross*, who was famed for his charitable deeds.

The name of Gillray's print was *Temperance enjoying a Frugal Meal*. It sent laughter rippling along Bond Street: 'A triumph,' passers-by might have muttered. 'Gillray's best yet!' But this wasn't Gillray's only gift to the royal family. For beside this Silas Marner was quite a different figure. As Londoners glanced through the bow window, the next thing they laid eyes on was a bulbous, bulging, spherical form.

This was, to the delight of the wide-eyed crowd, the bloated belly of George's eldest son and heir, the Prince of Wales. The Prince could not have been more different to his father. While the King lived by the mantra 'Waste not, want not,' Prince George was the epitome of excess. He frittered away vast sums of public money buying clothes and art, entertaining lavishly and showering gifts on family, friends, lovers, servants and total strangers. Sometimes he even paid off his pals' debts.[5]

Much of his pocket money went towards the renovation of Carlton House, a London pad on Pall Mall with direct access to St James's Park. It had been a pretty epic 21st birthday present from his parents; however, with a forgiving father, a generous Parliament and a flexible budget, Carlton House became a sinkhole for public money. Had George been alive today, he would have had all the latest fads: underground pools, spa complexes, private cinemas. For Carlton House had every room imaginable, all needing sumptuous decoration: the Admiral's Room, the Armoury, the Blue Velvet Closet, the Bow Room, the Chinese Drawing Room and dozens more. Despite all this space, the Prince tended to stay in his bedroom for much of the day, where visitors would find him 'rolling about from side to side in a state approaching to nudity'.[6]

Unlike his father, Prince George had no sense of the value of money. And why should he when it was handed to him on a plate? When dealing with his builders, upholsterers, jewellers or tailors, he often didn't specify the job in hand until it was completed, so the bills totted up from vast amounts of unnecessary work. Walsh Porter, the socialite who managed the Carlton House renovations, once wrote to the Prince: 'Sir, I know full well, by observation, that the word "no" forms no part of Your Royal Highness's vocabulary.'[7] This corpulent, yes-man of a prince was – in every sense of the word – a Royal Seal of Approval.

The most epic demonstration of his profligacy came when the Prince finally became king. After sinking public money into the furnishings and renovations of Carlton House for 30 years, he gave up on the project and pulled the whole place down.*

Frugal George III – a man who restricted himself to three coats a year – was horrified at his son's gross excesses.[8] And he blamed the great Whig families for encouraging this profligate lifestyle. Charles Fox was the main culprit: the King believed he was playing a long game, and that he had latched on to the Prince for his own career, in the hope that the Prince would one day appoint him prime minister.[9]

To put the Prince's spending in proportion, the likes of the Bennet family, Jane Austen tells us, had an annual income of £2,000 a year. And at the Meryton Ball, 'the report which was in general circulation within five minutes after his entrance' was that Mr Darcy had an income of £10,000 a year.[10] In 1812, this would have been deemed an average income for the dukes, marquesses, earls, viscounts and barons that dotted the country, relying on agricultural rents from their land.

* The capitals and bases of the columns were used for the entrance of the National Gallery in its current location on Trafalgar Square, which first opened in 1838.

The King had six times Mr Darcy's income, with a private income of £60,000 per annum.[11] But by the summer of 1786, Prince George's debts stood at an eye-watering £269,878 (nearly £30 million in today's money), having almost doubled in eighteen months. It was equivalent to more than a quarter of the UK's annual non-military expenditure.[12] Much of this was paid off by Parliament. But within ten years, the debts had risen again. The Prince was constantly writing to his father, describing 'the peculiar and very embarrassed situation of my affairs, arising from the necessary expenses I incurred during the course of last year'.[13] In desperation, he agreed to marry; it was the only way to force Parliament to increase his annual income. When, aged 32, he tied the knot with his unfortunate cousin, Princess Caroline of Brunswick, the Prince brought with him staggering £630,000 in debt – around £67m today.[14]

Poor Princess Caroline. The union was doomed before she arrived, for George already considered himself a married man, having secretly married his mistress, Maria Fitzherbert, the year before, in the drawing room of her house in Park Street, Mayfair. The Reverend Robert Burt, who conducted the 'ceremony', was given £500 and the promise of a future bishopric.[15] But Maria was a Catholic, and such a union with a member of the royal family was illegal under the Royal Marriages Act 1772. The marriage was invalidated and Maria parted ways with her beloved.

When cousin Caroline turned up to be his Parliament-approved bride, George didn't bother to hide his repulsion: he immediately ordered a glass of brandy. At the wedding, he was so drunk he could barely stand up and after the birth of one daughter within a year, they lived separate lives. Caroline was even barred from his coronation in 1821 and she died just three weeks later.

Prince George was one of Georgian Britain's most detested figures. 'There never was an individual less regretted by his fellow-creatures,' *The Times* would reflect, just one day after his funeral. If he 'ever had a friend – a devoted friend – in any rank of life, we protest that the name of him or her has not reached us'.[16] They named him 'an inveterate voluptuary ... of all known beings the most selfish'.[17] Historian Ian Mortimer recently dubbed him 'one of the laziest, most vain, spoilt, arrogant, self-indulgent, profligate, uncaring and conceited Englishmen ever to have lived', labelling him a 'lecherous, drunken boor; a glutton, a prig and a snob'.[18]

And Gillray's print of him certainly makes us believe it. Here he is in his grand rooms, the unfinished colonnade of Carlton House just visible through the half-opened sash window. And it's lucky the windows are open, for inside resides the disgusting, corpulent frame of this 'Prince of Whales', or, as Gillray put it: *A Voluptuary under the horrors of Digestion.*

*A Voluptuary under the horrors of Digestion*, James Gillray, 1792.

And what a horror it is! He reclines in true Hogarthian style, unable to hold himself upright after his latest feast. He's tried to hack through an enormous piece of meat; clean bones are strewn across the table, decanters of port and brandy are almost empty and wine bottles roll around the floor. And now, in a serious affront to manners, he picks at his teeth with a fork. The impropriety of this shocked the Victorian writer, William Thackeray: 'Fancy the first young gentlemen living employing such a weapon in such a way!'[19]

To hammer home the point, Gillray redesigned the Prince's coat of arms in the candle sconce behind him. Below the traditional Prince of Wales ostrich feathers, the coat of arms has been altered. It shows the tools this prince holds most dear: a crossed knife and fork. And look closely at the golden candle holders, too: one is shaped as a glass, the other a bottle.

This excessive eating has taken its toll on the royal physique. Behind the Prince is a delicate collection of bottles, pretty in pastels. But these are not perfumes or smelling salts. They are medical potions: a poor doctor's attempts to rectify the damage done to the lumbering, swelling royal body. 'For the Piles,' one bottle is labelled, and 'Drops for a Stinking Breath,' reads another. Pinned beneath his overflowing, stinking chamber pot is evidence of financial affairs: 'Poulterers Bill … unpaid,' 'Butcher's Bill … unpaid,' 'Baker's Bill … unpaid.'

The Prince is truly repulsive, there's no denying it. But in this trail of clues, Gillray leaves a final moralising message. Behind the Prince is a portrait of Luigi Cornaro, an elderly, bearded man, sipping a glass of water. As a young man, Cornaro lived a hedonistic and licentious lifestyle. After a bout of ill health at 40, he followed the doctor's orders, took up a strict, low-calorie diet and never looked back. This was Cornaro's rebirth: he lived in vigorous health until the ripe old age of 98. So convinced was Cornaro by this lifestyle change that he wrote a book: *Discorsi della vita sobria*.* It was the original *How to Turn Your Life Around in 10 Days*.

* *Discourses on a Sober and Temperate Life*.

If only Prince George would take a leaf out of Cornaro's book, Gillray's print seems to say, there would still be hope. But this lazy glutton wanted nothing to do with the culture of 'improvement', and it's hard to believe he'd ever pick up a self-help book.

George was indeed a man of excess – but he was only the tip of the London iceberg.

## GREAT LUMP OF LOVELINESS

Every prima donna needs her chorus. Prince George was the same. In London, he found a bevy of pals among the nobility, prancing from pleasure gardens to the theatre, from print shops to Devonshire House, all in a bustle of feathers and farce.

While George III might have advised his children to follow the modus operandi 'Everything in moderation', the friends of the Prince of Wales preferred the mantra of 'Everything in excess'. Or, as Oscar Wilde is supposed to have said: 'Everything in moderation, including moderation.' The glass was never half empty or half full: it was full to the brim and spilling on the carpet. Take the prince's behaviour at a 1787 London ball:

> Lo! At twelve o'clock in reeled H.R.H. as pale as ashes, with glazed eyes set in his head, and in short almost stupified. The Duchess of Cumberland made him sit down by her, and kept him tolerably peaceful till they went down for supper, when he was most gloriously drunk and riotous indeed. He posted himself in the doorway, flung his arm around the Duchess of Ancaster's neck and kissed her with a great smack, threatened to pull Lord Galloway's wig off and knock out his false teeth, till some of his companions called for his carriage.[20]

Prince George's profligacy was rivalled and often surpassed by his friends: the aristos who electrified London with indulgences of epic proportions. Perfect material for the etching burin.

The London these lucky few inhabited is largely lost to time. It was a city whose streets were marked by great and grand ducal palaces. These included Northumberland House on the corner of today's Trafalgar Square, a mighty Jacobean pile, once the seat of the Percy family. It was later painted by Canaletto, but the house was demolished in 1874. Norfolk House stood on St James's Square, near the house where George III was born. There was Lansdowne House and Burlington House, Montagu House and Londonderry House. Manchester House is still standing in a recognisable form – now home to the Wallace Collection – as is Apsley House, on the great roundabout of Hyde Park Corner. But the grandest of them all, by far, was the London house of the Duke of Devonshire, a handy pied-à-terre when Chatsworth was becoming dull.

Devonshire House was built on a prime piece of real estate. If you ever find yourself spilling out of the Ritz after a mountain of triangular sandwiches and petit fours, cast your eyes over the road to Green Park Tube Station. This entire block, between Stratton Street and Berkeley Street, was taken up by the Cavendish residence. A great stately home, set back from the road, with three acres of gardens at the rear. Designed by William Kent in the Palladian style, the central block, an eleven-bay *corps de logis*, was flanked by two service wings, all looking in on a private court where guests could dismount from their carriages. Here resided the Duke of Devonshire and his notorious wife, Georgiana. Devonshire House became the Duchess's own private court, which meant it was also the centre of London's social scene. It was a magnet for politicians, royals and celebrities, who gathered for balls, assemblies and concerts, for dancing, gossiping and gambling. Even when Georgiana's best friend, Lady 'Bess' Foster, became the Duke's mistress, they continued the opulence happily, all living together under one roof.

The frills and feathers that bounced around Devonshire House were well suited to Rowlandson's dainty, frivolous style. In pen and ink, he captured another night in for the sisters Georgiana, Duchess of Devonshire, and Harriet Ponsonby, Viscountess Duncannon, who were born into the illustrious Spencer family. The girls have converted the drawing room of Devonshire House into a private gambling salon, where the Prince of Wales and other such figures reduce the size of their fortunes. The game of the night is hazard, and Georgiana has tossed the dice in the air, with the company on tenterhooks to see the result. It was an expensive hobby for the Duchess: by 1789, she was more than £60,000 in debt – over £6 million in today's money.

Perhaps Georgiana shouldn't have thrown away her family fortune with such nonchalance. In 1924, less than 130 years later, the ninth Duke of Devonshire faced over £500,000 of death duties and Devonshire House was demolished. Siegfried Sassoon felt this loss deeply, penning his melancholic poem 'Monody on the Demolition of Devonshire House'. He had enjoyed gazing into the ducal residence and imagining how 'Byron rang the bell and limped upstairs' and mourned as he watched it pulled apart by workmen, leaving 'not one nook survived to screen a mouse'.[21]

*A Gaming Table at Devonshire House*, Thomas Rowlandson, 1791.
Metropolitan Museum of Art, Rogers Fund, Transferred from the Library, 1941

But the nobility of Regency Britain cared little for the future, or even for tomorrow. They lived unapologetically in the moment.

Isaac Cruikshank's swipe at the feckless English upper class came in an eight-panelled account of a night away at Belvoir Castle. The heavy drinking has taken its toll on the guests, lost in turrets and towers and struggling to find their way to their rooms. 'Why Jack,' an older man exclaims, 'what wickedness have you been at – you have a woman's cap on!' 'Have I uncle,' the nephew replies, '– and if I don't mistake, this is an under petticoat about your shoulders.'

Another young gentleman, wandering the corridors in the early hours of the morning, has fallen upon his knees. 'Shew me to bed,' he declares to a lady, 'or give me something to drink – great lump of loveliness – devine Cherry-bum, – hear me! – give me some drink, thou mighty Castle Spectre!' But this was no ghost: 'Bless your honour,' she exclaims, 'I am only the cook.'

*The Humours of Belvoir Castle or the Morning After*, Isaac Cruikshank, 1799.
Royal Academy of Arts, London Library of Congress,
Prints and Photographs Division, Cartoon Prints, British

Gillray, too, delighted in nosing behind the closed doors of blue-blooded society. And what better way to demonstrate the composure and elegance of his social superiors than by embodying – or parodying – the style of mighty Joshua Reynolds himself? Gillray drew inspiration from two of Reynolds's most celebrated works.

The first is an ode to the aristocratic Montgomery daughters, Barbara, Elizabeth and Anne, who were often nicknamed 'the Three Irish Graces' for their natural beauty and Irish roots. Here they are frolicking among a pastoral landscape, decorating a statue of Hymen, the Greek god of marriage and fertility, with flowers. The second painting was a portrait of another celebrated society beauty, Lady Sarah Bunbury, who had attracted the attention of the future King George III in her youth. She went on to wed Sir Charles Bunbury, and it was during these years that she was made the subject of Reynolds's canvas. Here we see her dressed in some sort of Greco–Roman garb, giving her own votive offering to the sacrificial fire of the three daughters of Zeus: Aglaea, Euphrosyne and Thalia.

Gillray took Reynolds's lofty neoclassical pretensions and ran. Sprinted, in fact. For while he gave us five fashionable ladies proffering their own votive offerings, these were not the idealised beauties of Reynolds's sycophantic airbrushing. Gillray took Reynolds's delicate, porcelain women and injected some life. Gillray's women were *real* women. Big, busty and boisterous. Some wrinkly, some bony, some chinless. Like boarding school mothers, they were manageable alone, but terrifying en masse.

For this was *La Belle Assemblée*, the finest ladies of London society. There's the rotund, overstuffed Mrs Albinia Hobart, paying her own offering to the god of love.* And coming up at the rear is Lady Sarah Archer, famed for her riding skills and, according to Gillray, always with whip in hand.

* We previously met Albinia on a seesaw with the Duchess of Devonshire in Rowlandson's 1784 election satire.

*Lady Sarah Bunbury Sacrificing to the Graces*, Joshua Reynolds, *c.* 1765.
Art Institute Chicago, Mr and Mrs W.W. Kimball Collection

*La Belle Assemblée*, James Gillray, 1787.


There couldn't have been a more blatant spoof of the Royal Academy's lofty pretensions. In fact, the satirists had started ruffling the feathers of serious art circles. In 1795, the history painter James Barry wrote a letter to the Dilettanti Society, furious that London was infected by 'the profligate caricatura furniture of print shops, from Hyde-Park Corner to Whitechapel'. The caricatures were so debased and so damaging, Barry thought, that it would better to have no art at all: 'Better, better far,' he wrote, 'there had been no art, than thus to pervert and employ it to purposes so base, and so subversive of everything interesting to society.'[22]

The writer, John Corry would have agreed that caricatures were a dangerous, corrupting force. In 1800 he argued that the print shops were 'so gratifying to the fancy of the idle and licentious' that they 'must necessarily have a powerful influence on the morals and industry of the people'.[23]

But the printsellers would have been delighted to know they were causing a fracas in such important circles, and they began fuelling the fire with greater vigour. Next, Gillray came for the 'conversation piece', a favourite genre of Gainsborough and Zoffany. This was a pompous style of painting that captured families of the nobility relaxing in their stately houses, tending to pets, taking tea or playing instruments. The paintings were supposed to achieve informal elegance. But Gillray's conversation piece, *The Pic-Nic Orchestra*, was far from refined.

*The Pic-Nic Orchestra*, James Gillray, 1802.
Metropolitan Museum of Art, Harris Brisbane Dick Fund, 1917

His sitters are a choice selection of aristocrats, who were well known for their amateur musical concerts. Gillray gives us the band in full swing: Lord Cholmondeley on flute, Lord Mount Edgcumbe on cello, Lady Buckinghamshire on keys, Lady Salisbury on trumpet, Colonel Greville on violin. But this is no scene of balance and proportion: tiny Lord Mount Edgcumbe is dwarfed by the giant

Lord Cholmondeley, the enormous Lady Buckinghamshire, and his very own cello. There's not much harmony here either, for Lady Salisbury appears to be engaged in a horn-blowing competition, determined to be victor.

Gillray wasn't the only one who found farce in these musical amateurs. Just a week before, a notice from the *Morning Post Gazetteer* was outraged at Lord Cholmondeley's behaviour. How appalling that 'an English Earl, one of our hereditary legislators', would play the flute in public, the reports cried, and 'waste the breath that should be used in discussing our laws, to produce sounds from a piece of wood to tickle the ears of the tabbies!'[24]

The elephant in the room is, of course, Lady Buckinghamshire, that magnificent globe spilling over the piano stool. Gillray seemed particularly fond of creating impossibly plump, spherical women. The bulbous Buckinghamshire was certainly low-hanging fruit for Gillray's etching burin.

It was the same story for Elizabeth Billington, one of the most celebrated opera singers of the time, who was also famed for her stout physique. She was in the centre of a scandal; when her private letters were published, Joseph Haydn was amazed to find that 'you couldn't get a single copy after 3 o'clock in the afternoon'.[25] She was in high demand: the managers of Drury Lane and Covent Garden theatres squabbled over her performances. And of course, she was immortalised by the great artists of the age.

First, Mr Reynolds gave us Elizabeth Billington as society wished to see her. Reynolds cast her as Saint Cecilia, the patron saint of music. He made her a doe-eyed goddess who is passive, mute and slimmed down to resemble the ideal woman of the era.

But Gillray didn't have time for airbrushing. He gave us the real 'Betsy' Billington. She is stout and majestic, gorgeously curvaceous and swathed in luxurious, gold-trimmed drapery and plumes of feathers. What's more, her mouth is open – she's actually singing. Not just singing heartily, but singing from the bottom of her lungs, throwing

*Mrs Billington as St Cecilia*, James Ward, after Sir Joshua Reynolds
Yale Center for British Art

forward every ounce of strength to reach those notes. For this is Billington at her best: the moment she 'astonished the audience' with an impossibly tricky 'new bravura song'.[26] The Covent Garden opera-goers were treated to four minutes of devilishly difficult trills, of passages climbing higher and higher up the octaves, her crystal-clear voice filling the room. Would glasses begin to smash? the audience might have wondered. Would Billington faint? Would she explode? In Gillray's print, he shows every sign of the endeavour: her cheeks are ruddy with the exertion, her mouth wide open and, to steady herself, her head is thrown back, with one hand holding her bosom and another outstretched for balance. And out of her mouth comes the angelic sound itself: swirling lines floating up and away.

*A Bravura Air. Mandane*, James Gillray, 1801.
Metropolitan Museum of Art, Harris Brisbane Dick Fund, 1917

Unlike Reynolds's Billington, Gillray's take is honest, unapologetic and far more powerful. She is a musical maestro in command of London's stage, captured in all her sweaty, ruddy-faced glory. In Gillray's print you can actually feel the power of her voice.

In another print, Gillray even cast Billington as a 'siren', whose voice was so powerful she had the great Duke of Portland in the palm of her hand. Out blast her notes, delivered with total control: 'ha, ha, ha, a, ha, a, ha, a, ha', up and up they fly into the air 'he, he, he, ho, o, o, o, ha, o, ho, o, o, o'. It's hard to imagine Reynold's Billington putting on such a formidable display.

*The Bulstrode Siren*, James Gillray, 1801.
Digital Commonwealth: https://ark.digitalcommonwealth.org/ark:/50959/2z111k31x

Billington's performances were no doubt deserving of Gillray's satires, but she was not the only flamboyant character in London society. Her audience members were a spectacle in themselves, who followed some of the most ridiculous fashions in history.

One trend which became popular in the 1790s was for women to pad out their stomach. It was 'an exact representation of the state of pregnancy ... accompanied by a complete display of the bosom – which is uncovered and stuck out by the sash immediately below it'.[27] On seeing such fashions in the streets, one Dutch gentlemen took it to heart: 'Ah, God help their poor parents,' he wrote, 'how miserable they must be upon perceiving the situation their daughters are in.'[28]

But this was soon overtaken by the *beau monde*'s next obsession. All the faff of hoops, bustles, whalebones, stays, petticoats, stomachers, corsets, powdered hair and coiffures were out. Classical antiquity was in. It was shockingly risqué, with young ladies donning what might appear to us to be cotton nightdresses. They were low-cut, high-waisted dresses and – God forbid! – exposed the arms.

But most shockingly, the muslin, cambric or calico used to make them was near-transparent and unapologetically clingy. 'Female dress of the present fashion, is perhaps the most indecent ever seen in this country,' reported the *Sporting Magazine* in July 1794. 'The *breast* is altogether displayed, and the whole drapery, by the wanton management of the wearers ... is said to *cling* so to the figure that nothing can be said to be completely concealed.'[29] Jane Austen, writing to her sister in 1801, described the intrigue of one evening: a friend was 'at once expensively & nakedly dress'd; – we have had the satisfaction of estimating her Lace & her Muslin.'[30]

One glance at Gillray's *The Graces in a High Wind* gets the point across. Muslin and calico might look graceful enough in the safety of a ballroom, but how would they stand up to the elements? Was this really suitable attire for the Great British weather? One glance at Gillray's print tells you the answer: everything is on display here,

*The Graces in a High Wind*, James Gillray, 1810.
National Portrait Gallery

each curve of every bosom and pear-shaped hip are fully exposed by blustery winds. Far too explicit to be deemed graceful.

Gillray delighted in sartorial commentary. In *Following the Fashion*, he gave us two women dressed in the height of 1794 style. The first is tall and impossibly slim ('a Soul without a Body'), the second is short and squat ('a Body without a Soul'). But both are drowning in enormous puffs of material, huge scoop-like straw bonnets and feathers as big as a palm leaf.

*What would our ancestors think of the latest fashions?* wondered Isaac Cruikshank. In one of his best prints, he gave us two fashionable ladies, gazing at each other in astonishment. But while one lady is from 1796, the other has travelled forward in time from 1556. This lady of Queen Mary I's court is decked in an enormous ruff and swathes of heavy fabrics and is shocked into dumb silence by the clingy attire of the later fashionista.

The stylish members of polite society were evergreen material for London's satirists, but they weren't the only gang in town. Beneath this layer of froth and diaphanous drapery, London was swarming with a ruddy-faced hoi polloi, who inhabited the back streets and alleys surrounding Covent Garden. It was here that Rowlandson, Gillray and Cruikshank found a wonderland of delights. It is time, dear reader, to venture forth into this belly of the beast, the seedy underbelly of the capital.

# 9

# *What a Picture of* Life *Was There!*

## TWENTY-FOUR BUMPER TOASTS

By the late 1790s, the printsellers were as important to London's fabric as the bustle of a coffee house or the gentle curve of the Thames. No longer loose threads lying in the sewing basket, they were woven into the city's ever-growing tapestry, telling the story of each other and their fellow city-dwellers. The tapestry that emerged was one of vivid colour. For Covent Garden was the throbbing, thriving, bohemian heart of the city, whose artists lived and breathed its endless life, laughter and licentiousness.

These were the streets that had made the late Samuel Johnson declare in 1777 that 'when a man is tired of London, he is tired of life; for there is in London all that life can afford'.[1] This was the London where grown-ups behaved like students. Where, one night, Dr Johnson was awoken by his friends shouting at his bedroom window, demanding he joined their 'ramble'. 'What, is it you, you dogs!' he retorted, 'I'll have a frisk with you.'[2] Despite his protestations, he was persuaded to join. At 3am they 'sallied forth together into Covent-Garden'.[3] Johnson, being in a charitable mood, offered to help the grocers set up morning shop, but this was politely declined.

So, he drank a bowl of his favourite 'Bishop' liquor and rowed some 2 miles to Billingsgate, just next to the Tower of London.

But London was growing rapidly and, by the end of the century, it was teeming with more hustle and bustle than Dr Johnson ever saw, and bursting with 1 million inhabitants. Charles Lamb, a resident of Fleet Street, described the city to his friend, William Wordsworth:

> The lighted shops of the Strand and Fleet Street; the innumerable trades, tradesmen, and customers; coaches, wagons, playhouses; all the bustle and wickedness round about Covent Garden; the very women of the town; the watchmen, drunken scenes, rattles; life awake, if you awake, at all hours of the night; the impossibility of being dull in Fleet Street; the crowds, the very dirt and mud, the sun shining upon houses and pavements; the print-shops, the old-book stalls, parsons cheapening books; coffee-houses, steams of soups from kitchens; the pantomimes, London itself a pantomime and a masquerade, – all these things work themselves into my mind, and feed me without a power of satiating me. The wonder of these sights impels me into night-walks about her crowded streets, and I often shed tears in the motley Strand from fulness of joy at so much life.[4]

'What a picture of *life* was there!' remarked Isaac Cruikshank's son, George. 'It was *all life*!'[5] where laughter and eccentricity were integral to the wonderful every day. This was the city where everything and anything caused a fracas – for example, take 5 January 1797, when the hatter John Hetherington stepped out wearing a bold fashion choice: a top hat. It was the first time anyone had done so in the city. Londoners were beside themselves. Such 'shiny lustre' did its best 'to frighten timid people' and 'several women fainted at the unusual sight, while children screamed, dogs yelped and a younger son of Cordwainer Thomas was thrown down by the crowd which collected and had his right arm broken'.[6]

The beating heart of this circus was Covent Garden, the place I'm lucky enough to be writing this book from. My evening runs take me along Pall Mall, past Buckingham Palace, round St James's Park (sometimes stopping off at the Two Chairmen pub), back along Whitehall, past the National Gallery, up the Strand and back up Drury Lane. Would Gillray be a good running partner? I sometimes muse. He wouldn't talk much, which would suit me just fine. Rowlandson would probably turn up late, nursing a hangover, but would run with vigour, gossiping all the way. Cruikshank would be wearing Lycra and a Fitbit, still jogging at the traffic lights.

But these running partners would be surprised at how much London has changed. 'The King's put a new facade on Buckingham House, I see,' they would remark after seeing Buckingham Palace. 'What's that medieval monstrosity?' they would quip while jogging past Parliament. 'Is that bloke on the column supposed to be Nelson?' while weaving through Trafalgar Square. But as we finished off at Covent Garden, they would exclaim with joy: 'Ah! St Paul's Church. Why, that hasn't changed a bit! Glad to see you left that alone!'

Indeed, the piazza of Covent Garden is pretty similar to what Gillray, Rowlandson and Cruikshank would have known. It was built by the Earl of Bedford for the parishioners back in the days of Charles I. According to Horace Walpole, one of the eighteenth century's great writers and art historians, the Earl instructed Inigo Jones that the church be built on the cheap: 'I would not have it much better than a barn,' to which Jones replied: 'Well, then, you shall have the handsomest barn in England.'[7] The result was an exercise in Vitruvius' ideas of the Tuscan order: frugal, sombre and built to last.

Perhaps the Earl hoped this magnificent church would become the centre of solemn worship. He might have been surprised to know that it would become a hotbed of London revelry. If you'd been wandering past St Paul's Church at 10pm on a weekday in 1796 and headed towards the river – down Henrietta Street and then round to what is now Chandos Place – you would have heard riotous sounds.

*The Brilliants*, Thomas Rowlandson, 1801.

From the upstairs window of the White Swan tavern would've come raucous toasts drowned out by hearty cheers and bellowing laughter and glasses smashing and banging on tables. If you listened carefully, you might hear some familiar voices. For in the joyful throng were our good friends Thomas Rowlandson and Isaac Cruikshank.

They were part of the Brilliants Club, a private club dedicated to getting absolutely plastered, according to Rowlandson's etching of 1801. The club had only three rules and they were very straightforward. First, 'each member shall fill a half Pint Bumper to the first Toast'.* Second, 'after Twenty four Bumper toasts are gone round† every may fill as he pleases'. Third, if anyone breaks these rules, they must drink a 'bumper of Salt and Water'. Unsurprisingly, Rowlandson's scene is mayhem: toasts are being declared from every side of the table, some are drinking and some are vomiting. And

* To fill a glass 'bumper' meant to fill it to the brim.

† In other words, after twelve pints.

several hours later, Rowlandson and Cruikshank would stagger back to their lodgings just a few minutes away.

There were plenty of clubs like this in London. Some intellectual, some musical, some political. Rowlandson's friends were part of the Sublime Society of Beef Steaks, where members wore waistcoats with brass buttons bearing the words 'Beef and liberty'. A leading member of this society, the Duke of Norfolk, was known to consume fifteen steaks in one meal.[8]

Another group, the Anacreontic Society, was a subject of Gillray's copper plate. This society attracted amateur musicians who caroused in the name of Anacreon, the Greek poet. 'While snug in our Club-room we jovially "twine",' Gillray's print tells us, 'the myrtle of Venus with Bacchus' wine.'

Each meeting, they sang the society song in a four-part setting. Next, there were 'various celebrated Catches, Glees, Songs, Duettos, and

*Anacreontick's in Full Song*, James Gillray, 1801.
National Portrait Gallery

other Vocal, with some Rhetorical compositions, till twelve O Clock'.[9] But, as Gillray's print shows us, the festivities raged on into the night for those with enough stamina. Here, eight members remain, the clock reading 3.40am. Some sing, some snore and a dog howls. Empty bottles and glasses are still overflowing: the party is far from over.

Rowlandson would have been familiar with such chaos. One of his prints – perhaps a fond memory of his youth – shows three students visited by two elderly men, who are throwing their hands up in disbelief. But are these students hard at work? Nose in a book? Silently ruminating? No such diligence is found here: these students are in a drunken slumber. The table is covered with a large punchbowl and drinking glasses. Mortarboards litter the floor. But, as if to say, 'Such is life', Rowlandson adds a quote from Cicero: '*O Tempora, O Mores!*'* Heavy drinking and raucous conviviality were essential to this era of excess.

*O Tempora, O Mores!* Thomas Rowlandson, 1787.

* 'Oh the Times! Oh the Customs!'

And despite the wars in France, the politicians were keen to lead the frivolities with some of their own biblical drinking sessions. On Wednesday 24 January 1798, a birthday celebration for Charles Fox was held at the Crown and Anchor tavern. The *Morning Chronicle* reported the events the next day:

> The annals of British Liberty do not record an instance of so large a Meeting of its friends as was held yesterday at the Crown and Anchor Tavern on the occasion of the festival of Mr Fox. The capacity and arrangements of that immense Tavern were put to the proof for dinner was served without confusion or disorder to near 2,000 persons assembled to testify their affection for the virtues of this illustrious Statesman or to rally under the standard of his political opinions. It was the Feast of Liberty and the enthusiasm of the company corresponded with the sentiment that animated their souls.[10]

But on Friday 26 January, the *True Briton* printed a report 'from a *sober* corespondent':

> WEDNESDAY, in pursuance of the Public Advertisements, a concourse of people assembled to celebrate the Anniversary of Mr Fox's Birthday. The large Room at the Crown and Anchor as well as the other rooms, were filled at an early hour. It is supposed about 1400 persons were assembled on the occasion. The dinner was served up in a manner very unpleasant to the generality of the Guests, and a greater scene of noise and confusion was scarcely ever witnessed upon any occasion – greater even than on former meetings of the same nature. Small Beer and Porter were in perpetual demand, and occasioned no small outcry during the dinner.[11]

Rowlandson was still one of the Three Jolly Dogs, with his old pals Henry Angelo and Jack Bannister. Angelo, the son of the famous fencing master, was now running his father's Angelo's School of Arms, teaching London's fashionable society how to wield a foil. Bannister, the prankster of the Royal Academy Schools, was now the most popular comedian of his day. He commanded the stages of the Drury Lane Theatre and was well on his way to becoming the manager. These old friends were regularly joined by Henry Wigstead, the chap who had worked on the Brighton Pavilion and travelled with Rowlandson on his drawing trips. Peter Pindar, the satirical writer who made his name making a mockery of the Royal Academy, was another recent addition to the gang.

'Well, I do remember sitting in this comfortable apartment,' Henry Angelo recalled, 'listening to the stories of my old friend Peter Pindar, whose wit seemed not to kindle until after midnight, at the period of his fifth or sixth glass of brandy and water. Rowlandson, too, having nearly accomplished his twelfth glass of punch, and replenishing his pipe with choice *Oronooko* tobacco, would chime in.'[12]

Rowlandson's obituary would confirm this: he 'indulged in his predilections for a joyous life, and mixed himself with the gayest of the gay'.[13] He also took part in the typical vices of the day. Like the Prince of Wales and the Duchess of Devonshire, he was familiar with hard drinking, gambling and promiscuity:

> [Rowlandson] was known in London at many of the fashionable gaming houses, alternatively won and lost without emotion, till at length he was minus several thousand pounds ... he had frequently played throughout a night and the next day; and that once, such was his infatuation with the dice, he continued at the gaming table nearly thirty six hours.[14]

Rowlandson was, according to friends, 'unhappily, much addicted to games of chance'. For those who tried to talk him out of it, the warning was 'spare your sympathy and advice also ... for that Tom Rowlandson was, is, and ever will be incurable'.[15]

But historians must be thankful for this habit. His financial perils resulted in a prolific output of work. 'I think it may safely be averred,' Henry Angelo remarked, 'that [Rowlandson] has sketched or executed more subjects of real sciences, in his original, rapid manner, than any ten artists, his contemporaries, and etched more plates than any artist, ancient or modern.'[16]

Rowlandson was also a regular at 'low life' pubs like the Bell near Furnival's Inn, the Coal Hole off the Strand and the Coach and Horses by Somerset House. Blokey pubs filled with tradesmen, shopkeepers and labourers. Here, he might smoke his Oronooko tobacco in a long, white ceramic pipe. Once finished, these were tossed away; many were flung into the Thames, along whose banks they can still be found today. It was these establishments that Rowly and Gillray put the world to rights over a bowl of punch, as Angelo recorded:

> They would, perhaps, exchange half-a-dozen questions and answers upon the affairs of copper and aquafortis; swear all the world was one vast masquerade; and then enter into the common chat of the room, smoke their cigars, drink their punch, and sometimes early, sometimes late, shake hands at the door – look up at the stars, say it is a frosty night, and depart, one for the Adelphi, the other to St James's street, each to his bachelor's bed.[17]

## THE COUNTENANCE OF MEN AND BEASTS

The circus of merriment swirling around the piazza of Covent Garden had always been a magnet for artists, engravers, wits, writers, dramatists and actors; towards the end of the century, they were joined by framers, print shop owners and auctioneers. Joshua Reynolds lived in Leicester Fields* until his death in 1792, and Josiah Wedgwood

* Today's Leicester Square.

and Thomas Chippendale set up on St Martin's Lane to sell their porcelain vases and fine furniture.

In 1793, Joseph Farrington recorded one particularly productive meeting with his fellow Royal Academicians in the Covent Garden piazza. 'The meeting of the Academy,' he wrote in his diary, 'did not break up past twelve o'clock, when Hamilton, Smirke, and myself went to the Bedford Coffee House, where we found Tyler, Rooker, Dance, Lawrence, Westall', all the most respected Royal Academicians. 'We staid till four in the morning.'[18]

This city provided endless subject matter for its artists. Not the timeless *ideals* preached by the Royal Academy, but the timeless *folly* of mankind itself. Rowlandson, in particular, was interested by everything and everyone – from dissolute aristocrats to the vast body of the poor.

He painted taverns with broken candles and glowing fires and snoozing dogs and empty bottles on the floor. He went into the streets to find scrawny old men singing from song sheets, soot-drenched chimney sweeps leaning against rails or rotund soldiers wallowing in coffee houses. There were rakes and Macaronis, prostitutes and mistresses, cits* and sots. They would be smoking tobacco and playing billiards and drinking gin and gambling away fortunes in taverns and coffee houses and back alleys and bawdy houses and the clubs of St James's. No one was safe from the satirists' Big Brother eye.

To make order of the chaos, Rowlandson developed his own cast of archetypes: the quack doctor, the physician, the politician from a rotten borough and the bawdy-house mistress. They were immediately recognisable to print shop visitors: 'That's you! And that one

* A 'cit' was an insulting way to describe a member of London's merchant class.

with the heaving bosom looks just like Aunt Caroline!' Rowlandson found delight in forcing opposites together – pairing up the young and old, tall and short, fat and thin, elegant and brutish, dark skin and light skin, respectable and ruinous, country bumpkin and gritty Londoner, healthy and sick, living and dead. Perhaps he read the 1788 rule book for caricatures, which pronounced that 'contrast alone will sometimes produce a ludicrous effect'.[19]

And to make the most of this cast of misfits and juxtapositions, Rowlandson didn't just look to the man on the street. He looked to the dog in the gutter, the lion in the wardrobe. The entire animal kingdom, in fact. He made pages of drawings comparing human figures with their animal counterparts: a beady-eyed man with a sheep, a fashionable lady with a peacock, an ugly woman with a duck, a tight-faced schoolmaster with a fish, a lecherous man with a lizard and a rugged farmhand with a cow.

In the streets of Piccadilly, Rowlandson didn't see a street of pedestrians, he saw a zoo alive with characters of avine, bovine, leonine, lupine, elephantine, equine and feline tendencies. And like Leonardo da Vinci, Ghezzi and Carracci had done before him, Rowlandson hoped to reveal something of their internal workings by exaggerating their external features.

This wasn't just an artistic tool. There were all sorts of scientific theories about grey matter swirling around during this time. In 1791, the scientist Franz Joseph Gall was grappling with one of the greatest mysteries of modern science: the brain. Gall tried to identify different parts of the brain. What if – he considered – these parts of the brain alluded to different personality traits? And wouldn't these show up as bumps and bulges on your skull? And wouldn't this change the shape of your face? And, if you worked out a systemic form of categorising these, wouldn't you be able to tell that someone was clever, or stupid, or careless, just by looking at them?

Gall was determined to get to the bottom of this baseless theory, building up his own collection of skulls, head casts and brain casts.

*Comparative Anatomy*, Thomas Rowlandson, 1800–1825.

He initially called the practice 'Cranioscopy', from cranium, meaning skull, and *scopos*, meaning vision.*

* Today, this dubious practice is known as 'phrenology', from *phren*, meaning mind, and *logos*, meaning study. With the blessing of proper medical knowledge, we know phrenology to be a pseudoscience, happily confined to the past. Although it was in its infancy in Rowlandson's time, by the late Victorian age, phrenology developed a sinister edge, encouraging gender and racial stereotypes through 'scientific evidence', which were used to inform theories of criminology. By the twentieth century, such theories were used by eugenicists to argue certain racial groups had lower intelligence. This was put into practice most notably

Rowlandson was well aware of Gall's theories, later dedicating an entire copper plate to the mad scientist. In Rowlandson's print, Gall's macabre collection of model heads are labelled 'Lawyers, thieves & murderers', 'Poets, dramatists, actors', 'Philosophers, statesmen & historians'. Rowlandson had clearly read extensively on the subject, including Giovanni Battista della Porta's 1586 work, *De Humana Physiognomonia*. Rowlandson wrote in a note-to-self that the author 'observed the resemblances between the countenances of Men & Beasts and has extended this enquiry furthest. He as far as I know was the first who rendered this similarity apparent buy placing the countenances of men & beasts beside each other – Nothing can be more true than this fact.'[20]

As the ideas of physiognomy developed, and caricature along with it, there was also a significant growth in membership of some peculiar clubs, peppered up and down the country, which revelled in any strange 'Marks and Signatures which Nature seems to have set upon' the face of a man. A series of 'Ugly Clubs' were set up, hoping to make 'every one sit down content in his own Carcass'.[21] Where nature had thought to make an ugly face, the only solution was to 'be merry upon the Occasion'.[22] Only ugly people could be members and thus the entry requirements were peculiar: 'The prominence of a candidate's nose, and the length of his chin, especially if they should happen to meet together like a pair of nutcrackers,' was an open door to membership. Likewise, those blessed with 'a large Carbuncle, Potato Nose' would have preference over those with a 'Roman or King William's'.[23]

Alongside an intellectual fascination with physiognomy, Rowlandson no doubt shared this cheerful, reasoned view of ugliness. It's no surprise that crowds became a happy home for Rowlandson

by the Nazis in the Second World War, who used the body measurements of Jewish people and other minority groups as 'evidence' of their supposed biological inferiority, which would be used to justify the Holocaust, one of the most abominable episodes of cruelty in human history.

to put his reading into practice. One of the best crowds for scientific dissection was to be found in the theatres of Covent Garden, where the characters were neatly segmented into boxes, galleries and pits. This was a perfect set of models. Here, Rowlandson could compare and contrast everyone from King George and Queen Charlotte to plain tradesmen and scholars. They betrayed expressions of shock and sorrow and delight, some snoozing, some canoodling.

All were captured by Rowlandson's hand, dancing across cream laid paper. Freeing himself from the restraints of the copper plate and etching burin, Rowlandson began favouring black and brown ink washes, emboldened with watercolour and graphite. Drawing, painting and sketching at every moment and catching the moments of London's brilliant pantomime before the next one appeared.

## MEDICAL HOCUS POCUS

Gillray and Cruikshank also revelled in the comedy of everyday life. They churned out prints of sleepwalkers in a nightcap and nightshirt, wandering down the stairs while in the grip of REM. There were women urinating in the street, crying: 'Blast you, what are you staring at?' There was a gout-stricken foot, throbbing pink, with a vicious demon digging its barbed fangs and sharp teeth into the naked flesh.

Gillray took position 'from his vantage-ground in St James's Street' and 'commanded a battery the volleys of which constantly rattled amid friend and foe'.[24] He found medical mishaps leant themselves to such ridicule in particular. One of these related to cowpox and the work of the physician Dr Jenner. Cowpox was a mild viral infection affecting cows, that would cause a few weeping spots on the animals' udders, but nothing more serious. It was often caught by milkmaids, who would fall unwell but soon recover. But what caught the attention of Dr Jenner was the country lore that claimed the same milkmaids who had recovered from cowpox never caught smallpox.

Were these folk tales true? In 1796, Jenner conducted an experiment. He rubbed cowpox into the arm of James Phipps, the eight-year-old son of his gardener. Young James Phipps, who had never had cowpox or smallpox, became immune to both. Jenner's miraculous discovery was filled in a vaccination report.*

But the anti-vaxxers were vitriolic. Some opposed the process on religious grounds, believing that it was wrong to overturn the will of God. Other traditionalists were suspicious of change. And there were some who feared mixing animal and human matter. What kind of monstrous bovine mutations would occur?

Leading the campaign of fake news and disinformation was Benjamin Moseley. He thought up an entire set of maladies with their Latin equivalent: he warned of Cow Pox Face (*Facies Bovilla*), Cow Pox Itch (*Scabies Bovilla*), Cow Pox Scaldhead (*Tinea Bovilla*) and Cow Pox Farcy (*Elephantiasis Bovilla*). He described the cases of Sarah Burley, 'whose face was distorted, and began to resemble that of an Ox; and Edward Gee who was covered with sores, and afterwards with patches of Cow's Hair'.[25]

This sort of news was irresistible to the satirical minds of the printmakers, and Gillray soon set to work on *The Cow-Pock – or – the Wonderful Effects of the New Inoculation!* Taking us to the vaccination centre of St Pancras, Dr Jenner is treating his patients with a bucket of 'Vaccine Pock hot from ye Cow'. The scene is chaos. The vaccine's results are immediate: sprouting out from cheeks, noses, arms and foreheads, and tearing through clothes, are horrible mutations of tiny prancing cows and sturdy pairs of horns.

In fairness to the 1790s anti-vaxxers, there was good reason to be suspicious of medical treatments. There was plenty of 'medical hocus-pocus' going around.[26] The most famous instances of this were the practices of two Americans, Elisha and Benjamin Perkins, who managed to convince much of high society that their treatment

* The lexical origins of 'vaccination' being *vacca*, the Latin word for 'cow'.

*The Cow-Pock – or – the Wonderful Effects of the New Inoculation!*, James Gillray, 1802.
Library of Congress, Prints & Photographs Division

could cure all manner of ills, from rheumatism, gout and lockjaw to tumours, sprains and headaches.

The treatment they popularised was the use of 'tractors': two three-inch metal rods with a pointed end, 'tractors' coming from the archaic definition meaning 'that which pulls'. The magic power came from them being unusual metal alloys (although, in reality, they were made of plain old steel and brass). After applying the points to the inflicted part of the body for twenty minutes, they were said to draw off the noxious electrical fluid that lay at the root of suffering, leaving the patient 'perfectly cured'.[27] Londoners fell for it hook, line and sinker: the Perkinean Institute was established in Frith Street in Soho and a public dinner to celebrate its opening was held at the Crown and Anchor.[28]

Elisha Perkins may have had dubious medical knowledge, but he was a genius of marketing. His son, Benjamin, brought the device to London and packed the *True Briton*, the *Morning Post* and *The Times* with adverts; it seems likely he got in touch with Gillray to dedicate a copper plate to the scam. Gillray's print captured the moment of treatment, as Elisha Perkins himself applies the electrical tractors to zap the hopeful patient. 'As soon as the surgical prospector begins to use his diving rod on this rich copper mine,' wrote a contemporary journal regarding Gillray's plate, 'a powerful tremor shakes the whole mountain of flesh and fat like an earthquake. Bright sparks tackle and spread out in electrical showers the nose and nostrils.'[29]

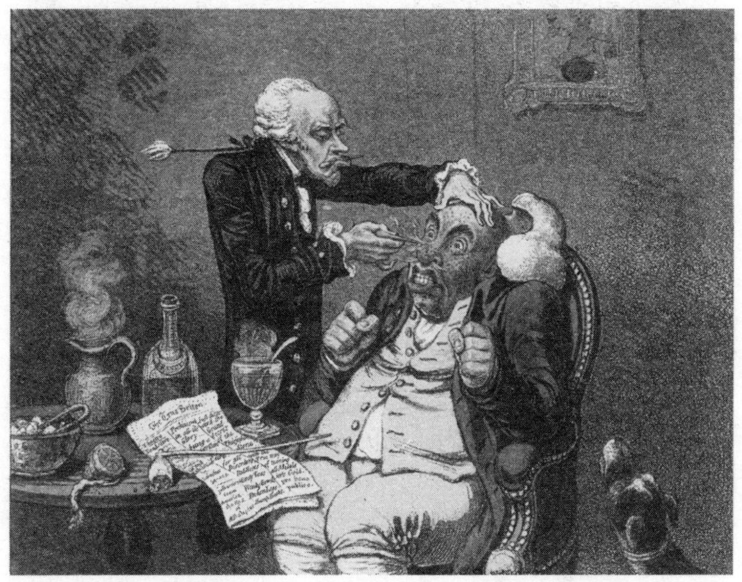

*Metallic Tractors*, James Gillray, 1801.
Digital Commonwealth: https://ark.digitalcommonwealth.org/ark:/50959/2z111j559

While Gillray was clearly a sceptic, Perkins was no doubt delighted at the coverage: after all, there's no such thing as bad publicity.

## A DISMAL UNINHABITED PLACE

But how did these printmakers settle in this eruption of animation, this revelry of ribaldry?

After living on the Strand for just a year, Rowlandson took a lease with 83 years left to run in December 1792. This was big a step up, Rowlandson's 'new address, new me' moment. For he now was part of the Adelphi complex, one of the most fashionable addresses in London.

Built between 1768 and 1772, the Adelphi was the ambitious brainchild of Scottish brothers Robert and James Adam.* Located between the Strand and the Thames, this was the first neoclassical building in London; it contained eleven large houses, all with glorious south-facing views over the river. They were raised high above the water, for underneath was a layer of busy wharves used by tradesmen, where goods were loaded and unloaded from the crafts on the river. The main terrace attracted a smart crowd. It boasted the headquarters for the Society for the Encouragement of Arts, Manufactures and Commerce and a number of the big cheeses of London society. David Garrick, the celebrated Shakespearean actor and playwright, and friend of Samuel Johnson, lived on the terrace until his death in 1779. The Attorney General Sir Archibald Macdonald moved into No. 8 in 1792, and the Solicitor General, Sir John Freeman-Mitford, had No. 1 from 1794. And behind the terrace, the Adelphi complex continued: Robert Street and John Adam Street had rows of large, handsome brick houses.

And now Thomas Rowlandson was joining the Adelphi crowd. His new pad was the basement of No. 2 Robert Street, which was a twenty-year-old development when he moved in. The previous leaseholder was the late Captain Sir George Richardson, who had travelled the world and made his fortune on the *Pigot*, a sailing ship chartered by the East India Company. It was in Richardson's old basement on Robert Street – once used for servants' quarters, kitchens, larders and sculleries – that Thomas Rowlandson set himself up. It was a maze of nooks and crannies, with access to cellars to store liquors and a vault

* *Adelphi* being the Greek word for 'brothers'.

under the street for coal. The estate agent ad would have described it as 'a well-connected, quirky basement flat in a sought-after area'.

It was not until Thomas moved in that he realised the downsides of storing drawings and watercolours in a basement a mere stone's throw from the Thames. The watercolours were up against a four-pronged attack of vermin, damp, flooding and subsidence. The environment was pretty horrendous for someone working from home. The basement backed on to a cobbled track which had a constant stream of loaded carts and wagons, supplying the wharves below. The air in Rowlandson's rooms would have been thick with coal dust and the smell of smoke, horses, sewage, dead fish and offal. Every day in London, the thousands of horses dropped twenty-two pounds of dung, each.[30] And to test all of poor Rowlandson's senses, he was subjected to sleep with the London soundscape. 'The clatter of the night coaches had scarcely ceased, before that of the morning carts began' wrote one visitor. 'The dustman with his bell, and his chant of dust-ho! succeeded to the watchmen; then came the porter-house boy for the pewter-pots which had been sent out for supper the preceding night; the milkman next, and so on, a succession of cries, each in a different tone, so numerous, that I could no longer follow them in my inquiries.'[31]

But these dismal conditions were the least of Rowlandson's problems. It seemed the Adam brothers had seriously underestimated the levels of the Thames, and the vaults and basements of the complex were soon awash with floodwater. The rate return of April 1794 includes a note that 'Thos Rowlandson' had 'removed to James Street No. 1'.[32]

It was only temporary: Tom had upped sticks and moved back up the hill towards the Strand, while his basement dried out. But the winter of 1794–5 brought over frost and heavy rainstorms. In mid-February 1795, the Thames spilt over again. By 1797, it seemed Rowlandson had reached his limit. The rate inspector marked that the basement was empty, 'a dismal uninhabited place', and 'likely to continue so'.[33] Rowlandson had moved in permanently to an attic in James Street, in an attempt to get as high up and far away from that infernal river.

A sketch of Rowlandson at the time shows him sporting a large pile of wavy hair, tied back in a cue* at the back.[34] He had a long nose and large hooded eyes. He comes across as a serious, contemplative man, lost in his own thoughts. Historians might say it is a classic depiction of the troubled satirist, mentally untangling the troubled world around him. Possibly. But considering Rowlandson's drinking antics, it seems more likely that he had been in the Shakespeare's Head tavern the night before and was facing the miserable consequences.

*Portrait of Thomas Rowlandson*, John Raphael Smith, undated.

* A low ponytail.

And on the topic of the previous night's pleasures, perhaps Rowlandson was thinking of the fairer sex. His sketches from tours of Hampshire showed all sorts of flirtations with buxom girls, and he needed no excuse to cheekily lift a skirt or add a saucy joke. But what of anything long term? Did he have a belle at this point? It's impossible to say either way, as the evidence that we have is thin.

The only possible suggestion of any love affairs comes from two handwritten notes, on the reverse of one of Rowlandson's drawings. The first reads: 'My Dear Rowlandson / I shall be at home and alone, if you will favour me with a call I shall be happy CN.'

At home and alone! Whoever CN is, they might as well have written *Come hither!* A reply from Rowlandson was scribbled below: 'Dear Bess / Am Obliged to dine out shall not be able to call on you before ten o clock.'[35]

Late night visits to Bess? What presumption! What impropriety! Who was this Elizabeth? There are a few candidates. There were three printsellers: Elizabeth D'Archeray of St James's Street, Elizabeth Jackson of Marylebone Street and Elizabeth Bull of Ludgate Hill. Was he really mixing work with pleasure? Disappointingly, the likely candidate was most probably Elizabeth Howitt, his *sister*, who now lived at 4 Old Compton Street.[36]

## THIS IS A FOOLISH AFFAIR METHINKS

And what of the laconic Gillray. Did he find a sweetheart? According to those who knew him, he was a catch: an 'extremely well-informed and widely read man, pleasant in company, with an effervescent wit'.[37] He was a man who kept himself to himself: 'No one would guess this gaunt, bespectacled figure, this dry man, was a great artist.'[38]

If Gillray did have a lover, he didn't bother to look very far, certainly not outside Covent Garden. Not outside his own street, nor even the print shop itself. By the 1790s, Gillray was working exclusively for Hannah Humphrey. By 1793, he had moved in, taking a room above Hannah's shop – a development that no doubt raised a few eyebrows among Rowlandson and his fellow gossips.

We know little about Hannah. She stars in a single Gillray print, portrayed as a jolly, bespectacled lady, engulfed with ribbons and bonnet, enjoying the conviviality of a game of whist. She is square-faced, with a small, tight mouth. She was about fifteen years older than Gillray, earning her the nickname 'Old Mother Humphrey'. Angelo recalled that she was 'not much given to the melting mood'[39] – read into that what you will. But from all accounts, she was a 'good friend and kind landlady',[40] and her letters show she was a shrewd, straight-forward person of simple taste. It seems that it was Hannah who kept young James on the straight and narrow.

By 1793, Gillray was probably lodging above her shop – first at 18 Old Bond Street, and then, at 37 New Bond Street in 1794, when she moved. He was certainly lodging with Hannah in 1797 when they set up shop at 27 St James's Street (the year of his mother's death) where he lived until the end of his life. Mrs Humphrey and her maid, Betty, were 'all the world to [Gillray]',[41] although this was more

Detail from *Two-Penny Whist*, James Gillray, 1796.

because 'they saved him the trouble of thinking of household affairs' than down to passion.[42] And, it seemed as if Gillray was prickly to work with; he was 'highly sensitive to criticism'.[43]

Nevertheless, Hannah put up with him, and he repaid her tolerance in unusual ways: in 1793 Gillray gave her a mahogany fire screen decorated with tiny caricatures. It was marked 'Jas Gillray, 1793, / For his old friend and / Publisher H. Humphrey, / as a mark of respect / and esteem.'[44] Letters between the two indicate an increasing affection, as things are taken up a notch from 'Dear Gillray' and 'yours sincerely', to 'Dear Gilly' and 'your affectionate friend'. The editor of *The Caricatures of Gillray*, printed in 1824, was clearly suspicious:

> Gillray, it is said, had more than once made nuptial overtures to the mistress of the house, which had not been refused. Indeed, it was asserted that they once proceeded to St James's Church to be made one the hold bands of matrimony, but, that on approaching the door of the sacred place, he whispered to the good lady, 'This is a foolish affair methinks, Miss Humphrerys [*sic*]—We lived very comfortably together, and we had better let well alone,' when turning upon his heel, he returned to his old quarters, and went coolly to work on his copper.[45]

A disappointing day out for Hannah, no doubt.

Despite flirting with tying the knot, there was, it was said, never any impropriety between the two. The same writer stated that despite living together for so many years 'report never whispered aught to the moral disparagement of Gillray [or] Miss Humphrey'.[46] The arts writer George Stanley, who would have been familiar with Gillray and Humphrey as a young boy, confronted the rumours: 'It had been whispered that there was a liaison between Gillray and Mrs Humphrey not essential to their relation as designer and publisher'. But he emphatically denied them, his evidence coming from the authority of 'persons of strictest morals ... at whose family table

Gillray and Mrs Humphrey dined on Christmas Day regularly for more than the last twenty years of his life'.[47]

It was a more straightforward tale for the Cruikshank clan, who were happy and prosperous. By 1794, they'd nestled into family life at 117 Dorset Street, Salisbury Square, just beside St Bride's Church on Fleet Street. Isaac and Mary had two young sons: a five-year-old named Robert, and a two-year-old name George, who were 'constantly devouring' the adventures of *Robinson Crusoe*.[48] It was a sociable home with printmaking at the heart of family life. While their father etched the copper from his designs, the boys were allowed to help their formidable mother with the hand-colouring and lettering.

Isaac enjoyed entertaining and would recount stories of his upbringing in Edinburgh or his father's experience at Culloden. He loved having a stream of interesting guests: the young George Dawe regularly dropped in, a man who would later make his name painting 329 portraits of Russian generals for St Petersburg's Winter Palace. And they had visits from Mungo Park, the famed explorer, who would enchant the young boys with tales of jungles, wild animals, witchcraft and daring escapes from his expeditions in Africa.

But the Cruikshank boys didn't need to head to Africa for daring adventures. They didn't need to go further than their own street. For London was a jungle in itself: a tangle of exotic specimens, rare species and dangerous predators. A delicate ecosystem where Gillray, Rowlandson and Cruikshank were top of the food chain. And as the century came to a close, Gillray was getting peckish.

# 10

# *A Wonderland of Delights*

## A PUZZLE OF PORTRAITS

Rowlandson's pen-and-ink sketches of Covent Garden's hoi polloi would certainly have ruffled the Royal Academy feathers. But stylistically, in terms of the way he marked out his characters, he hadn't ventured far. He had a 'lightness and daintiness of touch which was his peculiar gift, bringing all the graces, sparkle and animation of the French school'.[1] His street sellers had classical poses. His raucous drinking scenes could be mistaken for the preparatory studies of a great conversation piece. His sketches danced with big ideas of art – some sublime, some picturesque. His country townscapes would happily tick the pastoral idyll.

But Gillray had cut ties with the fine art tradition. Whether he had taken a lot of snuff, or overdosed on coffee, or became intoxicated by the smell of raw sewage that filled London's streets and wafted up to his bedroom window, Gillray's art had got *weird*. From his modest lodgings above Hannah Humphrey's shop, he was producing some of the most creative and shocking art ever to have graced the streets of London. To be Gillrayic was to be cutting edge, to be avant garde. He was the Tracy Emin, the Damien Hirst, the Banksy of his day.

This evolution started at the beginning of the 1790s, in the midst of French revolutionary carnage. Gillray seems to have mentally saved a digital image of a mathematical diagram, inspired by Euclid's famous text, *Elements*. 'A Sphere, is a Figure bounded by a Convex surface; it is the most perfect of all forms.' But a plane is 'a perfectly even & regular Surface, it is the most Simple of all Figures'. A plane vs a sphere, then.

Gillray imagined a print showing William Pitt, who was tall and thin, with the society hostess, the perfectly plump Albinia Hobart. What if you lined up the two images of the diagram and the people on Photoshop? And what if you selected the merge button?

Click. Fifteen seconds of watching the spinning wheel. Merge complete.

The result was masterful: Pitt was stretched out to become the plane; Mrs Hobart puffed up to become a sphere. Her heaving bosom, bulbous tummy and enormous bottom fill it up perfectly. And to keep Mrs Hobart upright (and save her the indecency of rolling around), she is wheeled in on a trolley. Her beady eyes have fallen on her victim, who she pushes up against. This is the other half of Euclid's pontificating, the plane. Playing this role is the tall, thin and terribly straight Prime Minister William Pitt. With his hands in his pockets, and an expression of nervousness, he appears unsure about how to deal with this enormous woman, who is determined to have her way.

Gillray was eager to try his new skills again. What about when Pitt, on entering his ninth year as prime minister, was accused of usurping the prerogatives of the Crown? Would Gillray turn Pitt into a thief, perhaps? Stealing the Crown jewels from the Tower of London? Or sitting on a throne of his own making? Or changing his email sign-off to include HRH? No. Gillray took two opposing scenes. One was a stinking, hot, fermenting cowpat, the other the crown of George III.

Click. Merge. The crown became the dunghill. And out of this dirt grew a large 'Toadstool'. But this horrid 'Excrescence', this great 'Fungus' growing off the rotting crown was the morphed face

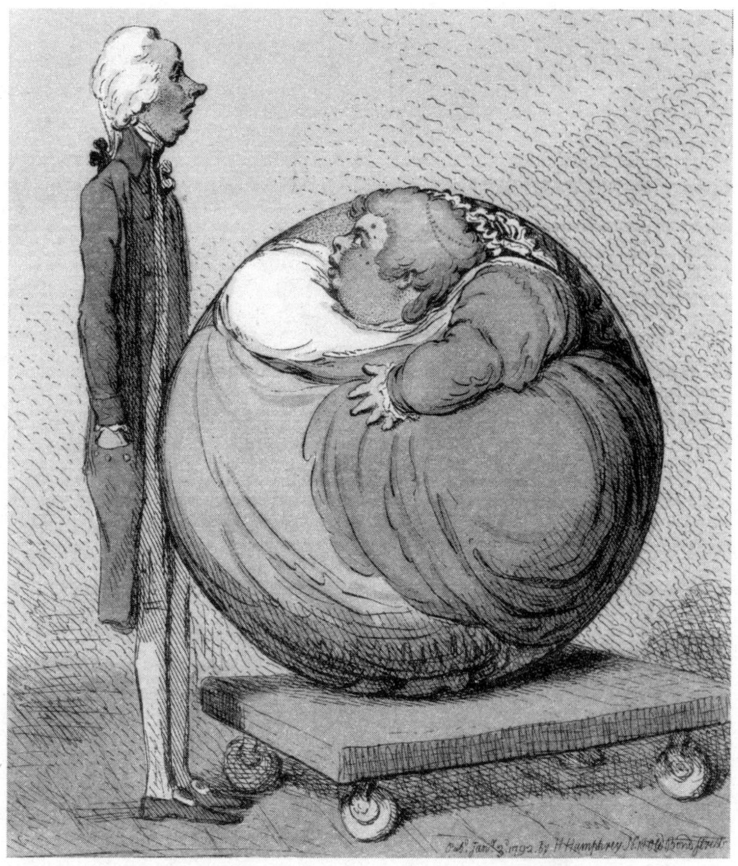

*A Sphere, projecting against a Plane*, James Gillray, 1792.
Digital Commonwealth: https://ark.digitalcommonwealth.org/ark:/50959/2z111j851

of William Pitt, his long nose and double chin perfectly filling the requirements of a prime mushroom.

Soon, Cruikshank took a leaf out of Gillray's weird book. In one print, he gives us an oddly shaped hourglass. But rub your eyes and take a second glance. This same print has become a 'puzzle of portraits': silhouettes of the prime minister and the King. Once Cruikshank had tricked your brain and ruined your eyesight with

*An Excrescence; a Fungus; alias a Toadstool upon a Dung-hill*, James Gillray, 1791.
Yale Center for British Art

optical illusions, he began playing God. He merged human and insect DNA. The results were terrifying: the specimen had the body of a locust and the head of a Pitt – a creature that would have thrived in Bosch's nightmarish underworld.

These surrealist sparks caught on with other printmakers too. One up-and-coming London satirist, John Nixon, began morphing his characters into packs of playing cards. His humorous sketches converted 'spades, hearts, clubs, and diamonds, into grotesque figures and groups, which he designed with a whimsicality of appropriation'.[2]

*A Puzzle of Portraits*, Isaac Cruikshank, 1794.

*The Political Locust*, Isaac Cruikshank, 1795.

In the 1790s, the wonderland of London's print shop windows were exciting beyond belief: this was an age when images on the street were such a rarity that a new pub sign was worth a visit. Their surrealist visions were – and still are – unsettling.

It might have been the Golden Age of British Satire, but perhaps the Gillray gang could also be known as the First Surrealists, too. Even in the twenty-first century, with our eyes adjusted to the weirdness of Salvador Dalí, graphic design and every kind of CGI fantasy visual Hollywood can cook up, these visions are still unnerving.

## LOOK, MUM, I'M ON TV!

It's no surprise, then, that such surrealism was incredibly powerful. These prints could be dangerous, pulling down reputations that had taken years to build. But they could also be harnessed and shaped, putting young upstarts on the political map. For a new MP, being featured in a Gillray print said that you were 'in' the political bubble. An establishment seal of recognition.

One politician who was particularly aware of this was a chap named George Canning, an ambitious 25-year-old with 'lively wit' and a mop of hair that 'a raven might have envied'.[3] As Canning began his political career, snuggling up to Pitt, he made a concerted effort to network himself into a Gillray print via a mutual friend, the Reverend John Sneyd. On 21 August 1795, Canning wrote in his diary, full of hope: '[Sneyd] tells me that Mr Gillray the caricaturist has been much solicited to publish a caricature of me and intends doing so. A great point to have a good one.'[4]

But on inspecting the print in question – and realising he was nowhere to be seen – Canning 'fell a crying, and could not be comforted till the housekeeper brought him a slice of bread and butter sprinkled with sugar!'[5] This young man was not one to fall at the first hurdle, however. He understood the political game well enough,* pestering Sneyd later that year: 'Have you heard anything from Mr Gillray lately? And do you know how soon after my *coming in* I am likely to *come out*?'[6]

Such persistence did not bear fruit, and by January 1796 Canning was in despair. He wrote to Sneyd again: 'I have seen in the window of Mrs Humphreys … the Print of the death of Wolf† and have looked with trembling anxiety for something that I might acknowledge as a resemblance of myself. But not finding such a thing, I had concluded the project *in my favour* to be abandoned.'[7] Poor trembling Canning!

Gillray, who was in the '*jaws* of rheumatism', had in fact already apologised to Sneyd: 'I regret with you that Mr Canning did not make his *debut* in Mrs H's window in so excellent a print.'[8]

Canning couldn't bear it. He pressed Sneyd to arrange another meeting with Gillray, but 'without its appearing to be at my instance or with my *formal assent*': essentially, 'please introduce me to Gillray, but *don't let him know I asked*.'[9] Sneyd tried this more devious approach. He arranged for Gillray to drop off a frame at Canning's office during his 'breakfast hour', instructing him: 'If you can take the drawing to his house … any morning about 10 o'clock … you will be let in, and thus perhaps make a friend.'[10]

As 10am came round each day, Canning must have tidied up his hair, donned his most impressive set of clothes and waited with great excitement for the frame exchange. But Gillray never turned up.

There had been a hiccup in the plan. Gillray was probably in his rooms at 37 New Bond Street when he received Sneyd's instructions. He may well have been reading Sneyd's letter when the sound of bellowing voices floated up to him from the print shop downstairs. These weren't the rounded vowels of London's fashionable elite, laughing and guffawing at their own folly. These voices were hoarse

* He later became prime minister.

† A satire of the great history painting by Benjamin West.

and hurried. A moment later, the pale face of Hannah Humphrey popped up around his doorway. 'Gilly, dear, I think you had better come downstairs.' The men had been sent by the Justice of the Peace William Addington. Gillray was arrested.

On 22 January 1796, the *Evening Mail* reported: 'On Saturday morning James Gillray, a Caricature Print-engraver, was brought before the sitting Magistrate; at the Public-office, Bow-street, charged with selling a certain burlesque Caricature Print, entitled "The Wise Man's Offering".'[11]

The print in question, which had been published by Hannah Humphrey the month before, was dubbed 'vile' and 'most obscene' by the *Oracle*, which declared pompously that 'decency is shocked at the subject'.[12] But this print, which mocked the Prince of Wales, was *gentle* compared to Gillray's other works. And although Hannah had published the print, Samuel Fores was arrested as the publisher.

So, why on earth was Gillray arrested? And Samuel Fores, too? The answer lay with the justice of the peace who initiated the prosecution, William Addington. He was known to be impulsive and 'never remarkable for his accuracy'.[13] The whole thing was a farce. No charges were taken forward. The issue was swept under the rug, perhaps with Canning's help, and Gillray returned to Hannah's for some well-deserved TLC.

But coming nose-to-nose with a sitting magistrate was a nasty shock, and as good a lesson as any to toe the line when it came to politics. The Gillray–Humphrey team began working on a campaign sponsored by Sir John Dalrymple, with a goal to 'rouse all the People to an active Union against that Invasion'.[14] Dalrymple was fiercely patriotic: 'All Weapons' were needed to defend the country – 'except those which the French use'.[15] He employed Gillray's services, but 'charged him not to introduce a single Caricature, or indulge a single sally that could give pain to a British Subject'.[16] Gillray was happy to oblige.

Later that year came one of Gillray's most ferocious pro-government prints: a peek into the future at the 'Promis'd Horrors of the French Invasion'. It is indeed a vision of horror: the September Massacres playing out on London streets – St James's Street is overrun with bayonet-wielding French soldiers, the Cabinet and royal family are massacred, St James's Palace is ablaze, Pitt is being whipped (by Fox, of course) and a guillotine is set up at Brooks's Club.

But most importantly, this was the moment that Gillray finally gave Canning his *debut*. Was he going to be the hero of the scene, fighting off French soldiers with volleys of plum puddings? Not quite. He swings from a rope outside White's Club: Canning the hanged man.

But it didn't matter. This was Canning's 'Look, Mum, I'm on TV' moment. Eighteen months of anticipation were over. Now, he was in Gillray's cast of characters, and it would only be three months until his next appearance.

*Promis'd Horrors of the French Invasion, or Forcible Reasons for negotiating a Regicide Peace*, James Gillray, 1796.
© Chronicle / Alamy Stock Photo

Canning's follow-up finally came on 21 January 1797. Gillray was tinkering with scale again. Here is Pitt in the House of Commons, but this Pitt is a giant, towering high above the galleries of the chamber in a lilac coat. The only seat big enough for him is the canopy above the Speaker's Chair, and he straddles it, with a lanky leg on either side. His pockets are bulging with guineas and papers ('Volunteers, 200,000 Seamen, 150,000 Regulars'), and he amuses himself with a toy globe, on which France is disproportionately large and Britain puny and obscure.

While Pitt is consumed by the momentous task ahead of persevering with the French Revolutionary Wars, he is oblivious to the squabbles of his tiny MPs. He hasn't noticed his enormous left foot crushing the leaders of the opposition: Erskine, Sheridan and Fox. And he rests his right foot on Wilberforce (still waiting with 'Slave Trade' reforms in his pocket*) and tartan-clad Henry Dundas, a man who dominated Scottish politics in the late eighteenth century, earning him the nickname of 'Henry the Ninth'. And the tiny man kissing the foot of the Great Pitt? The up-and-coming George Canning.

If Gillray had ever held reservations about Pitt and his politics, he was reassured for now. Could there be a better argument for Pitt's position? He is depicted as a colossus of British politics, with the globe in his hand and money and troops spilling out of his pockets. He even wears a coat of regal purple. The Tory peer Lord Bateman seemed to agree: 'The Opposition are as low as we can wish them,'

* For two decades, Wilberforce campaigned tirelessly for Parliament to pass a law ending the slave trade, presenting a bill for abolition each year between 1789 and 1806. Meanwhile, the abolitionist cause was growing into a popular mass movement, driven by the campaigns of Thomas Clarkson and the writing of Olaudah Equiano, among others. Josiah Wedgwood's medallion, of an enslaved man kneeling in chains asking: 'Am I Not a Man and a Brother?' became an international symbol of the abolitionist movement.

*The Giant Factorum amusing himself*, James Gillray, 1797.
Digital Commonwealth: https://ark.digitalcommonwealth.org/ark:/50959/2z111h995

he wrote to Gillray. 'You have been of infinite service in lowering them, and making them ridiculous.'[17]

And Pitt needed every ounce of support he could get, for a month later, the country was thrown into turmoil once more.

## LAND OF THE LEEK

For most Britons, there was nothing remarkable about the evening of Wednesday 22 February 1797. Rowlandson was probably settling into a large chair at the Coach and Horses, puffing away at a pipe, with another bowl of punch on the way. He tossed his head back in laughter at Jack Bannister's titbits of gossip, hot from Drury Lane Theatre. Down the road at Devonshire House, Georgiana Cavendish was announcing to the Prince of Wales that another round of cards was in order: 'You must stop worrying, Prinny, you know Parliament will pay up.' Over in Buckingham House, George III and Queen Charlotte had been asleep for hours, ready to attack the day at 7am, fuelled by a boiled egg.

Pitt was sinking into his chair in front of a roaring fire, nursing a glass of port, wondering how to tackle the diminishing value of banknotes. As a result of overprinting to fund the war effort, each note was gradually losing its value. This had resulted in several runs on the banks – in Newcastle-upon-Tyne, Sunderland and Durham – a great rush of people trading in their banknotes for gold before they became worthless. It was a perilous path. If this continued, the Bank of England's coffers would soon be empty. What would his father, the great Pitt the Elder, have done? Gillray, too, was considering the crisis, deliberating with Hannah Humphrey whether it was time to trade in their own banknotes for gold. And down the road, Cruikshank and his son George were preparing copper plates for another commission for Samuel Fores.

But none of them could have known that 250 miles away, on the Pembrokeshire coast, their worst fears were being realised. Scrambling up the rocky cliffs of the Carreg Wastad Bay in the dead of night were 1,400 sworn enemies of Britannia. The French were invading.

The conquerors were led by William Tate, a 44-year-old Irish–American colonel who had served during the American War of

Independence. The men he commanded were a ramshackle bunch: most were untrained and many were ex-convicts. They wore British uniforms, dyed a brown-black colour, which gave them the menacing nickname, *La Légion Noire*.

However, these attackers weren't fully focused on the task ahead. When they broke into a local farmhouse about a mile inland, although their orders were to gain ground, set up camp and maintain a position, the farmhouse was stashed with booze (probably pillaged from a wreckage of a Portuguese ship) and *La Légion Noire* became uproariously drunk. They rampaged around the house in true looting style – burning window frames, stealing a clock and, most impressively, cutting up bedding to make trousers (clearly, scaling the Welsh cliffs had left some members exposed).

When Tate ordered his unruly invaders to forage for food and get hold of some horses, they couldn't help but loot a bit here, plunder a bit there. It was an embarrassing, amateur disaster. British troops marched to Fishguard and, by the evening of 23 February, Tate was trying to talk his way to an unconditional surrender. It was accepted the next morning. The invasion force was kept under lock and key in the most secure temporary accommodation: the local pubs. They were then formally imprisoned and returned to France the following year in a prisoner exchange. What a gap year!*

The objective of the invaders had been to capture England's second city, the great port of Bristol. But in truth, this force was nothing more than a distraction, designed to disperse and divert the British defences for as long as possible. It was the third prong in an attack launched by the French general Lazare Hoche. The goal was to join

* As tradition goes, a British invasion must be marked with a tapestry. In 1997, to mark the bicentenary of the event, 70 Fishguard locals stitched a 30-metre-long tapestry. The fabric was bought in a Greek market, packed into holiday suitcases and brought back to Wales. Now, the tapestry, backed with Velcro strips, is on permanent exhibition at Fishguard Town Hall. A fine memorial to Britain's last invasion.

forces with the British radical groups pushed underground by Pitt's heavy hand and unleash revolutionaries across the country that would uproot the established order.

But like the Armada sent by King Philip of Spain in 1588, Hoche's invasion force fell foul of British weather. The majority of the invading forces were sent to Ireland, with 15,000 troops dispatched to support the Society of United Irishmen. But, in an echo of 1588, the weather was on Britannia's side: it was the worst winter in living memory. The French ships were tossed in rough seas and battered by ferocious winds, many losing their anchors as cables snapped. The invasion was called off and the fleet returned to Brest, battling storms, fog and British patrols. The other prong of the attack was a contingent destined for Newcastle. But after being lashed by the tempestuous North Sea, facing lousy discipline and outbreaks of mutiny, they called it a day and returned to France.

The attempted French invasion was a complete failure, but it sent shock waves through Britain. It had been believed that if an attack would be made, it would be directed on the east coast. Henry Dundas, secretary of state for war, had stated with confidence: 'The coast of the Bristol Channel, St George's Channel & the North of Scotland demand such peculiar and great arrangements to attack them, that they probably do not enter into the contemplation of an Enemy, who has greater objects to aim at nearer at hand.'[18]

Seeing the government so clearly caught on the back foot, Londoners grew anxious. Meanwhile, with national debt piling up, Pitt ordered the Bank of England to issue paper banknotes rather than gold. Anxiety burst into panic. Londoners rushed to convert their banknotes into gold before they lost their value, leaving the banks dangerously short of bullion. With roughly twice as many notes in circulation than the value of the actual gold reserves, the bank was on a fast track to bankruptcy.

Pitt pushed through a Bank Restriction Act, suspending these 'specie payments' with immediate effect. This meant that, by 1814, the banknotes in circulation would have a face value of £28.4 million, backed by just £2.2 million of gold.[19] Richard Brinsley Sheridan, the Irish playwright and MP, was disgusted at Pitt's handling of the crisis. Sheridan stood up in the Commons and 'made a fanciful allusion to the bank', describing her as 'an elderly lady in the City, of great credit and long standing' who had 'unfortunately fallen into bad company'.[20]

Such an analogy was enough to set Gillray's mind whirring. Soon the print shops were adorned with a haggard old woman dressed in one of history's most blingy outfits, made entirely of banknotes.

Whether this old woman had such concerns is unlikely, for this was the Old Lady of Threadneedle Street: the personification of the Bank of England. In Gillray's print, an ultra-lanky Pitt reaches into her pockets, trying to distract her with a kiss. But this old lady is not to be charmed. 'What, have I kept my Honor untainted so long,'

*Political Ravishment, or The Old Lady of Threadneedle Street in danger!*, James Gillray, 1797

she cries, her arms flung out, 'to have it broke up, by you at last? O Murder! Rape! Ravishment! Ruin! Ruin! Ruin!!!'

Pitt may have had control of the Commons and more than fifteen years of premiership under his belt, but the closing years of the eighteenth century were fraught with peril. The ongoing war with France was becoming ruinously expensive, draining the coffers dry. It had put any other issues – the abolition of the slave trade or administrative reforms – firmly on the back burner. And when the country needed it most, the Royal Navy was facing crisis. Grumblings about pay and conditions broke out into full-blown mutiny, first near Portsmouth and then in the Thames Estuary. Invasion, banking crisis, mutiny. In 1797, Britain was in a sorry state.

## GREATLY PROVOCATIVE TO SOMNIFEROUS ORISON

Thomas Rowlandson dealt with the situation in the best way he knew: he headed for the seaside. 'In coaches, chaises, caravans and hoys,' Londoners would 'fly to the coast for daily, nightly joys, And all, impatient of dry land, agree, With one consent to rush into the sea'.[21]

Rowlandson, impatient of dry land, took to the waters with the families of Henry Angelo and Henry Wigstead. It was a dismally wet summer, but the party seemed to make the most of it. They stayed with a gouty retired naval officer, Captain John Urry, at his large house at Yarmouth. The captain had made his own preparations for war: he'd painted a magnificent set of *trompe-l'œil* defences on his garden wall, ready to strike terror into any French adversary.

The group enjoyed a 'dashing passage to Hurst' – an artillery fortress looking out across the Solent.[22] Then there was a fishing expedition – although like every group holiday, the party split. Mrs Wigstead stayed with some of the children, who were 'left behind owing to their fears of the water'.[23]

While bumbling about the Solent, the party might have noticed the presence of a vast Dad's Army of volunteers, preparing themselves for French invasion.[24*] And had Rowlandson taken the group to Portsmouth, he might have pointed out the rows of prison hulks that no doubt filled the children with unease. For inside the ships were hundreds of prisoners of war packed together like sardines in dark, dank, disease-ridden squalor.

As the rainy holiday came to a close, Rowlandson and Wigstead appeared keener than ever to take a break from family life. They set off on another of their drawing expeditions to relive their youthful adventures. But choosing a destination was tricky: Spain had declared war on Britain in October 1796, Ireland was about to break out into open rebellion, and war was popping up in every corner of Europe. A sunny mini-break on the continent was out of the question. Instead, they stayed on home turf and reconnected with their Romantic sensibilities, popularised by William Gilpin's 1786 work, *Observations, Relative Chiefly to Picturesque Beauty*. It was time to discover the picturesque, and for this, they followed in the recent footsteps of J.M.W. Turner and William Wordsworth. They headed to Wales: the Cambrian mountains were calling.

'We left London in August, 1797, highly expectant of gratification,' Wigstead wrote in his diary. 'I was induced to visit this Principality with my friend Mr. Rowlandson, whose abilities as an artist need no eulogium from me.'[25] Off they sped by coach through St Albans, Daventry, Coventry, Birmingham and Wolverhampton. The country had certainly changed since their sketching trip of 1783. Wigstead wasn't enamoured by these country towns, many showing the early signs of industrial change (Birmingham was 'by no means an agreeable object to a picturesque eye').[26]

* By 1800, they were nearly 400,000 strong – more than twice the size of the standing army.

They crossed the border at Welshpool, taking 'leave of the luxuries on the other side of the Severn'.[27] They were unimpressed by their lodgings: a 'cockloft, at the very brink of a step-ladder staircase'.[28]

Perhaps things would improve at the Welsh mountains, the artists hoped. Here they would experience the 'fixed, abysmal, gloomy, breathing-place' that Wordsworth had felt.[29] The misty mountains and their 'roar of waters, torrents, streams'.[30] So moving were his walks up Snowdon, Wordsworth hoped 'they ne'er Fade from remembrance!'[31]

Rowlandson and Wigstead's travels through the Welsh mountains would certainly never fade from remembrance, albeit for quite a different reason. The artists made some of the journey on hardy mountain ponies. Rowlandson's sketch of the travails, entitled *An Artist Travelling in Wales*, reveals that the Londoners were put through their paces by the expedition.

*An Artist Travelling in Wales*, Thomas Rowlandson, 1799.

Firstly, the pony is so small that the artist's feet (probably those of disgruntled Wigstead) brush the ground. And while he tries to balance on this stocky beast as it clambers down the rocky mountainside, he clings on to his artist's paraphernalia: a sketchbook, a colour box, an easel and a paint set. To add to the nightmare, the heavens have opened and Wigstead's tiddly umbrella is putting up a poor defence against the elements.

The artists faced heavy rain and fog throughout the trip – brilliant for the Romantic aesthetic but poor for morale. It would have been a business-ending Tripadvisor review: Corwen, a pretty market town, was condemned by Wigstead as the 'most miserable of all miserable Welsh villages'.[32] The accommodation was the final straw:

> Nor can the bad accommodation at most of the receptacles for the traveller, and the insolence and inattention of their proprietors, joined to the filthiness of their attendances, be sufficiently censured. No possible excuse can be made for the dirtiness, everywhere predominant. Water is every where in abundance, but the rooted laziness of the commonality will never suffer proper use to be made of it.[33]

The artists returned to London after their rainy Welsh holiday like many since: regretful, remorseful and glad to be home.

## A MAD BULL IN A CHINA SHOP

Once Rowlandson had escaped the Welsh rain, he returned to a London print scene that was by now a serious money operation. 'There are now I believe,' judged William Blake in 1800, 'as many Booksellers as there are Butchers & as many Print shops as of any other trade. We remember when a Print shop was a rare bird in London.'[34]

At the turn of the century, London was the de facto centre of the satirical print trade in Europe. It was now so lucrative that it attracted the attention of one of the great entrepreneurs from the continent: Rudolph Ackermann.

Ackermann was born near Leipzig, in Saxony, in 1764, making him the same age as Isaac Cruikshank. He had a humble start in life, being the sixth child of a saddler, Barthel Ackermann. Rudolph was a bright young boy, who thrived at the Latin school at Stollberg, but, without the financial means, was forced to apprentice with his brother Friedrich, who was also a saddler. Here he learnt to draw and engrave, and in 1782, he upped sticks and headed to Dresden, then Paris, to design carriages. He first stepped foot in England in 1787, aged 23, where his career thrived. Soon he was designing grand coaches for the likes of George Washington.

But from 1795, Ackermann directed his focus on the London print trade. He opened a drawing school at No. 96 the Strand, then, in 1797, moved to larger premises at No. 101 the Strand. This was the magnificent Repository of Arts: the new hub of London's commercial art scene. He commissioned and published new portfolios of prints and drawings (such as Rowlandson's Welsh sketching trip), and sold books and art materials: watercolours, papers, pens and inks.

Ackermann wasn't the only insect drawn to the bright lights of the print shop windows. There were swarms buzzing to London. One was a country artist, George Murgatroyd Woodward, seeking his fortune in the big smoke. He'd impressed his Derbyshire neighbours by sketching 'all the comical *gaffers* and *gammers* of the country round',[35] and soon they gave him a showbiz nickname: he was 'commonly designated by his merry associates' as Mustard George.[36]

For this ambitious young man, living in the countryside was 'like a mad bull in a china-shop'.[37] He escaped the provinces to make his name in London and soon became the new darling of the print scene. He had all the qualities needed to grow a fan base. Lambasting the

French? Tick. Witty wordplay? Tick. Outrageous ribaldry? Tick. Tick. Tick. Soon he was working for the big names – Ackermann, Holland, Humphrey – and the great Rowlandson was etching his designs. Mustard George made it look easy.

Indeed, he took things easy, too. He spent a lot of time with a pipe and tankard in Offley's Cyder Cellar in Henrietta Street. Or sometimes it was the Blue Posts tavern, the Hole in the Wall or the Brown Bear, often in the company of Rowlandson.[38]

Another old face was back on the scene, too. William Holland 'continued publishing satirical prints', wrote the *Morning Post*, 'following his release from jail'. Still trading from 50 Oxford Street, he transformed the back room of his shop into a gallery. It cost one shilling to enter, and punters could have an exclusive look at the latest satirical designs. The name of this new endeavour was simple but brilliant: the Laughing Lounge.

At the close of the century, the London print trade was on fire. Not only had Gillray fine-tuned the art of satire, he had dived into the world of the surreal and pushed and pulled and twisted its possibilities to redefine the satirical genre. Close behind were Rowlandson, Mustard George and Isaac and Mary Cruikshank, and their boys, Robert and George. Then there were the bevy of printmakers: Hannah Humphrey, Samuel Fores, William Holland and, more recently, Rudolph Ackermann. They were all experts in their trade. Humphrey, Fores and Holland had spent decades with their fingers on the pulse of the nation: lampooning Pitt and Fox, poking fun at George III and his family and even the man on the street. And now, they were attracting continental talent and nurturing an international fan base.

Such innovation was paying dividends. Satires were being printed on jugs, mugs and tobacco jars. Gillray's prints in particular were reported to be 'very well received by the public ... You will always see dozens of people standing outside the shops which sell these caricatures.'[39] Some of his work entertained 'the entire country ... for days'.[40]

And it wasn't just in Britain. When the engraver Abraham Raimbach was travelling from Paris to London in 1802, he noted that the Commissary's Office in Calais 'was decorated with a great number of Caricature prints ... I believe all of them imported from England'.[41]

A French art journal reported that 'English engravers being so numerous, their productions have become a pretty significant branch of commerce for England. Many of them are exported to foreign countries and especially to Germany, where English caricatures are sold, despite the fact that people there are familiar with neither the people nor the facts that make up their subject.'

The reason for the German enthusiasm was largely down to a subscription journal. The *London und Paris*, established in 1798, set out 'to entertain, to amuse and to recount' with news from the two capitals: the 'playgrounds of fashion which rule the world'.[42] Every little titbit was reported: social life, gossip, customs, fashions, Parisian crime, English xenophobia, how the French walked around parks, what to think of Charles James Fox. And of course, the latest prints.

The Germans couldn't get enough of English satirical prints, and they simply adored each 'witty rocket fired from Gillray's burin',[43] and wanted all the updates of Hannah Humphrey's business too: 'Mistress Humphrey', the Germans were informed, 'had exhausted her entire, very considerable supply after only a few days.'[44]

Gillray was their favourite. He had an 'extensive literary knowledge of every kind', which combined with 'his extremely accurate drawing; his ability to capture the features of any man ... his profound study of allegory; the novelty of his ideas and his unswerving, constant regard for the true essence of caricature',[45] which made him a bestseller. His work was so compelling, Germans found it now impossible not to 'picture Pitt as a broomstick with a turned-up nose', or 'Fox as a well-stuffed pig'.[46] In fact, Gillray was considered 'the foremost living artist in his genre, not only among Englishmen, but among all European nations'.[47]

Could our British satirists rise any higher? What more could they do? Where could they go? At this point, they might well have thought the bulk of their lifetimes' work was done. That they'd probably peaked. A few more years until a steady retirement, perhaps. However, they couldn't have been further from the truth, for their greatest project was only just beginning.

The next victim of the London satirists was a young Corsican officer making his name on the European scene. I hope you're sitting comfortably, for the next act is quite a spectacle.

Ladies and gentlemen, please welcome to the stage ... Napoleon Bonaparte.

# *Act III*

# 11

# *The First Kiss This Ten Years*

## GO THE DISTANCE

'Ajaccio is the prettiest town in Corsica,' wrote James Boswell, the Scottish lawyer and biographer of Samuel Johnson, when he visited the Mediterranean island in 1765. 'It hath many handsome streets, and beautiful gardens, and a palace for the Genoese governor. The inhabitants of this town are the genteelest people in the island.'[1]

A short walk from the sparkling blue sea, up a cobbled street named Rue Saint-Charles, a four-storey town house stands in the heart of Ajaccio. It is rendered in pale yellow, with large windows and pale blue shutters. If you had been passing just before noon on 15 August 1769, sweltering in the heat and serenaded by the lazy whirring of cicadas, you may well have been startled by a piercing scream. And then, after a moment of uneasy silence, the crying of a newborn baby.

This babe was the second surviving child of Carlo and Letizia Buonaparte, a family from the *haute bourgeoisie*, or upper middle class. Their newborn son was named Napoleone, after his great-uncle, although he would be known to the world as Napoleon. 'She was on her way home from church when she felt labour pains,' Napoleon said of the event, 'and had only time to get into the house, when I was born, not on a bed, but on a heap of tapestry.'[2]

A younger brother for Giuseppe (later known as Joseph), the boys would be joined by a gaggle of siblings: Luciano (Lucien), Maria-Anna (Elisa), Louis, Maria-Paola (Pauline), Maria-Annunziata (Caroline) and Girolamo (Jérôme). Their mother possessed a devout Catholic faith and was a formidable guiding force. 'To my mother,' Napoleon would say, 'I owe my fortune and all I've done that's worthwhile.'[3]

As Letizia kept an eye on this merry brood, playing in the dappled sunlight outside Casa Bonaparte, she was unaware that the exploits of these rascals would fill the history books. For these children would one day sit on the thrones of Europe: one would become emperor, three would be kings, one would be queen and two would be sovereign princesses.[4]

The Bonaparte children grew up happy and carefree, surrounded by a large, loving family but against a backdrop of political violence and disorder: Corsica came under French rule the year Napoleon was born. 'I was born when the country was perishing,' he later recalled. 'Thirty thousand Frenchmen vomited onto our coasts, drowning the thrones of liberty in seas of blood, such was the odious spectacle which first met my eye. The cries of the dying, the groans of the oppressed, the tears of despair surrounded my cradle from birth.'[5]

At the age of nine, young Napoleon was whisked away to 'the continent', not to return for almost eight years. He was sent to a French school, where the headmaster described him as 'a thoughtful and gloomy character. He had no playmate and walked about by himself... He had ability and learned quickly ... If I scolded him, he answered in a cold, almost imperious tone: "Sir, I know it."'[6] Although he arrived speaking only Corsican* and Italian, he learnt French within three months, and was subsequently admitted to the

* Corsican is a language spoken on the island of Corsica. It is closely related to Italian, particularly the Tuscan dialect.

Royal Military School at Brienne-le-Château, deep in the rolling hills of the Champagne region.

The school, one of twelve feeder schools for the main military academy in Paris, was run by monks, who made it deliberately austere. The boys had small, unheated cells, with a straw mattress and a single blanket. Napoleon spoke with a thick Corsican dialect (pronouncing 'ou' instead of 'eu' or 'u') – an easy joke for his classmates, who were the polished and confident sprogs of the French aristocracy. They nicknamed him *La Paille au Nez*, 'straw up the nose', which rhymed with 'Napoleone'.[7] While he found some comfort in tending a small vegetable patch in the school grounds, his only other option in these bleak circumstances was to become a fully fledged bookworm.

Napoleon withdrew to the school library and, without friends of his own, acquainted himself with the greats of history: Caesar, Diderot, Cicero, Voltaire, Erasmus and Livy.[8] He dived into Polybius' chronicles of the Sack of Carthage. He poured over Plutarch's accounts of Alexander the Great. Soon he could recite whole passages from Virgil. This reading equipped him for life: 'The reading of history', Napoleon later explained to the Marquis de Caulaincourt, 'very soon made me feel that I was capable of achieving as much as the men who are placed in the highest ranks of our annals.'[9]

All this big thinking seemed to have left its mark: Napoleon had a 'docile expression, mild, straight-forward, thoughtful'.[10] A school report at the end of his five-and-a-half-year stint reported he 'would make an excellent sailor'.[11] But Napoleon didn't heed this advice, opting to go for the artillery instead; this was partly because his mother didn't like the idea of him sleeping in a hammock, and partly to make use of his mathematical brain.[12] Having passed his exams, Napoleon left the spartan cells of Brienne in October 1784 (the same year William Pitt won his first election), and landed a place at the *Ecole Militaire* in Paris. In this monumental complex of palatial facades on the banks of the Seine, Napoleon spent a year training to become an artillery officer.

He graduated on 28 October 1785, beginning a brilliant career as a second-class lieutenant. He was good – very good, in fact. The type who would be talked about as 'a real asset'. He would always outdo and constantly outperform his rivals, climbing higher and higher up the promotional ladder. It was an unstoppable rise. In 1793, he became brigadier general. In 1795, when a new constitution placed executive power in a five-member Directory, Napoleon became a direct adviser to the top brass. By 1796, aged only 27, he was commanding the French Army in Italy and forcing Austria and its allies to make peace.

It was enough to catch the attention of the British public, who rushed to commission portraits of the latest dashing young hero, seen to be setting Italy on a course of liberation. But it was a short-lived love affair, for by 1797, Napoleon was becoming Britain's new public enemy number one.

In 1798, the name 'Bonaparte' was regularly appearing in London's papers, for Napoleon was leading a campaign to seize the Ottoman territories of Egypt and Syria. Although far from the green fields of England, this was a direct attack on British interests, for the true aim of the campaign was to cut British trade links with India. It was an audacious move: in one fell swoop, Napoleon had become the most unpopular man in London.

In late July 1798, the French Navy moored up in the shallows of Aboukir Bay at the mouth of the Nile, not far from Alexandria. The threat level was considered low, and many of the crew were sent ashore to find food and supplies. But these French ships were *canards assis*. For a British fleet had got wind of the French location and, after taking 'a good stock of French Beef to sea', closed in on the enemy.[13] As the sun set over the murky waters on 1 August 1798, Admiral Nelson, the leader of the British fleet, ordered an immediate attack on the formidable French Mediterranean forces. Nelson knew this was make or break. 'Before this time tomorrow,' he told his men before battle commenced, 'I shall have gained a peerage or' – in the case of his death in battle – 'Westminster Abbey'.[14]

At 5pm, Nelson made the signal to clear the ships for action and position windward of the enemy fleet. At 6pm, he 'hoisted the Bloody Flag at his main topgallant mast head, and made a signal for the ships to form a line in the best manner they could, and engage the enemy as they came up'.[15]

The fighting was ferocious. Soon the bay was filled with flying broadsides and pistol shots. As French mizzen rigging became tangled in British jib booms, ships tried to stay afloat in perilously shallow waters.* The air became thick with smoke, as creaking booms lurched and swayed and finally crashed down into the watery graveyard.

In the chaos, a chunk of iron – probably blown off the side of a French ship – flew straight at Admiral Nelson and struck him in the temple. With hot blood streaming down his face, he was taken below deck to await his fate at the hands of the ship's doctor. A chaplain was called, and Nelson's mind probably wondered which plot they'd give him at Westminster Abbey. But incredibly, the wound was stitched up and Nelson returned to the upper deck at around 10pm.

The scene before him was worthy of Homer. The French flagship *L'Orient* was under heavy fire and the French admiral, François-Paul Brueys, who had lost both legs in the battle, had himself strapped to an armchair on the quarterdeck. With tourniquets on both stumps, Brueys continued to direct the fight until a cannonball blew him in two halves.[16] *L'Orient* went up in flames as its captain, Commodore Casabianca, lay mortally wounded. His ten-year-old son, still following his father's instructions, refused to leave his station, staying put until the bitter end. He was later immortalised in the poem 'Casabianca' by Felicia Dorothea Hemans, which opens with the lines:

* Contemporary reports stated some points of Aboukir Bay were just 4 fathoms deep, or 7.3 metres. The French flagship, *L'Orient*, had a draught of over 8 metres.

The boy stood on the burning deck
Whence all but him had fled,
The flame that lit the battle's wreck,
Shone round him o'er the dead.[17]

At around 11pm, flames licked the magazine of the 120-gun flagship. *L'Orient* blew up immediately, melting the tar sealant on the hulls of nearby ships and releasing a deadly shower of oak splinters. The explosion was heard twelve miles away and swallowed all in its vicinity.[18] It was a moment immortalised in George Arnald's magnificent painting, *The Destruction of 'L'Orient' at the Battle of the Nile, 1 August 1798*.

*The Destruction of 'L'Orient' at the Battle of the Nile, 1 August 1798*, George Arnald, 1827.
National Maritime Museum, Greenwich, London

## A RAVENOUS NATION

The following evening, as Nelson surveyed the bay of smoking hulls, drifting aimlessly among the shallow waters, he knew that this was not just a defeat. This was a total annihilation. Eleven of the thirteen enemy ships had been captured or destroyed, and the French Army were stranded in the blistering heat of the Egyptian desert. Napoleon fled, thwarted. His ambitions in Egypt had gone up in smoke. All the French could claim to have laid hands on was the Rosetta Stone.*

A glorious naval victory was just what the Britannic doctor ordered: 'In a trace it calmed all the huffing and puffing of the ever-more-heavily-burdened Briton, who was now taxed from head to toe.'[19] As the German commentators noted, Pitt must have had a 'friendly guardian angel' who intervened at exactly the right time to cheer up the grumbling Englishman: 'an excellent sop to silence the old grumble-gizzard'.[20]

As news of the battle reached London on 2 October 1798, all that huffing and puffing and grumbling and moaning about being taxed to the eyeballs was replaced with wild celebrations. There were 'Night Illuminations in every Street' and 'Mobs throwing Squibs' – a type of firework, splashing the city with hissing and pops and sparks.[21] In light of such japes and jollification, Rudolph Ackermann set

* On 15 July 1799, Napoleon's soldiers were digging foundations for a fort in Rashid, or Rosetta, a town 40 miles east of Alexandria. They came across a rock, which, after some dusting down, revealed a set of ancient symbols, carved on the surface during the Hellenistic period. But the Rosetta Stone, as it came to be known, was much more than merely a beautiful relic: this was the key to understanding the ancient world. The text was carved in three languages, enabling the likes of Jean-François Champollion to decipher Egyptian hieroglyphs for the first time. The French were soon defeated by the British, who brought the Rosetta Stone to London in 1801. It has been on public display at London's British Museum since 1802, where it remains to this day. Perhaps Gillray, Rowlandson and Cruikshank saw it there.

*Admiral Nelson recreating with his Brave Tars after the Glorious Battle of the Nile*, Thomas Rowlandson, 1798.

Rowlandson to work to commemorate the events on the Nile and capitalise on the public celebrations.

The first piece was a magnificent hand-coloured etching of the heat of the battle. A once-mighty French ship, *La Sérieuse*, lists dramatically, with sailors jumping desperately to the waters from the hulk or clinging to broken masts. In the background, *L'Orient* has exploded, with masts and men flying high into the air amid smoke and flame. The British sailors aboard Admiral Nelson's ship, HMS *Vanguard*, wave their caps in delight. And in another of Rowlandson's prints, the after-party is in full swing. Nelson, his head bandaged, sits above the deck while sailors dance and swig with lashings of beer and piles of bread.

In light of this British success, patriotic Isaac Cruikshank couldn't help but take a swipe at the leaders of the Whig cause, with their long-held sympathies with France and her revolutionary habits. The setting of Egypt gave the printmakers a new toolbox to work with. It was all exotic, exciting and dangerous, and, like the director of *Live and Let Die*, they brought in a crocodile at any opportunity.

Londoners who peered through the window of Samuel Fores' print shop on 7 October 1798 were greeted with a remarkable scene: two crocodiles with the heads of Fox and Sheridan stitched onto their scaly skin. Their keeper, 'the gallant Nelson', brings home 'two uncommon fiery French Crocadiles from the Nile as a Present to the King'. And as the Foxites blub streams of crocodile tears, presumably for their past efforts to champion the French cause, it is hard to feel sympathy. 'Come along you Hypocritical dogs,' Nelson cries out merrily.

*The Gallant Nelson bringing home two uncommon fierce French Crocadiles from the Nile as a present to the King*, Isaac Cruikshank, 1798.
National Maritime Museum, Greenwich, London

A couple of weeks later, Gillray produced a print showing a fat Englishman gorging on an enormous feast. A feast so huge that he declares: 'What! ... where do you think I shall find room to stow all you bring in?' But this was no Double Big Mac with extra fries: this was a once-in-a-lifetime meal. The waiters? British admirals, wearing aprons over their glistening uniforms. The food guzzled up by this lucky Englishman? Captured French ships piled high on golden plates. 'In comes Nelson with nine conquered warships,' the German reporters wrote, 'and all the glory of his victory at Aboukir, which he now serves up under the greedy gaze of a ravenous nation.'[22]

*John Bull taking a Luncheon: – or – British Cooks Cramming Old Grumble-Gizzard with Bonne-Chére*, James Gillray, 1798.
National Maritime Museum, Greenwich, London

Nelson serves a dish of 'Soup and bouilli' and '*fricassée* à la Nelson'. A tempting 'bill of fare' is peeping from this pocket: 'List of French ships – Taken, Burnt and destroyed'. Behind him comes Lord Howe, proudly presenting a Spanish '*Fricandó* à la Howe' – usually a rich Catalan beef stew, though in this image it takes the form of a captured ship. Mighty Admiral Warren brings the Englishman a delectable dessert – the failed French invasion force tossed around in Irish waters. In memory of the triumphant Battle of Camperdown,

Admiral Duncan brings forth some tasty morsels: two fat 'Dutch cheeses' and other delicacies 'à la Duncan'.

And who was this lucky chap, stuffing himself with *confit de Frigate*?

This was a man, created by Gillray, to represent the British people. If *sans-culottes* were established as the epitome of French degradation, what kind of figure stood on the shores of England, overlooking the white cliffs of Dover? Why, it was that ruddy-faced bumpkin you might spot propping up the pub bar. The chap who wears a stained tweed coat in the town, bringing the smell of the countryside with him, too. He's not the *pinnacle* of high society, but he's a good egg, nonetheless, with decent British common sense. And so jolly!

'Another pint, John?' the barman would ask, to which he would chuckle: 'Go on, then. I've been doing honest work all day, and a deep ol' sip of ale is just what any Englishman deserves.'

John Bull was a puppet-project of the satirists to represent the people of Britain. It was an idea created from the old paperwork of Mr Hogarth and pumped up with implants of Englishness and fillers of jollity to quench the thirst of the turn-of-the-century patriotic zeal. He was moulded and shaped to look the part. John Bull was to be a handy satiric weapon. For the fight at Aboukir Bay was merely the hors d'œuvre of what was to come.

## THE FIRST KISS THIS TEN YEARS

As Napoleon fled Egypt, Britain was keen to organise itself while France was on the back foot and formed the Second Coalition with Austria and Russia. Meanwhile, the French government was in crisis. Napoleon returned to Paris and, seeing the leaders flailing and pondering, seized his chance. On 9 November 1799, the Directory was replaced with the French Consulate and Napoleon became first consul in a bloodless coup d'état. Most historians see this as the moment that ended the French Revolution and paved the way for the rise of the First French Empire.

As Napoleon stepped into the corridors of power, it was time for another great man to take his leave. Across the Channel, the 1800 Act of Union, which united the Kingdom of Great Britain and the Kingdom of Ireland, was causing friction. Pitt believed the act meant that Catholics should be admitted to Parliament. King George found this incompatible with his coronation oath, declaring anyone who supported it would be his personal enemy. On 14 March 1801, after eighteen years in Downing Street, Pitt resigned. George Canning followed suit, leaving office too, and without his patrons in power, Gillray's government pension of £200 a year was terminated.

Henry Addington took on the mantle of PM, leading a feeble administration. 'Pitt is to Addington', it was said, 'as London is to Paddington.'[23] Peace talks began between Britain and France and the Treaty of Amiens was signed on 25 March 1802. How long peace would last was another matter.

For wealthy Britons, peace meant 'Shopping in Paris!', 'Pack your bags, dear!', and 'Oh joy! We'll have lovely clothes again!' Brits flocked to the City of Light while they had the chance. Fox stayed for three months.

The French took their chance to pop across the Channel too. In May, a certain Madame Tussaud arrived in London with her young sons, Joseph and François. She arrived laden with portraits and waxworks,* ready to present them at the Lyceum Theatre. And on 5 July 1802, another exciting spectacle threw Londoners into a frenzy of excitement.

For several hours 'all the metropolis was in an uproar; many accidents occurred, and many depredations were committed'.[24] No doubt

* Marie had cast many of these waxworks from the severed heads of victims of the French Revolution, including those of the Princess de Lamballe and Louis XVI.

Rowlandson and his cronies were in the thick of the chaos. The crowds were heading north to Marylebone, where Prince George, the Duchess of Devonshire and 'an immense number of nobility' had gathered at Lord's Cricket Ground.[25] They were there to watch the 'famous aeronaut' André-Jacques Garnerin, a French balloonist. He was to set off from the cricket pitch, impress the crowd with the parachute in flight, and hopefully float back down again to whoops and cheers.

But things didn't quite go to plan: 'From the extreme density of the atmosphere the balloon was out of sight in three minutes after the cords were cut, and left one of the most immense multitudes ever assembled in the metropolis gazing on the wide expanse.'[26] As the crowd squinted into the clouds, the balloon rose a mile and a half above ground. Fifteen minutes later, it landed seventeen miles away near Epping Forest.

The possibility of this off-piste landing had been considered in the risk assessment: Prince George had written a letter of recommendation to reassure surprised locals that these were not 'necromancers coming from the clouds' – nor the latest French invasion force – and could they alert the 'notice of any gentleman in whose neighbourhood he may happen to descend'.[27]

Garnerin delighted Londoners with several balloon ascents that summer and autumn, one of which was etched out in copper plate by Isaac Cruikshank. On this occasion, in a gesture of goodwill between once-feuding nations, a Tricolour and Union Jack fly from the basket, and now the balloonist is accompanied by Madame Garnerin (who is balloon-like herself). Indeed, the spectators express concern at the weight of this added cargo. 'Jack she'll never rise,' whispers one, 'she's as heavy as two Aldermen.'[28] Another advises the spectators to 'make sail for no man's land' as soon as the cables are released.

Despite these unkind quips at the expense of Madame Garnerin, such Anglo–Franco flirtation inspired a Gillray *amuse-bouche* entitled *The first Kiss this Ten Years!* Here was Britannia, a jolly and rotund

*The First Kiss this Ten Years!*, James Gillray, 1803.


woman, receiving a peck on the lips by a lanky and sardonic Citizen François.

He charms her with a little bit of raunchy *je ne sais quoi*: 'Madame, permittez me,' François swoons, 'to pay my profound esteem to your engaging person! & to seal on your divine Lips my everlasting attachment!!!' Britannia appears to be charmed: 'Monsieur, you are truly a well-bred Gentleman! ... you make me blush ... you Kiss so delicately, that I cannot refuse you.' But a knowing side-glance reveals an underlying suspicion: 'Tho' I was sure you would Deceive me again!!!'

Gillray's bouncing buxom Britannia was right to be suspicious: the Peace of Amiens was short-lived. As Napoleon hit the headlines with reports of his relentless ambition and energy, the printmakers of Piccadilly refocused their acerbic wit on the latest mover and shaker of the world stage. The nation's enemy was no longer the *sans-culottes* of Republican France, but this wildly ambitious despot who had sprung out of nowhere.

It was time to up the ante. Gillray applied himself 'almost exclusively to sharpening the national spirit of hostility against the foreign enemy'.[29] From 1 January 1803, as diplomatic promises were falling like dominos, Gillray added an extra bit of *spice*.

It all started on the steps of the Tuileries Palace. Gillray's Napoleon, surrounded by a gang of looming grenadiers, is waiting for the new Austrian envoy, who is expected to pay his respects. The ambassador does indeed bundle along in his carriage, but he's got no intention of actually stopping; he's more interested in taking snuff than meeting Europe's newest upstart.

And here, immortalised by a copper plate, is the moment that Napoleon realises the snub. His reaction is extraordinary. This is no great statesman, calm and dignified in a moment of crisis. Napoleon is fuming at the insult: he flings his arms and legs out like a helpless child. He erupts into a frenzied rage, spluttering words in French and English, hardly able to string a sentence together: 'Ha, diable! – va't 'en! Impertinent! – va't 'en! – is dere von Man on Earth who not Worship little Boney? – Soldats! aux Armes! revenge! – ah sacre dieu! – je suis tous Tremblans.'*

But most peculiarly, this Napoleon has been cut short. He is not just slouching. He is the height of a small child. Why did Gillray do this? No one had mentioned Napoleon's height before. Sometimes, it's true, his personal guard, all very tall, would loom over him, and he might have appeared relatively short. But Napoleon was 5 *pieds* 2 *pouces*, the equivalent of 5 feet 6 inches in English measurements

* This roughly translates to 'Ha, devil! – go away! Impertinent! – go away! – is there a Man on Earth who does not Worship little Boney? – Soldiers! to Arms! revenge! – Oh God! – I'm all shaking.'

*German nonchalence; – or – the Vexation of Little Boney*, James Gillray, 1803.
Digital Commonwealth: https://ark.digitalcommonwealth.org/ark:/50959/2z111j81x

at the time, or 167.5cm.[30] I know what you're thinking – 'So he *was* short! It's true!' – but this was above average height for the time. In fact, Napoleon would probably have stood taller than Nelson, who was described as 'small', 'not a tall man', and around 5 feet 5 inches.[31]

Gillray was yet to know it, but he had just made history. The title of the print was *German Nonchalence: – or –* and more importantly – *the Vexation of Little Boney*. The myth of Napoleon as a short man was cemented in the British psyche, and the character of Little Boney was born, a character who would outshine Napoleon himself.

# 12

# *Maniac Ravings and Low Scurrilities*

## ALL-YOU-CAN-EAT PLUM PUDDINGS

On 18 May 1803, Britain, once again, was at war with France. The nation was infected with 'scarlet fever'. The patriotic Cruikshank family felt compelled to do their bit. Putting their etching burins to one side, Isaac joined a Bloomsbury volunteer troupe, while fourteen-year-old Robert and eleven-year-old George drilled alongside him with blackened mop handles and toy drums. Not long afterwards, young Robert was sent to sea as a midshipman in the East India service.[1]

Gillray wasn't marching the streets, but patriotism was pulsing through his veins nonetheless – he was the son of a Fontenoy veteran after all. His weapons were his copper plates, and it was time to muster his troops. On 24 May 1803, he fired off another attack. This print was inspired by an incident that was widely reported by London society. Napoleon had stormed out of a meeting with the British ambassador in a fit of rage, acting in 'total want of dignity as well as of decency'.[2]

This full-blown toddler tantrum was immortalised in Gillray's *Maniac Raving's – or – Little Boney in a Strong Fit*. With fists clenched and a face contorted with fury, Napoleon stamps on the piles of British newspapers, which are strewn among other casualties of his irascible temper: a chair, table, a (now-broken) globe and a huge plumed cocked hat. And out come his lashings of fury in great long tongues of white-hot flame: 'Oh, English Newspapers!!!', 'Treason! Treason! Treason!', 'Insolence of British Parliament', 'Oh cursed Liberty of ye British press!', 'Invasion! Invasion!', 'Four Hundred & Eighty Thousand Frenchmen', 'British Slavery – & everlasting Chains!'

*Maniac Raving's – or – Little Boney in a Strong Fit*, James Gillray, 1803.

The world's most powerful man was being reduced to a terrible toddler. This was punchy stuff, and it went down a storm in the frenzied panic of 1803. For Napoleon was focusing all his efforts on a British invasion. 'With God's help,' he claimed, 'I will put an end to the future and very existence of England.'[3] Using the proceeds from the sale of Louisiana to the Americans, Napoleon financed an invasion fleet to set up camp on the cliff tops of Boulogne. In total,

170,000 Frenchmen prepared to cross the Channel: Britons had every reason to lie awake at night.[4]

Frenzied and sleepless, Gillray's fan base went wild when a new print went up: 'If men be fighting over there for their possessions and their bodies against the Corsican robber,' one spectator noted, 'they are fighting here to be first in Ackermann's shop and see Gillray's latest caricatures.' This was the Beatlemania of the day: 'The enthusiasm is indescribable when the next drawing appears; it is a veritable madness. You have to make your way in through the crowd with your fists.'[5]

On 26 June 1803, Hannah Humphrey delivered again. If pedestrians could get a look in through the heaving crowd, they would have seen a familiar figure. Here was George III peering at a tiny man in his hand. But this was no toy soldier or model. Much to their delight, this was Napoleon. Cast as characters from *Gulliver's Travels*, Bonaparte plays Gulliver and George III takes the King of Brobdingnag. Addressing Napoleon as 'My little Friend Grildrig', George III informs him that he considered the French to be 'the most pernicious, little odious reptiles that nature ever suffer'd to crawl upon the surface of the Earth'.

This 'pigmy effigy strutting the palm of our good old King' went down a storm; 'the heads of the gazers before the shop-front of Mrs Humphrys were thrust one over another, and wedged so close, side by side ... Nothing could be more amusing that to listen to the remarks of the loitering crowd.'[6] George III was mostly concerned that he was shown wearing the wrong clothing: 'Quite wrong, quite wrong, not [wig] with uniform!!!'[7]

Despite the King's concerns, a month later, Gillray imagined what Napoleon might look like '48 hours after Landing' on the British coast. It was a dismal prospect. His haggard head is spiked on the pike of a delighted John Bull, who cries out: 'Ha! My little Boney! – what do'st think of Johnny Bull now? – Plunder Old England! hay? ... ravish all our Wives & Daughters! Hay – O Lord help that silly

"My little friend Grildrig, you have made a most admirable
"panegyric upon Yourself and Country, but from what I can
"gather from your own relation & the answers I have with
"much pains wringed & extorted from you, I cannot but con-
-clude you to be, one of the most pernicious, little-odious-
reptiles, that nature ever suffer'd to crawl upon the surface
of the Earth."


*The King of Brobdingnag, and Gulliver*, James Gillray, 1803.
Metropolitan Museum of Art

Head! – to think that Johnny Bull would ever suffer those Lanthorn Jaws to become King of Old England's Roast Beef & Plum Pudding.'[8]

And Isaac Cruikshank was backing up Gillray's campaign with prints showing jovial British citizens reacting to the invasion fears. Cruikshank gives us scenes of Brits heartily drinking damnation to all Corsican usurpers. 'I wish he'd come!' one cries. 'Zounds, how we would Tar & Feather him,' with suggestions of, 'we would send our old women to take him by the Nose'. And Cruikshank struck

*Bonaparte, 48 Hours after Landing!*, James Gillray, 1803.
Library of Congress

another blow by giving us Napoleon terrorised with nightmares: he is approached by the ghost of King Louis XVI, who points at his crown and declares: 'That's Mine!!!'

While the print shops released a shower of satirical arrows to bring down Napoleon's reputation, he was still on the rise. On 2 December 1804, aged 35, Napoleon crowned himself Emperor of France in a lavish ceremony in Notre Dame. Was there anything that could stop this man's mighty ambition?

*Dreadful Fears of Invasion!!*, Isaac Cruikshank, 1803.

## AN INSATIABLE APPETITE

As reports of the new Emperor filled the papers, three important pieces of news in the first weeks of 1805 may well have caught the attention of Hannah Humphrey and James Gillray.

Firstly, the newspapers were splashed with stories of a carpenter from Horsham, who paid fourteen shillings for the most patriotic all-you-can-eat deal around: an unlimited supply of plum pudding. The *London Courier and Evening Gazette* reported: 'The man was daily served with a sufficient quantum of this favourite old English food, and managed in the course of the week, to devour forty-six pounds, averdupouis!'[9]

Another snippet of news that may well have piqued Gillray's interest was a letter published in *The Times* on 15 February 1805. In a carroty offering (the stick being an invading force lining the coast at Boulogne), Napoleon wrote a letter to King George III in a bid for peace. 'The world,' the new Emperor wrote, 'is sufficiently large for our two nations to live in it.'[10] The great globe was only just big enough for the two nations to share, it seemed.

And thirdly, on 21 February 1805, had Gillray been sitting in on a Parliamentary session, he would have heard the oratory of William Windham. This MP questioned whether (with the regular army already fighting overseas), the 500,000 Dad's Army volunteers could fight off a Napoleonic invasion. 'It was impossible,' Windham exclaimed, 'to make an army out of a painted army, or what merely looked like an army ... You might as well suppose, that flour and eggs and butter and plums, would make a plum-pudding, as that men alone would make an army.'[11]

Could world politics really be changed with the ingredients of a plum pudding? Gillray might have mused. How funny that the Horsham carpenter and the Emperor Napoleon shared the same insatiable appetite. The one devouring a plum pudding, the other devouring the globe, refusing to share.

Somewhere in this blur of plum puddings and globes and enormous appetites, Gillray's vision clicked into focus. On 26 February 1805, his most enduring work went up in the window of 27 St James's Street; Londoners were presented with the most famous cartoon in history: *The Plumb-pudding in danger; – or – State Epicures taking un Petit Souper*.

This was such a momentous print that the German commentators felt some context was needed: 'In more than a quarter of all English caricatures the subjects are shown guzzling, or (which amounts to the same thing for true English diners) smacking their lips in pleasure. For the English are a nation of eaters. All travellers describe with amazement the assimilative powers and enormous capacity of the typical English stomach, which the German can seldom match.'[12] Looking closely at Gillray's latest print, they recommended, 'no reader should take up this joke on an empty stomach'.[13]

*The Plumb-pudding in danger; – or – State Epicures taking un Petit Souper*, James Gillray, 1805.
Library of Congress

There is, indeed, plenty of chomping, chewing and munching in this one. Napoleon and Pitt, who once threatened each other with total destruction, have made friends at last. They've even joined each other for dinner. It's a tête-à-tête that would have made the most remarkable restaurant booking in history. Pitt is calm and confident, dressed in military attire and a cocked tricorn hat. His dinner guest, Monsieur Bonaparte, is stockier and smaller with a large hooked nose and twitching eyes. He's sporting the uniform of the French Imperial Army, and he is dwarfed by an enormous bicorn hat with towering feathers.

The pair tuck into what appears to be an enormous steaming boiled pudding: a 'juicy, round, delicious-looking plump raisin dumpling'.[14] But the raisin marbling of this steaming orb sketches out the shapes of countries and continents of the globe. It's a clever analogy: a visual representation of Britain and France's dominance of the world. Napoleon has sliced off Spain, France, Holland and most of Europe. Pitt has gone for the Atlantic Ocean, the Americas and the West Indies. A Shakespeare misquote hammers home the greed of these politicians: 'the great Globe itself and all which it inherit is too small to satisfy such insatiable appetites.'

German commentators, writing in the journal *London und Paris*, were most concerned at Napoleon's portion: 'Unless his carving knife suddenly grows blunt,' they reasoned, 'he will soon have Africa below and Heaven only knows what else on his plate!'[15] With prescient logic, they predicted where such an appetite would lead: 'Any stomach with room for a snack like this first mouthful will surely want second and third helpings! Woe then to us poor Germans ... we shall probably come to grief very soon.'[16]

Napoleon himself was well aware of the power of caricature. He was furious at Gillray's attacks and had even tried to have a clause inserted in the Treaty of Amiens to ban them.[17] He tried his own retort: 'Have caricatures made,' he instructed Joseph Fouché, his minister of police. 'An Englishman, purse in hand, entreating the various Powers to take his money ... The immense attention which the English direct to gaining time by false news show the extreme importance of this work.'[18] But none of France's satirists – who risked committing *lèse-majesté*,* and incurring the wrath of the secret police – ever matched the power or vitality of their London equivalents.

A year after the *Plumb-pudding* triumph, Gillray put Little Boney in the kitchen as a gingerbread baker. But this was no ordinary kitchen, and these were no ordinary gingerbread. This bakery contained quite an incredible piece of equipment: a 'New French Oven for Imperial Gingerbread'. Riding on rumours that Napoleon was preparing to put his relatives and favourites in positions of power, Gillray cast him as Chef Bonaparte. Out of the furnace, he draws a

* This phrase comes from the Latin *laesa majestas*, meaning 'injured majesty'. It describes any act that insults the dignity or authority of a sovereign power, spanning from a minor insult to the crime of treason.

freshly baked batch of kings, a play on his new role as 'king-maker' of Europe. Below the oven lies the residue – an 'Ash Hole for broken Gingerbread', where Spain, Italy, Switzerland, the Netherlands and Austria lie in pieces – swept to destruction by the Corsican broom.

*Tiddy-Doll, the great French-Gingerbread-Baker; drawing out a new Batch of Kings*, James Gillray, 1806.

As Napoleon expanded across Europe, London's satirists let their minds run wild. They threw all their ideas at him: he was an earthworm, an earwig, a pest, a baby, a matador. They even rewrote his life story, changing his origins in the lovely townhouse in Ajaccio to portray him as a 'Ragged Headed Corsican Peasant'.[19] Napoleon was happy to clear up the confusion: 'There are genealogists who would date my family from the Flood,' he explained, 'and there are people who pretend that I am of plebeian birth. The truth lies between these two. The Bonapartes are a good Corsican family, little known because we hardly ever left the island, but much better than the coxcombs who take it upon themselves to vilify us.'[20]

Rowlandson imagined him as a Corsican spider, trapping flies in his deadly web. These insects – from Venice, Italy, Hamburg, Prussia and Hanover – are soon to be devoured by the Arthropodal Napoleon with 'unbounded ambition'. The Turkish Fly, sporting a jewelled turban, squeals: 'I am afraid it will be my turn next.' The weird little John Bull with four wings has more resolve: free from the clutches of the Corsican trap, the British fly is still able to buzz and bombinate to its heart's content, gleefully singing out: 'Ay you may look Master Spider but I am not to be caught in your web.'

*The Corsican Spider in His Web!*, Thomas Rowlandson, 1808.
Metropolitan Museum of Art, The Elisha Whittelsey Collection, The Elisha Whittelsey Fund, 1959

But more powerful than any of these, the idea of 'Little Boney' was sweeping the continent. Gillray's prints were so instantly effective that within less than a decade, Napoleon's reputation had been tainted for ever. When the Emperor looked back on his life's work while in exile on Elba, he is said to have considered that Gillray's prints did him more damage than a dozen British generals.

## LOW SCURRILITIES AND STALE JOKES

On 10 March 1805, there was an almighty explosion on St James's Street. It came from a skinny man, who had just wrenched the cork from an old bottle of sherry. The pressure that had built up over the years was so immense, the liquid inside burst out and fired high into the sky. Whoosh!

But this man wasn't just another ASBO moping around the streets, looking for trouble. In fact, he wasn't really on the streets at all. This man was Pitt the Younger, and the explosion of froth and fizz was to be seen in the Gillrayic attack hanging in Hannah Humphrey's window.

The print in question takes us to what appears to be a wine cellar, with rows and rows of bottles. But this is no ordinary cellar. This is some sick, psychedelic science experiment. For in these bottles are the heads of Pitt's political enemies, fizzing and fuming at their imprisonment. There's Fox, labelled 'True French Wine', and his fellow Whig MPs: William Windham, labelled 'Brandy and Water' and George Tierney, labelled 'a Glass of All-Sorts'.

They watch as the bottle of Old Sherry – containing the head of Sheridan – explodes before them. Out burst 'Old Puns', 'Groans of Disappointment', 'Stolen Jests', 'Invectives', 'Lame Puns', 'Loyal Boastings', 'Dramatic Ravings', 'Low Scurrilities', 'Stale Jokes' and 'Fibs, Fibs, Fibs!'.

This is no wine cellar, but the House of Commons itself. And we are hearing another of Sheridan's long, rambling pontifications.

'Tho' he does not very often address the House,' Gillray tells us, 'when he does, he always thinks proper to pay off all arrears ... like a Bottle just uncork'd bursts all at once, into an explosion of Froth & Air ... whether they have any relation or not to the Subject under discussion.'

*Uncorking Old Sherry*, James Gillray, 1805.
Library of Congress, Prints & Photographs Division

There was good reason for the politicians to be frothing at the mouth. The peace proposals Napoleon had offered in January 1805 had been rejected, and preparations for the invasion of Britain pressed on. Napoleon declared the English Channel was 'a ditch which will be leaped whenever one has the boldness to try', and this boldness seemed to increase by the day.[21] Meanwhile, the French made ground on the Italian peninsula, which led to the coronation of Napoleon as the King of Italy. On 11 April 1805, Austria, Sweden, Britain, Russia and a number of German states, known as the Third Coalition, declared war on France. Napoleon diverted his gaze away from Britain to the Austrian advance on French-controlled Bavaria. Phew!

But while the Third Coalition fought it out on land, the seas held more promise for Britannia's fortunes. At 10am on Monday 4 November, the tiny topsail schooner HMS *Pickle* dropped anchor two miles off Falmouth.

The captain, Lieutenant John Lapenotière, was on an urgent mission. Within an hour, he had rowed to shore. And within an hour of landing, he was on a post-chaise, heading for London. No time could be lost, for this man carried news. Thrilling, terrible, incredible news. It was to be delivered, according to the instruction of Admiral Cuthbert Collingwood, 'using every exertion, that a moment's time may not be lost in their delivery'.[22]

Lapenotière flew across the country at full speed. Leaving the pirated creeks of Cornwall behind, he raced along the winding lanes of Devonshire and through the wide valleys of Somerset. As soon as his horses tired, after ten or fifteen miles, they were swapped. After 271 miles, 21 changes of horses, and 37 hours later, he arrived in a fog-shrouded London. At 1am on Wednesday 6 November, the lieutenant burst into the board room of the Admiralty, dishevelled and exhausted.

'Sir,' he announced to William Marsden, first secretary to the board of Admiralty, 'we have gained a great victory, but we have lost Lord Nelson!'[23]

On 21 October 1805, the British Navy had destroyed the Franco–Spanish fleet at Trafalgar, just off the southern coast of Spain. Lapenotière had come as quickly as he could to deliver the news. His haste was generously rewarded, including a promotion and a gift of a silver spice sprinkler from the King. Pitt soon received word from Admiral Collingwood that 'twenty sail of the line captured … The most decisive and complete victory that ever was gained over a powerful enemy'.[24]

It was the Battle of the Nile all over again, but twice as great. The victory at Trafalgar was a much-needed morale boost. The public's patriotic zeal was only fuelled by stories of the heroic Admiral Nelson, caught by a musket ball fired from the French ship *Redoubtable* as he stood on the quarterdeck of his flagship, HMS *Victory*. Any problems Pitt had been facing were temporarily swept under the carpet. On the night of the Lord Mayor's banquet, no one cared to dwell on the fact that Pitt faced the rise and rise of Little Boney, or a Herculean wartime financial burden, or the cracks in his own weak ministry.

Instead, he was toasted as 'the saviour of Europe', to which Pitt gave what Arthur Wellesley considered 'one of the best and neatest speeches I ever heard in my life'.[25] 'I return you many thanks for the honour you have done me,' began Pitt, 'but Europe is not to be saved by any single man. England has saved herself by her exertions and will, as I trust, save Europe by her example.'[26] Short and sweet.

But those few words were to be the last time Pitt's mighty oratory was heard in public. For although he seemed in fine health at the Trafalgar celebrations, he was suffering bouts of illness – headaches, attacks of gout, sickness, nausea, stomach pains and loss of appetite. He was whisked away to Bath on 7 December 1806, spending Christmas at 2 Johnson Street, taking the waters and continuing to receive visitors for official government business.

For the fate of Europe hung in the balance. By mid-December news of a great battle was reaching London. It was rumoured to be another great victory, and Pitt held his nerve. But from 29 December

1805, the terrible truth was trickling out via the London newspapers. In ten hours of fighting, the Austrian and Russian armies had been annihilated by Napoleon at the Battle of Austerlitz. Pitt's eighteen-month effort to assemble the Third Coalition had been destroyed in a single day.

The disastrous news of Austerlitz crushed Pitt's spirit. His health continued to decline. So much so that he missed the grandest state occasion of the era: the five-day national mourning of Admiral Nelson.

Nelson's body had returned aboard HMS *Victory*, preserved in a barrel of spirits. When it arrived at Chatham, 'no variation appeared in the body, excepting that the lips and the ancles were a little discoloured'.[27] Nelson was dressed for the final time: 'A shirt, a pair of silk stockings, and his lordship's uniform breeches were put on the corpse.'[28] As the admiral had requested, the coffin was made from the mast of the French ship, *L'Orient*, which had been blown to pieces at the Battle of the Nile, eight years before. It was 'six feet in length, but rather narrow; the outside was covered with black cloth, and the inside lined with white silk, stuffed with cotton'.[29]

Nelson's body lay in state in the Painted Hall at Greenwich from Sunday 5 January; 15,000 mourners came to pay their respects, 'and numbers went away unsatisfied'.[30] On Wednesday 8 January, a monumental procession took the body up the Thames to Whitehall, where 'the shore was lined with thousands of spectators – every hat was off, and every countenance expressed the deepest regret felt at the loss of so great a hero. Not a vessel was suffered to disturb the procession. The decks, yards, rigging, and masts of the numerous ships on the river, were all crowded with spectators – the number of ladies was immense.'[31]

The following day, London came to a silent standstill as Nelson's cortège made its way from Whitehall to St Paul's. The funeral carriage and coffin were followed by 8,000 regular soldiers. Rows and rows of private carriages followed: 'The commoners went first, then the Peers, beginning with Barons, and closing with Dukes, next, the

Princes, and last, the Prince of Wales.'[32] Among those in the vast, silent crowd were Isaac Cruikshank and his son, George. They stood at Ludgate Hill to watch the coffin pass, then rushed back to their top-floor studio to etch what they saw, producing a frontispiece for *Fairburn's Edition of the Funeral of Admiral Lord Nelson*.[33]

After three and a half hours, the procession arrived at St Paul's Cathedral. Under the great dome, the congregation sat in tiered circle seating. And in the centre was the coffin itself, 'placed on a stool, covered with black, and with gold tassels'.[34] Suspended above was 'an immense octangular lanthorn' of 'nearly five hundred lamps' filling the cupola with light.[35] After the service, with solemn chants from Purcell and divine anthems from Handel, 'the body was placed on a platform, and solemnly descended by balance weight, twenty feet to the vault beneath'.[36]

## POOR, POOR P

For the Cruikshank family, this time of national mourning was especially hard. Since 1803, their eldest son Robert had been living a life on the ocean waves, after signing up to serve on the East India Company's ship *Perseverance*. Nothing remarkable occurred until, at some point in 1805, the family's worst fears were confirmed. News reached London that Robert had perished on duty.

Yet things weren't quite as they seemed. Robert Cruikshank had been a strong-willed young man, with a mind of his own. After coming to blows with his captain, he was left behind on the island of St Helena in the South Atlantic as punishment. On official records, he was listed as presumed dead. After hiding from press-gangs, he befriended the governor of the island and found safe passage back home. He strolled into the family house on Dorset Street in early 1806.[37]

Imagine the scene. Solemn Isaac, working on his coppers, thinking of nothing but his boy lost at sea. Mary Cruikshank, sobbing and sniffing as she checked through the accounts. George and his sister, Eliza, colouring the prints, paralysed by grief at the sudden loss of a sibling. And in this fog of gloom, a voice comes up from below: 'Mother? Father? I'm home!'

As the Cruikshanks celebrated, a painfully thin William Pitt returned to his London house in Putney Heath. Pitt's niece Lady Hester Stanhope was shocked: 'He was supported by the arms of two people, and had a stick, or two sticks in his hands, and as he came up, panting for breath … I retreated, little by little, not to put him in the pain of making a bow to me, or of speaking.'[38] Canning wrote to his wife that Pitt's illness was 'nothing specific but weakness, total exhaustion, inability to eat any thing, and an extinction of voice after a quarter of an hour's attempt at conversation … Poor, poor P.'[39]

On the night of 22 January, Pitt's condition deteriorated. He was muttering and mumbling and sometimes, with his mind still in the Commons, crying: 'Hear Hear!'[40] The following afternoon, at about 2.30pm, he exclaimed: 'Oh, my country! How I leave my country!'[41] From that point he remained silent and still.

On 23 January 1806, 25 years and eight months after he had first entered the House of Commons, William Pitt passed away. He was 46 and utterly worn out. It seems he suffered from peptic ulceration of his stomach. Today, this could be cured in a few days. The Duke of Wellington blamed 'long and previous exertions in the House of Commons', and the heavy drinking prescribed by the doctor, 'by deluging his stomach with port wine and water, which he drank to excess, in order to give a false and artificial stimulus to his nervous system'.[42]

The death of Pitt was another major blow for a nation still in mourning for Admiral Nelson. Even Fox admitted there was 'something missing in the world – a chasm or blank that cannot be supplied'.[43]

A coalition government was pulled together led by Pitt's cousin, Lord Grenville. It was known as the Ministry of All Talents, but dubbed by Gillray the 'Broad Bottoms', probably in relation to the rather wide posteriors possessed by the governing members. In the sudden power vacuum, politicians began jostling for office, which soon featured in a Gillrayic attack, *More Pigs than Teats*, in March 1806. Here were the 'new litter of hungry grunters'.[44]

Fox was offered the post of foreign secretary, which, after two agonising decades on the sidelines, he accepted. Finally, he could prove his French sympathies were right all along. He was 'sure that two civil sentences from the Ministers would ensure Peace'[45] and set about conducting peace talks with Charles Maurice de Talleyrand-Périgord, the French foreign minister with whom he had become friends during his visits to Paris.

But it soon dawned on Fox that friendship and conviviality counted for little when carving up global plum puddings. 'Charley Fox eats his former opinions daily,' commented John Rickman, a government official. It was embarrassing, to have everything he'd argued for proven wrong so quickly: 'He should have died, for his fame, a little sooner; before Pitt.'[46]

While he failed to push through either Catholic emancipation or peace with France, on 10 June 1806, Fox tabled a bill that lay close to his heart. It stated: 'This House, conceiving the African slave trade to be contrary to the principles of justice, humanity, and sound policy, will, with all practicable expedition, proceed to take effectual measures for abolishing the said trade.' The Foreign Slave Trade Bill would come into force in 1807.[47]* Fox wrote that:

> So fully am I impressed with the vast importance and necessity of attaining what will be the object of my motion this night, that

* Finally, in 1807, after one of the first and most successful public campaigns in history, Parliament abolished the slave trade. The tally at that date, since 1662, of African people purchased by British and British colonial ships totalled an estimated 3,415,500. Of course, although the British ended their slave trade in 1807, slavery itself continued in the British colonies until full emancipation in 1833.

> if, during the almost forty years that I have had the honour of a seat in parliament, I had been so fortunate as to accomplish that, and that only, I should think I had done enough, and could retire from public life with comfort, and the conscious satisfaction, that I had done my duty.[48]

Just eight months after the death of Pitt, Fox died at Chiswick House on 13 September 1806. An autopsy revealed a hardened liver, 35 gallstones, and around seven pints of transparent fluid in his abdomen.

In just a year, Britain lost not only the mighty hero Nelson but also the bulwarks of British politics of the past two decades. Pitt had dedicated his life to political service. He had captained Britannia through the tempestuous storms of the Regency Crisis, the French Revolution and the Napoleonic threat. And all the while, despite endless attack from satirists on all sides, Fox provided a rigorous and unrelenting opposition, keeping the Prime Minister and King to account, and never letting them off the hook. Both men delivered their ideas through some of the greatest oratory this country has ever heard.

Britons must have felt a confusing jolt at the loss of these three leaders. But nowhere was this felt more than in the print shops of Piccadilly. Hannah Humphrey, James Gillray, Thomas Rowlandson, Isaac and Mary Cruikshank, William Holland and Samuel Fores had lost their main characters. The stars of the show, Pitt, Fox and Nelson, had suddenly been whisked away, with no understudies and no worthy replacements. The artists may have had the artistic skills to make the prints, but Pitt and Fox provided the electric content – and they always had done. What was the London print trade without them? What was a ship without wind in its sails?

As 1806 came to a close, there was one question that would have kept the satirists awake at night: would they survive the years to come?

# 13

# *Advantages of Wearing Muslin Dresses*

## CATCH ME WHO CAN

So, was this it? Was it time for Hannah Humphrey to pack up shop? Was Rowlandson to find work as an assistant at the Royal Academy Schools? Was Samuel Fores about to transform his shop into a coffee house?

Not quite. Despite the sudden exeunt of the major characters, there was still plenty for the satirists to feast on. With Britain no longer the focus of Napoleon's plans, years of pent-up tension and anxieties about invasion were released: London burst into a wondrous frenzy of innovation.

Had you wandered down Pall Mall on 28 January 1807, you'd have witnessed the city's first fully operating streetlights being switched on. Or had you perused the papers in March, you might have read about the opening of the docks at Rotherhithe, a precursor to the first three miles of the Grand Surrey Canal. The public were treated to another delight in July 1808. On a site just south of today's Euston Square Tube Station* was the 'steam circus', showing off the latest

* University College London's main campus, to be precise.

invention of the Cornishman Richard Trevithick. For just one shilling, the public could board the steam locomotive, *Catch Me Who Can*, and race around the track.

It wasn't just an era of innovation. It was an era of daring. At 5am on 27 November 1809, the most audacious hoax in London's history began. A chimney sweep turned up for work at 54 Berners Street, just north of Oxford Street. The maid turned him away as no sweep had been expected. Another sweep came, who was once again turned away. Soon came another, several more, until twelve chimney sweeps had turned up, all under the impression that they were due for work. Yet, none of them had been sent for.

But the sweeps were only the start. Next came coal wagons, deliveries for wedding cakes, apothecaries, surgeons, lawyers, fishmongers, shoemakers, haberdashers, hatmakers, butchers' boys, vicars, priests and undertakers. There was a queue of pianos, organs and bespoke coffins waiting outside the door. All loitered outside 54 Berners Street, all under the impression they had been called for work.

Soon enough, the streets became madly congested and the city was brought to a standstill. Crowds gathered to watch the bizarre spectacle: the governor of the Bank of England, the lord mayor of London and even the Duke of Gloucester turned up to gawp. By mid-afternoon, it emerged that these hundreds of tradesmen had been the victims of an elaborate hoax: 'It turned out that letters had been written to the different trades people, which stated recommendations from persons of quality.'[1]

Indeed, opposite 54 Berners Street, one young rascal watched the drama unfold in delight. Theodore Edward Hook had bet a guinea that, within a week, he could make any house in London the most talked about in the city. To win the bet, he sent out 4,000 requests and orders to tradesmen and professionals, requiring them to present their services at Mrs Tottenham's house. With his winnings secured, Hook left for the countryside and kept a low profile, never to be convicted of his mischievous crime.

It was Berners Street's busiest ever afternoon. You might have soon wanted to escape the crowds. If you'd walked south, crossing Oxford Street, you'd have found yourself strolling through the heart of Soho, Wardour Street. At No. 73, two voices may well have floated from the open door.

The duo in question were Thomas Rowlandson and his sister Elizabeth Howitt. Elizabeth was turning a new leaf and setting up a print shop of her own. The first years of the 1800s had been rocky for the Rowlandson siblings. Elizabeth had split from her difficult husband and the father of their three children, the etcher and painter Samuel Howitt. Samuel had been 'somewhat of a spoiled child – a wayward genius of a convivial soul and vivacious impulses'. But he was unthinking and selfish, especially when it came to drinking. Elizabeth had found him 'a trifle too given to yield to careless convivial company or the allurements which the hour might hold forth, oblivious of sober consequences to follow'.[2]

Thomas Rowlandson, too, had reason to grieve. Mary Chateauvert, his loyal, beloved housekeeper, and his last link to the happy years with Aunt Jane, had passed away. And the siblings' 75-year-old father, William Rowlandson, was causing trouble yet again.

Over the past fifteen years, William Rowlandson had built up a bleaching and laundering warehouse in Finsbury, known to locals as 'Rowlandson's Place'.[3] It was an impressive recovery from bankruptcy, but his gaze soon wandered from business matters to a local dressmaker, Ann Hall. Ann was half William's age, but she was an ambitious woman and attracted by the security of a profitable marriage.

They tied the knot in 1804. On 29 July 1805, William Rowlandson altered his will, and a month later, he died. The will soon made itself known. Ann was to inherit 'all my Estate and Effects of what kind and nature soever'.[4] William's children, Thomas and Elizabeth, received a shilling each: they had been deliberately disinherited. It must have been a source of great angst that a younger woman, fresh on the scene, had pocketed their father's fortune. Especially as recently divorced Elizabeth was facing a domestic crisis of her own, and Thomas described himself 'a trader and poor'.[5]

But Elizabeth and Thomas did not wallow in their misfortune. Elizabeth was soon welcoming punters at 73 Wardour Street, where she commissioned, coloured and sold prints. And Thomas was taking his career in a new direction. By 1807, he was settled in with a studio on the top floor of 1 James Street. Here he would take commissions – sometimes of his own designs, sometimes designs by others – which he could either etch and print on his own private press or take to an independent printer. He might colour the prints in the studio, or bundle them under his arm for a quick walk over to Wardour Street where his sister Bess would colour them. Most excitingly, he began publishing directly with outlets as far away as John Downes in Great Yarmouth, to whom prints would be delivered by waggon or coach.[6]

Perhaps this burst of industry and invention was no coincidence, for Rowlandson had found someone to put his affairs in order. Betsy Winter was employed to run his household, to dutifully clean his rooms, cook his meals and launder his linen. Betsy, a younger woman in her late thirties, came from West Wycombe, a town famed for stories of Sir Francis Dashwood's Hellfire Club. Cupid's arrow soon flew through the window of Rowlandson's studio. Thomas and Betsy fell in love. Perhaps it was therefore to be expected that Rowlandson went through a phase of producing particularly risqué prints at this time.

With a successful studio, a merry companion and a reliable network of sellers, things seemed to be looking up. Rowlandson enjoyed regular visits from his friends and clients, and with so many visitors going to and fro, it became quite the social scene. William Pyne, a fellow artist, wrote a sumptuous memoir named *Wine and Walnuts, Or, After Dinner Chit-Chat*. Several pages of this chit-chat was dedicated exclusively to anecdotes from the staircase of Rowlandson's James Street studio.

## AFTER-DINNER CHIT-CHAT

One episode featuring Rowlandson's stairwell began with a Scotsman named Caleb Whitefoord, an ex-wine merchant who had climbed the slippery slope of society to become the vice-president of the Society for the Encouragement of Arts, Manufactures and Commerce. The society was based on John Adam Street, also in the Adelphi complex; so it was no surprise that Whitefoord was a regular at Rowlandson's studio.

'Well, Sirs,' the memoir sets out, 'Master Caleb was on his way up the hill in the Adelphi, to his post at the Society of Arts, and who should he stumble upon at the corner of James Street, just turning around from Rowlandson's, but Master Mitchell.'[7]

Matthew Mitchell was a successful banker and a great friend and patron to Rowlandson. He was as rotund and jolly as he was wealthy: 'He was extremely well proportioned,' a friend recalled, 'and walked in what I have often heard the ladies of the *old school* style a portly manner.' He had a 'width of chin as large as Titus Oates's', and a 'set of large white teeth'.[8] If drawings were ever made of Rowlandson and Mitchell, 'Mitchell claimed the greater proportion' of the paper.[9]

With his wife Louisa, Mitchell darted between his three properties: one in London (in the Beaufort Buildings, where the Savoy Hotel now stands), one in Essex and one in Cornwall, where Rowlandson was regularly welcomed on his jaunts around the country.[10] It was a most agreeable life of conviviality and idle hours. Only one thing could break this man's jollity, which would leave him paralysed by fear: 'He could sit in a room without experiencing the least emotion from a cat; but directly he perceived a kitten, his flesh shook on his bones, like a snail in vinegar.'[11]

In this particular episode, on the streets outside Rowlandson's house, Mitchell had a portfolio of Rowlandson's latest works under his arm. Caleb Whitefoord was intrigued: 'Well, worthy Sir, what more choice bits – more graphic whimsies, to add to the collection at Enfield, hey? Well how fares it with our old friend Rolly?'[12]

The enormous banker set out to climb the stairs to Rowlandson's apartment, talking and panting as he went: 'Why yes, Mister Caleb Whitefoord, I go collecting on, though I begin to think I have enough already, for I have some hundreds of his spirited works; but somehow there is a sort of fascination in these matters, and – heigh – ha – ho – hoo ... – Bless the man, why will he live so high? – it kills me to climb his stairs,' Mitchell exclaimed, while 'holding his ponderous sides'. And after a breather, up again they went, still trying to keep up a conversation: 'I find something new, and am tempted to pull my purse-strings. His invention, his humous, his – oddity is exhaustless.'[13]

Caleb Whitefoord was happy to concur, 'Master Rolly is never at a loss for a subject, and I should not be surprised if he is taking a bird's eye view of you and I at this moment, and marking us down for game.'[14]

After Mitchell's meeting with Rowlandson, he bumped into Jack Bannister, the actor, and another artist, John Nixon, 'who was just popping in at Rowlandson's as Mitchell was rolling out'. On recognising a fellow member of his old club, the Sublime Society of Beef Steaks, Mitchell declared: 'Why, my worthy knight of the knife and fork,' and invited him for dinner. But, alas, the young man was already busy: 'I am engaged at the Beef-steak,' Nixon replied, pointing to his buttons impressed with grid-irons.

But the banker did not give up, probing Jack Bannister: 'Well do you come then, my old friend, none can be more welcome. You shall have a bottle of the best, and we will gossip of old times. Rolly has promised to come down – I would have taken the rogue with me, only that he is about some new scheme for his old friend Ackermann there, and says he must complete its within an hour.' But Bannister was occupied too, for he was on the stage at Drury Lane that night.

As Mitchell climbed into his carriage, full to the brim with provisions for the evening, the others sent their dearest regards: 'Take care how you step, for charity's sake, or you'll turn the carriage over, and all the turtle will be spoilt.' The lively party shook hands, wished him a pleasant ride and away he drove for Essex. And as soon at the carriage was on its way, Jack Bannister burst into hysterics, clasping his own sides: 'Ha – ha – ha – ha! Famine! What a picture of famine!'[15]

Just off the Strand was the perfect place for Rowlandson to be based, as he was just a stone's throw from Ackermann's shop, the Repository of Arts. This had a library 'nearly fifty feet in length … fitted up with great elegance and … furnished with a valuable and extensive collection of works'.[16] Ackermann was a great contact. Not only did he have a fondness for Moselle wine, he had an entrepreneurial spirit in his genes and was forever coming up with new concepts. In 1801, he had taken out a patent for the waterproofing of paper and cloth and opened a manufactory in Chelsea. Unfortunately, it was soon closed after the dishonesty of one of his partners cost him £1,000. But Ackermann was not one to fall at the first hurdle. He would bounce back with more determination than ever.

In 1804, a carriage of his design carried the Pope to Napoleon's coronation at Notre Dame. And in 1805, he was commissioned to design the funeral carriage and coffin of Admiral Lord Nelson. In 1806, he travelled undercover to Hamburg, Leipzig and Vienna, escaping French troops by disguising himself as a coachman. In 1807, he worked with the War Office to design a system of paper distribution. His model was an air balloon, built specifically to distribute British propaganda over Europe. On 24 March 1809, he became a citizen of the United Kingdom.

Besides this eclectic array of projects, some of the cogs of Ackermann's *Dragon's Den* brain were put into motion by investing in London's print trade. He began inventing all sorts of new schemes to mould the weird and wacky ideas of London's satirists into a serious commercial venture. The chaotic lives of the heavy-drinking artists were to be managed and ordered into a well-oiled caricature-creating machine.

First, he made use of what was already there. He called Rowlandson in to make 'counterproof' copies of his old designs. Rowlandson would wander down the stairs of his James Street address, pootle along the Strand and, after inspecting the lively windows of Ackermann's Repository of Arts, push open the door to begin work. Everything was set out for him – paper, a brush, vermilion ink, water, a saucer.[17] He was given a reed, which could be cut and shaped however he preferred. Then the work began.

Wielding a pen and a pot of gleaming ink, Rowlandson began carefully drawing over the outline of one of his old pieces, chosen by Ackermann. Then, while the ink was still shining, the paper was given to an assistant and placed on a fresh sheet of dampened paper. The two sheets were squashed together through a press, which would transfer the design onto the damp paper. *Voilà!* An exact copy! As many copies as could be made until the ink ran out. 'Then that original became useless, and Rowlandson preceded to reline the replicas, and to tint them according to the fancy of the moment.'[18]

Ackermann made a steady income from the sale of well-loved Rowlandson classics. But it didn't put him on the map. His great spark – his light bulb moment – came in 1806. It was the result of a waking nightmare. Mr Ackermann, the respectable chap that he was, imagined himself on a summer's day on the banks of a serene river. Leaving his clothes in a neat pile on the bank, he dives in and finds himself splashing and gliding among ducks and reeds and cool, clear waters. What bliss! What heaven! But on returning to the bank to get dressed, the successful, impressive Mr Ackermann discovers in horror that a passer-by has 'taken a sudden fancy to the cut of every article of [his] dress!'[19]

The vision of a nude Ackermann stranded in public was not one of his own invention. Nor was it – thank goodness – based on personal experience. This vision arrived from reading a book by Reverend James Beresford, a fellow of Merton College, Oxford. While pontificating on theology, Beresford penned *The Miseries of Human Life*, a light-hearted treasury of all the inconveniences and embarrassments of the wonderful every day.

Beresford asked his readers to imagine hundreds of embarrassing situations, including:

> Slipping your knife suddenly and violently from off a bone, its edge first shrieking across the plate (so as to make you hated by yourself and the whole company), and then driving the plate before it, and lodging all its contents – meat, gravy, melted butter, vegetables, &c., &c., partly on your own breeches, partly on the cloth, partly on the floor, but principally on the lap of a charming girl who sits by you, and to whom you had been diligently endeavouring to recommend yourself as a suitor.[20]

There were many Miseries of the Table: 'While swallowing a raspberry, discovering by its taste that you have been so unhappy as to occasion the death of a harmless insect!'[21] Or the Miseries of Social Life: 'Sitting down alone in a large party upon a sofa that makes an *equivocal* noise.'[22]

Beresford's book went down a storm. Surely, Ackermann thought, he could capitalise on this? Perhaps Mr Rowlandson could add to Beresford's quips with his scenes of ridicule? The plan was set. Soon, Rowlandson was darting between Ackermann's shop on the Strand and his own studio on James Street, checking proofs and revisiting drafts.

Rowlandson's take was perfection. He beefed up Beresford's work with charm. Take the scene of getting stuck in traffic: 'In going out to dinner, (already too late) your carriage delayed by a *jam* of coaches ... which choke up the whole street, and allow you at least an hour more than you require, to sharpen your wits for table talk.'[23]

But Rowlandson's vision wasn't just a M25-esque gridlock. This was literal chaos: carriages scaling the corners on just two wheels, passengers flying out of their seats, horses thrashing as dogs and street

*Miseries of London*, Thomas Rowlandson, 1807.

sellers and builders weaving in and out of the madness. Look down for one moment and you'll be flattened. Ladies heading to dinner set off looking presentable but, after an hour in Rowlandson's traffic jam, they'll look as though they've been dragged through a bush.

And what of parties in the countryside? There was also a Misery for them. What a nightmare it is 'going to a party to dinner, getting very tipsy, quitting the house in a Dark Night, and getting upon your Horse with your face towards the Tail and wondering during the few minutes that you are able to keep your seat, among the jeers of your companions, what Freak can have entered the Brain of the Beast to go backwards'.[24] For this piece, Rowlandson cast this unfortunate passenger on a reversing horse, as a parson, his pomposity pricked by his wig having fallen awry and his hat sent flying.

Rowlandson so delighted in Beresford's conceit that he also came up with his own. There was the elderly couple who reversed their gig into a china shop and the plump Mrs Figgs who fell through the floor of her carriage and exposed her naked bottom. Misery indeed!

*More miseries*, Thomas Rowlandson, 1807.

Rowlandson wasn't the only to one to lay into such petty outrages, tiny discomforts and minor humiliations: Gillray, too, enjoyed ridiculing society's mores. In *Advantages of Wearing Muslin Dresses!*, he takes us to a scene of afternoon tea, where the attendees are trapped by convention and pretension. Everything they do – from the way they laugh, or hold their fork, or enter the room – follows a set of rules. But the rule book doesn't make way for human error.

Behind one rather large lady is a fireplace, and somehow, a red-hot poker has fallen onto her dress, sending her muslin dress up in flames. As she jumps up in horror, the table overturns, sending boiling tea flying, crockery smashing, cats squealing, eyes widening and screeches of panic. Even the landscape above the fireplace depicts an erupting volcano.

Gillray never made a part two of this scene, but it would no doubt be an almighty breach of propriety: this buxom woman drenched in water, with the damp muslin clinging to every inch of her shape, half of it burnt to cinders. Avert your eyes, gentlemen!

*Advantages of Wearing Muslin Dresses!*, James Gillray, 1802.
Digital Commonwealth: https://ark.digitalcommonwealth.org/ark:/50959/2z111j47m

In another of Gillray's japes he takes us to a lavish breakfast parlour, decorated with gilt detailing in the shape of palm trees. Here are five gentlemen and a lady, tucking into boiled eggs, bread and muffins. It seems this is the house of a wealthy widow hosting her potential suitors – each trying to outshine one another with postulation and pomp. But this lady is about to commit a heinous act. She gets up from the table to request some more muffins, crosses the room and reaches out to tug a raspberry-coloured piece of rope. God forbid! A lady ringing a bell-pull!

Her five bad-breathed companions are shocked at such impropriety. In their haste to stop her, disaster ensues: crockery cascades to the floor, the boiling-hot urn crashes down, one man chokes on a muffin, another (whose wig has been speared by a knife) finds a muffin in his eye and a dog bites the knee of another unlucky suitor.

As the widow looks on in bemusement, one can't help but feel this was part of some kind of test. Which of these potentials could really cope in moments of crisis?

*Company shocked at a Lady getting up to Ring the Bell*, James Gillray, 1804.
Digital Commonwealth: https://ark.digitalcommonwealth.org/ark:/50959/2z111k65r

## A WALKING TURTLE

Ackermann was a heavyweight businessman. He was an establishment type who was keen to toe the line. His next project, *The Microcosm of London*, stepped things up a notch. It was a set of prints that would showcase London's most important buildings and prestigious institutions, designed to appeal to more sober tastes of London's fine society. Ackermann's exquisitely rendered prints would sit happily alongside a great oil painting; there were no prime mushrooms or plum puddings here.

But who was best to approach for this work? James Gillray was off the cards: he was working exclusively for Hannah Humphrey. Isaac Cruikshank's style was more suited for political cartoons. His son,

George, was showing impressive talent, but this was a big project that needed experience. Rowlandson was the obvious choice: he lived just down the road and could churn out a watercolour of London life in his sleep. But Ackermann wasn't satisfied. Rowlandson's figures were brilliant: such life, such character, such vigour. But his rendering of architecture was – well – *lacking*. He usually made do with a few sketchy lines and a watercolour wash.

It wouldn't cut the mustard for a high-quality, premium product. Ackermann's bright idea was to organise a collaboration: Rowlandson would do the figures and Augustus Pugin would provide the backdrop. He was an architectural draughtsman whose skills had been fine-tuned under the expert eye of John Nash. He was a small 46-year-old Frenchman who had fled from revolutionary disorder in around 1798 and settled in London.*

The collab between the pair was risky. Pugin was traditional, fussy and genteel. He was probably surprised to be paired with Rowlandson, who had recently been sketching the bare bottom of Mrs Figgs. But Ackermann was a man with a vision and a great eye for talent. 'Trust the process,' he might well have reassured Monsieur Pugin.

Both Rowlandson and Pugin did a lot of trusting. Merging their differing styles and approaches was tricky. Drafts and redrafts were issued. A passive-aggressive war was played out through curt and sarcastic notes. 'This group of figures to be left out,' Pugin wrote on Rowlandson's work, 'no figures in this Gallery', and, 'the figures near rather too small. The Master is more of a gentleman'.[25] Rowlandson gave his own feedback, too: 'With submission to Mr Pugin's better judgement, Mr Rowlandson conceives, if the light came in the other side of ye picture, the figures would be set off to better advantage.'[26]

* His more famous son would lead England's Gothic Revival with his sumptuous designs for the Houses of Parliament.

Creative differences were overcome. The result was a splendid account of London life, with magnificently rendered settings brought to life by lively characters. But they didn't all come at once. Ackermann got the public hooked by teasing them with four plates a month for the next two years, beginning on 1 January 1808. Finally, they were bound in three volumes containing all 104 hand-coloured aquatints and were put on sale for the grand sum of 13 guineas.[27]

But it wasn't always Ackermann who came up with the ideas. The third of his great publications sprung from a drinking session of Rowlandson's gang in late 1807. While mulling over a punchbowl and puffing away on a pipe of tobacco, the jovial Rowlandson was unusually mellow. He was so out of sorts that – according to Jack Bannister – a fellow boozer enquired: 'What are you about, Rolly?' 'Why, nothing in particular,' he replied, which wasn't altogether true, as he went on to explain: 'I think my inventive faculty has been very sluggish of late. I wish one of you would give a hint.'[28]

Rowlandson set out his dilemma. He had recently travelled through Devonshire and Cornwall with his patron, the jolly banker Matthew Mitchell. Rowlandson's idea was to create a character who endured a series of frolicking dalliances and rollicking adventures at inns and markets and turnpikes around the countryside. But Mitchell had got the wrong end of the stick and was rather hoping he might star as the lead of the series.

'What can I do for such a hero?' Rowlandson despaired. 'A walking turtle, – a gentleman weighing four-and-twenty stone, – for such scenes he is out the question. I want one of a totally different description.' Jack Bannister, used to working on London's stage, declared: 'I have it! You must fancy a skin-and-bone hero, a pedantic old prig, in a shovel-hat, with a pony, sketching tools, and rattletraps, and places him in such scrapes as travellers frequently meets with, hedge alehouses, second and third-rate inns, thieves, gibbets, mad bulls, and the like. Come,' he exclaimed, really warming up to it now, 'give us a sheet of paper and we'll strike off a few hints.'[29]

And so it was – according to the recollections of Jack Bannister – that Rowlandson's new hero, Dr Syntax, was born. He was a long-nosed, chisel-chinned rural pastor who set off one day on an old horse to tour the English lakes. Accident-prone, gullible and strangely likeable, Dr Syntax attempted to make his fortune from writing and illustrating a book about his travels.

When Ackermann received Rowlandson's portfolio of drawings of the Syntax adventures, he was delighted. He perused them one evening alongside the writer William Combe, who happened to have stepped into the shop. The two men laughed and snorted and guffawed at Rowlandson's latest. But always the entrepreneur, Ackermann considered how to make the most of the designs. What if some writer added verse alongside the images? Perhaps they could turn it into a story? They could feature the stories in the new *Poetical Magazine* and then publish a collective volume of the whole narrative. Ackermann was decided, and he offered the commission to Combe on the spot.[30]

Ackermann might have hoped this collaboration would be smoother than the Pugin–Rowlandson project. Combe was an old hack of impressive range. He'd spent a lifetime writing verses, satires, translations, epistolary novels, histories and even ready-made

*Doctor Syntax Drawing After Nature*, Thomas Rowlandson, 1812.
British Library HMNTS 11641.g.38

sermons. He was a handy Swiss Army knife in Ackermann's toolkit, ready to adapt to whatever was needed. For this gig, he wrote in octosyllabic verse and would 'regularly pin up the sketch against a screen of his apartment in King's Bench and write off his verses as the printer wanted them'.[31] Things started off well, but – as is inevitable with experienced creatives who have their own ways of doing things – the pair soon found themselves in disagreement.

Combe was a church man. He wasn't happy at Rowlandson's mockery of the nation's clergymen, some of whom were pictured swigging heartily from tankards, with their servants throwing up. 'If ridicule was the intention,' Combe declared, 'to such a plan I resolved not to lend my pen; I respect the clergy; and I determined to turn the edge of the weapon which I thought was levelled against them.'[32] So, Rowlandson's rowdy clergymen were cut – or at least, they were swigging slightly less heartily from their cups.

The result, published in 1809, was *The Tour of Dr Syntax in Search of the Picturesque*. It was another bestseller. It was enjoyed by Jane Austen, who wrote to her sister, Cassandra, while staying in Henrietta Street in March 1814: 'I have seen nobody in London yet with such a long chin as Dr Syntax.'[33]

## A MIRROR OF MIRTH

The London print scene was changing. At the smarter end of town, Ackermann was flying high on profits from his printing endeavours. He was bringing in big-name collaborations, producing material en masse and rethinking every process with the latest technology. His commissions tended to be print series, which would be carefully planned with multiple rounds of tweaks and edits to reach that premium standard. His tastes were more sober and prudish, too – a precursor to his Victorian successors.

At the lower end of the market, London print shops were being undercut by another corporate empire. But this was a Wild West by comparison to Rowlandson's gold standard. In 1805, Thomas Tegg set up his Apollo Library at 111 Cheapside, in the shadow of St Paul's Cathedral.

First and foremost, Tegg was out to make money. He was a man who made things happen, even if it meant cutting a few corners. When he heard that Nelson had been shot at Trafalgar, he commissioned an engraved portrait of the heroic admiral, quick as a flash. Then, he swotted up by reading the *Naval Chronicle*, bashed out an account of *The Whole Life of Nelson* and sent it off to press. Pitched at a reasonable price, Tegg saw 5,000 copies fly off the shelves.[34]

Sometimes he would republish classic books that were out of copyright. 'My line is to watch the expiration of copyright,' he later explained, 'and then produce to the public either current works at a cheaper rate.'[35] He was a serious wheeler-dealer with unscrupulous methods. When Tegg was halfway through reprinting Milton's *Paradise Lost*, the paper supplies ran out. Tegg printed *FINIS*, and send it off to the binders anyway.[36] 'Ol' trick of the trade,' he might have muttered, with a wink. Adapt. Improvise. Overcome.

Others remembered Tegg tearing out the pages of classic novels until they fitted the length desired, no doubt leaving many readers in a state of confusion. 'Didn't you *adore* the book, Henrietta; don't you think the final twist was just *shocking*!' To which readers of a Tegg edition must have nodded in bamboozlement, struggling to remember what on earth the twist in the final chapter was.

But while 111 Cheapside became a hub for cheap books, punters flocked for Tegg's satirical prints. He knew how to flatter his clients: 'Noblemen, Gentlemen, etc. wishing to ornament their Billiard or other Rooms, with Caricatures may be supplied 100 percent cheaper at Tegg's Caricature Warehouse.'[37] They were indeed dirt cheap: half the original price and half the original quality. Tegg would print on cheap paper or use old, worn-down plates that didn't pick up the ink properly.

But he commissioned original material, too. He got the star names on board from the start – Mustard George was a big coup, for he was now a celebrity comedian who had won the public's hearts. His prints were down-to-earth, full of double entendre and killer punchlines. What's more, Mustard George was a big drinker who was struggling to keep his finances in order. He'd been lodging at the Southampton Arms tavern on Chancery Lane and sometimes the Brown Bear – crawling up to bed after a drinking session, only to continue drinking the next morning. He spent as much as he earned. So, Tegg's cash-in-hand, cheap-and-cheerful approach suited him perfectly.

With Mustard George's designs, often etched by Isaac Cruikshank, Tegg created *The Caricature Magazine or Hudibrastic Mirror*, by G.M. Woodward. The prints of Mustard George were published weekly at affordable prices. Over time, these would build into a collection of nearly 500 plates in five volumes.

The covers of these magazines were full of five-star reviews – as imagined by Tegg himself. For there are characters delighting in the prints, exclaiming them 'the drollest things ever sent into our Country'. 'Come John,' a comely woman squabbles, 'let me look don't keep it all to yourself.' Another impressed customer bemuses: 'I wonder how they think of all these things.' Another squeals in delight at one of the characters: 'There be one exactly like our Exciseman.'

Soon, Tegg rolled out another publication, named the *Mirror of Mirth*, which was 'designed and engraved by Thomas Rowlandson, Esq.', including 500 plates by Rowlandson, Cruikshank, Mustard George and a few others. It was a viral success: Tegg had cracked the algorithm.

How far things had come, Rowlandson must have mused as he held this weighty compendium in his hands. How different the print world was now from when he'd made his debut as a young man. As he silently flicked through Thomas Tegg's *Caricature Magazine*, Rowlandson couldn't help but feel something was amiss. Something had been lost. These great catalogues looked gorgeous, but they were devoid of the spark and spontaneity of the 1780s content. These glossy compendiums had none of the thrill of day-by-day scoops, of jostling between publishers, of fans screaming at shop windows.

What's more, the trade was being swamped by two corporate empires: respectable Rudolph Ackermann, with his sober taste and considered approach, and Thomas Tegg, who would churn out whatever would sell, at whatever cost.

Was Hogarth's great legacy – to bridge the gap between high and low art and culture – coming to an end? Had the Golden Age of British Satire finally outgrown itself? Had the bubble burst at last?

In 1809, London was rocked by the juiciest social scandal the satirists could have dreamt of. This was to be the last hurrah.

# 14

# *The Crew to Pluto's Realm*

## *THE MODERN CIRCE*

Mary Anne Clarke was one of the world's greatest social climbers. Born the daughter of a tradesman, she charmed her way up the social ladder to become the mistress of Frederick, Duke of York, the commander-in-chief of the army and the second son of King George.

The Duke indulged his feisty young mistress with a fashionable lifestyle, which he soon came to regret: giving her an inch, she took a mile. Her careless extravagances became too lavish, even for the Duke. When he tried to cut off her allowance, she publicly blackmailed him by threatening to leak 'everything which has come under my knowledge during our intimacy, with all his letters'. What's more, word got out that Clarke had been bribed by army officers to help them gain promotion through her influence over the Duke.

Next, Mistress Clarke was called to the Houses of Parliament to testify. She stunned the crowd, batting off all allegations with ease. 'House examining Mrs Clarke for two hours,' noted Wilberforce in his diary, 'cross-examining her in the Old Bailey way – she was elegantly dressed, consummately impudent, and very clever: clearly got the better in the tussle.'[1]

The damage was done. The opposition benches, hungry to see the Duke's demise, embellished the rumours with aplomb, and a tsunami of new material flooded the London print shops from every satirist and printseller in town. 'The demand for this exciting pabulum,' wrote Joseph Grego some years later, 'was sufficiently eager to induce the caricaturist to bring out a fresh pictorial satire almost daily, and sometimes two or more appeared on the same day, while the "delicate investigation" was proceeding, and the public interest in the circumstances remained at a boiling heat.'[2]

Thomas Tegg commissioned over 50 designs from Rowlandson alone, eventually bundling them together as a catalogue. There were scenes of Clarke schmoozing the Duke over wine and dessert: 'I have a small list of promotions which I wish to be fill'd up immediately my Dearest,' she swooned, to which he replies: 'It shall be done my Darling.' There were dejected officers admitting: 'I did not think it would have been done so soon. I had promised at least a dozen promotions.'[3] There were even designs for a monument to be erected in Gloucester Place, with a cornerstone labelled: 'The Foundation of York Folly!'[4]

James Gillray cast Clarke as Pandora, opening a box of evils in the House of Commons. In the print, out fly hissing snakes labelled 'Deceit', 'Revenge', 'Perjury', 'Forgery', 'Lies', and 'Calumny', much to the delight of the opposition. And at her feet lie the notes for her tell-all confessions: 'Prices of Commissions', 'Forged Letters' and 'Scheme to destroy the House of Brunswick'.

And what of Isaac Cruikshank's contribution? The Cruikshank boys were now running their father's workshop from the top-floor studio of their four-storey terraced house at 117 Dorset Street.[5] Their father had developed a habit of spending long nights drinking, and it was taking a toll on his work. Luckily, his son George was brilliantly capable. At the age of thirteen, he was finishing off his father's work with titles, backgrounds, furnishings and dialogue.

He hoped to attend the Royal Academy (the great Romantic artist Henry Fuseli, considered him a worthy candidate), but the pressure of looking after his mother and running his father's workshop 'was so great that he had no leisure for the lectures or work of an art student'.[6] So, along with his brother Robert, the boys ran the studio, finishing off their fathers plates and etching the designs of others ('the washing of other people's dirty linen', as George put it).[7] George Cruikshank was an ambitious young man who hero-worshipped James Gillray. Although they were 'never admitted to personal familiarity', George believed he was, hands down, 'the prince of caricaturists'.[8]

The Mary Anne Clarke affair was the perfect time to put the up-and-coming Cruikshank's skills to the test. George and Robert probably helped produce their father's most effective print. Here, Mistress Clarke was dressed up in the Duke of York's military cloak, which is so billowing and roomy that it forms a tent to cover a crowd

*The Modern Circe, or a Sequel to the Petticoat*, Isaac Cruikshank, 1809.
Library of Congress, Prints & Photographs Division

of little men who cluster round her. 'Come under,' she cries, 'I've made it weather proof to shelter you all.' From her waist hangs a sign: 'Who'll buy good luck ... Who'll buy Promotion tickets here am I.' Entitled, *The Modern Circe, or a Sequel to the Petticoat*, it went up in Samuel Fores' print shop window on 14 March 1809, to the delight of his fans.

Just ten days later, drowning in this sea of satire, the Duke resigned as commander-in-chief of the army.

There had been such an exceptional flurry of prints surrounding Clarke's mischief, the satirists' take was news in itself. Isaac Cruikshank created a print showing Napoleon and the French generals flicking through a collection. As they pass around the prints they laugh heartily: 'Aha, dis be de great Commander at Dunkirk,' Talleyrand delights. 'Dere is nothing to be feared from such Petticoat Commanders,' concludes another. And another French officer admires a scene of some big-bottomed ladies. 'He he he, raise de Wind,' he cries, noticing the windmill behind them. The print was named *French Generals receiving an English Charge* – 'charge' being the French term for a caricature.

*French Generals receiving an English Charge*, Isaac Cruikshank, 1809.
Library of Congress, Prints & Photographs Division

The deluge of prints surrounding the Clarke affair was indeed a formidable, thundering charge, slicing through public reputations with cut-throat satire. At moments like this, the artists were the most powerful commanders in London. They sat in the director's chair, playing puppetry with great men, dressing them up, recasting them and rewriting their script at every change of scene.

They seemed an unstoppable, untouchable force. Yet, within two years, the heart of this force would be wrenched out, leaving an empty shell behind. As Gillray's followers surged forwards to catch a glimpse of Mary Anne Clarke in Hannah Humphrey's shop window, they had little idea that this was to be the final flourish. Not only was the game over: the whistle had already been blown.

## A DEPLORABLE STATE OF MENTAL ABERRATION

There were a few noticeable absences from the Mary Anne Clarke fiasco. Where was Rudolph Ackermann in all this? Or Mustard George? Ackermann had a reasonable excuse. He purposefully took no part in the scandal: the paperwork for his British citizenship was still being processed, and he was reluctant to antagonise the authorities at this crucial moment.[9] And Mustard George? His name was nowhere to be seen during the scandal. Was he working away on some other big project? his fans might have wondered. Had he escaped to the continent under a cloak of secrecy, to work on his next big commission?

This was no top-secret commission. Mustard George may have been the young darling of the print scene, riding the wave of celebrity, but he was secretly fighting a more private battle. His hand-to-mouth existence, with every penny spent on drink, had taken its toll at last. To his friends and colleagues, it appeared that all was well: the work was produced, he was always merry and always spending. But had anyone looked closely, they'd have realised he was staggering between taverns for a bed each night, clinging on by his fingertips.

By November 1809, the mirage evaporated. 'He went to the Brown Bear public-house in Bow-Street,'[10] the *Gentleman's Magazine* reported. He was 'in a coach, very unwell; and, though he had no money, Mr Hazard, the landlord, very humanely took him in, and paid the coachman, although he had no knowledge of him, except occasionally sleeping there'. On seeing George struggle to walk, his body disgustingly swollen, his arms and legs heavy as bricks and impossible to bend, the landlord 'procured a doctor to attend him, and rendered him every possible assistance'.

But it was too late. The doctor was powerless to save Mustard George. His heart, liver and kidneys were pickled in alcohol. There was nothing to be done but watch the glimmer of light fade from this creative spirit, a powerhouse of originality who had so much potential. George Woodward Murgatroyd 'only survived a short time, and died of a dropsy'. With no money to his name, he was at the mercy of the pub landlord who paid out of his own pocket: 'Mr Hazard had the corpse buried at his own expense.'[11] He died as he lived, felt Henry Angelo: 'In character, suddenly, with a glass of brandy in his hand.'[12]

The sudden death of 43-year-old Mustard George sent shock waves through the print shops of London. A 'lively grief' plagued his 'tender hearted associates',[13] horrified at the private anxieties their friend had silently battled through, secretly living with not a penny to spare.[14]

As James Gillray heard the news, working away in the upstairs rooms of Hannah's shop on St James's Street, he must have felt a pang of anxiety in his stomach. Thank goodness loyal Hannah was there to look after him. She was his saving grace. For James had been hiding his own secret, too. A secret that had tormented him for a couple of years.

A few months before, he had found his eyes getting tired. Old age, he had thought. Perhaps a one-off. Maybe he shouldn't work so hard. But these occasional bouts of blurry vision – which sometimes became altogether dark – were now more and more regular. Spectacles didn't help. The horrible truth couldn't be avoided any longer. Gillray knew it: he was going blind.

Just four days after Mustard George's death, Gillray signed off a copper plate, just as he had for the past three decades. It would be his last. Tormented by his inability to work, and probably tortured by his Moravian cynicism, this great artist fell helplessly into an uneasy mental state, somewhere between depression and deep sorrow. 'Poor Gillray,' wrote Angelo, 'at last sunk into that deplorable state of mental aberration, which verifies the couplet, so often quoted, wherein the consanguinity of wit to madness is so eminently proved'.[15] By the end of 1810, Gillray and his genius was all but lost to the world, a prisoner trapped in the realm of delirium.*

Gillray wasn't the only madman in London. In November 1810, the 27-year-old Princess Amelia – George III's youngest and favourite child – was suddenly snatched away by tuberculosis. The King was 'melancholy beyond description', playing out 'scenes of distress and crying every day'.[16] This grief marked the beginning of King George's end: it kicked off a bout of madness from which he would never recover.

George cut a pathetic, sorry figure at the age of 72. In his final ten years he would dress in a cotton nightshirt, his hair hanging loose and long over his shoulders. Sometimes silent, sometimes weeping, sometimes raging, he was losing his sight, his hearing and his mind. At one point he uttered the words 'I must have a new suit of clothes and I will have them black in memory of George III'.[17] This popular, dutiful king, who had carried Britannia through half a century of challenges, was a shadow of his former self: another madman in the attic. Before he was lost for ever, and fearful of his own terrible demise, the King acknowledged the need for a Regency Act. On 6 February 1811, George, Prince of Wales became Regent of the United Kingdom of Great Britain and Ireland.

* It has been suggested by fellow Gillray enthusiasts that the decades working with acid and chemicals could have contributed to this condition.

The Regency period had officially begun. One of the most hated men in the country now sat on the throne. Charles Greville, clerk of the privy council, would confide in his diary that 'a more contemptible, cowardly, selfish, unfeeling dog does not exist'.[18]

Of course, Prince George had always been a figure of ridicule, bouncing from one outrageous scandal to another. But he had always been balanced by the rational, reasonable, sensible King George III, the bulwark of Britain's greatness. With King George hidden away and Prince George ruling the country in all but name, his gross corpulence and blatant laziness were not so funny. And Gillray wasn't even around to bring him down a peg or two and make light of it all.

This was no doubt on the mind of patriotic Isaac Cruikshank, as he stepped out into the April 1811 sunshine a couple of months later. Perhaps this younger Prince Regent would put things in order, Cruikshank might have thought. It was the springtime after all, a time of hope; a time of new beginnings. 'Just popping out for a quick drink,' he may well have called up to his boys, working away at the coppers on Dorset Street. 'See you later!'

But the boys must have known, there was no such thing as a 'quick drink' these days, and they wouldn't see him later. Their father had made a habit of returning home staggering and slurring, and he would be thick in the head the next day. This evening was no different. Sitting with his old chums, Isaac would drink hard and fast, with conversation quick and slick and full of wit. Soon, there were drinking games, and then bets were being thrown across the table.

'If you can finish every tankard on this table, I'll take you to Drury Lane next week,' a crony possibly tossed to Cruikshank. Isaac was not one to give up in the face of a challenge. He drank, and drank, and drank, and won the bet. With congratulations and cheers, the fellow drinkers tripped out into the streets on their merry way, back to their wives and beds.

But after that session, Isaac Cruikshank slept deeper than usual. At sunrise, he slept through. At lunchtime, still he slept. When Mary left the coppers to wake her husband, she couldn't. For Isaac was not sleeping. Under the effects of alcohol poisoning, he was comatose. Over the following days, his family prayed for him to wake up. They waited for him to spring to life – they'd laugh it off, they imagined, and breathe a sigh of relief when he finally dusted himself down and returned to the studio.

But that day never came. Isaac Cruikshank never woke up. On 16 April 1811, Mary and her children headed a few doors down Fleet Street to St Bride's to bury their beloved father, his body ravaged by the bottle. It would have been a sorry sight, seeing Mary Cruikshank and her three children, Robert, George and Eliza, huddled together on that blustery spring afternoon.

Over in the smarter area of Piccadilly, yet another tragedy was unfolding. As the St James's Street pedestrians were passing a glance over to Hannah Humphrey's print shop, they well may have smiled at those famous bow windows, filled with Gillray masterpieces. But something seemed wrong. From the window above the shop a haggard man was staring out blankly, dead behind the eyes. Then he started leaning out – too far out. His leg appeared over the sill. And then the other. Suddenly, the man was falling, his arms flailing. Within a split second he hit the ground with a smack. A still, lifeless heap, just outside the print shop window.

A pause. Then the street erupted. Young ladies gasped in shock. Children were hurried away to protect their innocence. An old lady flew out of the shop, hysterically screaming, shouting, crying. A couple of young gentlemen tended to the motionless body. They carried the fallen man inside.

James Gillray survived his suicide attempt. But he lived on in a state of miserable despair. He never worked again, and, like King George, never recovered his mind. The go-to treatment for insanity at this time was to be sent to Bedlam madhouse, where the unfortunate patient would be chained up, kept naked and filthy in a damp, dark, stone cell, while paying visitors gawked and laughed at them. But Hannah Humphrey wouldn't let this happen on her watch. She continued to care for Gillray out of her own pocket. He was kept on the top floor of the St James's shop, his deranged face sometimes spotted 'fixed between the iron bars which guarded the attic bedroom in which he was confined during the several years of madness which preceded his death'.[19] A window of prints was no longer the only attraction at Hannah Humphrey's print shop.

## ABHORRENT TO THE FEELINGS OF ENGLISHMEN

Within eighteen months, the beating heart of the Golden Age of British Satire had been ripped out. Mustard George and Isaac Cruikshank had both died suddenly from drinking, not yet aged 50. James Gillray and King George were all but lost to the world. It was as if the satirical burst of the Mary Anne Clarke affair had surged the system and the electrics had blown, leaving only a few lamps flickering in the darkness.

Hannah Humphrey called in Rowlandson and young George Cruikshank to complete Gillray's unfinished plates. And Ackermann, suddenly without his star creatives, cheered himself up by splurging on the latest gadgets. In 1811, he became the first person in London to have his house lit by gas,[20] with lamps 'in the forms of the Greek honey suckle and other classic devices'.[21]

But shiny new technology couldn't keep away morbid thoughts. Ackermann and Rowlandson produced a 72-plate series named *The English Dance of Death*. Like *The Tour of Dr Syntax*, each had verses by William Combe with accompanying illustrations by Rowlandson. It was an account of the skeletal figure of Death springing up in people's lives without notice.

Some try to resist Death's arrival: 'Begone, & stay, till I invite you,' they cry. But it is futile. Sometimes Death appears relaxing in the family armchair, sometimes throwing random arrows as skaters slip and slide precariously, sometimes plucking a couple of children away at a family meal. A distraught mother bursts into her child's room, only to find Death rocking the cradle: 'Life is o'er: The Infant sleeps, to wake no more.' There are those who take a swim in a gentle stream, only to be drowned: 'Thus it appears a pond of Water May prove an Instrument of Slaughter.'

Rowlandson gives us Death in town, tending to regular victims: the infirm and elderly. There is the quack doctor, who has Death under his employment, working behind the counter mixing a 'slow poison' for the doctor's 'medicines'. There is the elderly genealogist looking at his extensive family tree: 'On that illumin'd roll of fame,' Rowlandson warns, 'Death waits to write your Lordship's name.'

*The Sot* (*The English Dance of Death*),
Rudolph Ackermann and Thomas Rowlandson, 1814.
Metropolitan Museum, The Elisha Whittelsey Collection, The Elisha Whittelsey Fund, 1959

Rowlandson showed us those in peril on the sea: while a great hulk sinks in tempestuous seas, a group desperately tries to row to safety. But the little boat is powerless in the great waves, already carrying rag-doll corpses on its crests. Their hopes for survival are dashed as Death appears on the helm, calmly holding out a timer, waiting to deliver 'the Crew to Pluto's Realm'. And for those who manage to reach shore, half drowned, but still breathing, Death waits patiently to claim his prize.

Rowlandson even etched the fate of his friends, Mustard George and Isaac Cruikshank: 'Some find their Death by Sword & Bullet,' went one verse, 'and some by fluids down the Gullet.' Another scene shows Death carrying a drinker away from the tavern: 'Drunk and alive, the man was thine, But dead & drunk, why, – he is mine.'

It wasn't just Rowlandson who felt his life's work slipping through his fingers. There was a sense that the country was falling apart. Over the past few decades, new technologies had been gaining momentum. 'Invention' and 'improvement' had been the buzzwords. Society had been moving forward. But it was obvious now – this progress had come at the expense of the old ways of doing things. By 1811, it was time to take a stand.

Skilled textile workers from Nottinghamshire, Yorkshire and Lancashire began heading out in the dead of night, breaking into factories and mills and smashing and burning mechanised looms and knitting frames – the monstrous objects that were taking their jobs. The workers, known as Luddites, were impressively organised, often meeting on the moors at night to practise drills and manoeuvres. Were William Pitt's nightmares finally coming true? Had the radicalism of the French Revolution finally found its footing on British soil?

It was surely on the mind of the prime minister, Spencer Perceval, when, the following year, as he headed through the House of Commons lobby, at 5.15pm on 11 May 1812, he was approached by a well-dressed man. The man raised a steel pistol and shot him at point-blank range. A bullet pierced his heart. He staggered forward, with a 'hoarse cry of "murder, murder"',[22] and fell on his face. He was pronounced dead within minutes.

The nation groaned in despair. This shouldn't be happening. An assassination was, as George Canning put it: 'Foreign to the character and abhorrent to the feelings of Englishmen.' Soon came the sermons questioning the 'state of the nation'. The mood was shifting. The country was ruled by the Prince Regent, a man who was universally despised. The weaving mills, those great beacons of progress, were being smashed by the mobs of angry workers. And now, the prime minister had been assassinated in the centre of British democracy. The country was going to the dogs.

And what's more, the Napoleonic Wars were emptying the nation's coffers. By 1814, Europe had been at war, on and off, for over two decades. Exhausted and war-weary, in March 1814, the Treaty of Chaumont was signed: Austria, Russia, Prussia and Great Britain bound themselves to fight together for the next twenty years. They would not stop fighting until Napoleon was finally overthrown. It was a depressing moment: if the battle really did drag on for another twenty years, they were only half-way through.

Luckily, a morale booster came in the form of Rowlandson's satires, as he filled the boots of his old friend Gillray. He began 'to take up the gauntlet against the dreaded Buonaparte, the great little Corsican, against whom Gillray had waged such savage warfare until his powers dwindled into vacancy'.[23] And besides him, 'George Cruikshank stepped valiantly into the place of the colossus of caricaturists, and carried on the combat with unflagging zeal and whimsicality on his own account'.[24]

The tables were turning for the Corsican upstart. Reading the news from London, George Cruikshank absorbed every detail with fascination. He loaded up his satires and fired them out, thick and fast. On 1 April 1814, this bright young artist had all the great generals of Europe in his command. He cast them as 'The Allied Bakers', and tasked them to fit the 'Corsican Toad in the Hole' in the oven.[25]

But bickering and confusion has infiltrated the kitchen. 'This door Sticks!' cries the Austrian Emperor, 'I don't think I shall get it open?!' To which the apron-wearing Prussian General Gebhard Leberecht von Blücher exclaims: 'Pull away Frank! you Keep us waiting!' Meanwhile, the King of Sweden calls out some advice: 'The Hinges want a little Russia Oil.'

Five days after the print was published, on 6 April 1814, the Corsican was finally forced into the oven: Paris capitulated and Napoleon had no choice but to abdicate his throne. It was a day that many thought would never come. Finally, the seemingly indestructible man was defeated. Finally, after the disastrous experiment of the French Revolution, the Bourbon monarchy could return. Louis XVIII, the exiled brother of the murdered Louis XVI, prepared to return to the world stage. London erupted into euphoria. The city was illuminated for three nights and white *cocades*, Bourbon flags and *fleur-de-lys* adorned the streets.

But what to do with Napoleon now? The mighty Emperor was now a 'pretty plaything for Ye Allies'. He was a 'Corsican shuttlecock', as imagined George Cruikshank in his print on 10 April, where he was bounced between badminton racquets. 'Bravo Schwartzenberg!' von Blücher cries, as Napoleon flies through the air between them, 'Keep the Game alive! Send him this way & d—n him I'll drive him back again.'

Napoleon was exiled to Elba, a Mediterranean island six miles from the Italian coast, and given a pension, hopefully never to return again. It was the end of an era. A chance to start afresh. A blank slate upon which to draw a line. The publisher William Holland certainly thought so. After three decades of dominating London's print trade, he packed it in. Perhaps it was the loss of his greatest talents, Isaac Cruikshank and Gillray. Perhaps he felt the country was falling apart. On 16 February 1815, he put an advert in the *Morning Post*:

> Cheap Caricatures and Other Prints. The large stock of caricatures and other prints of W. Holland, No. 11 Cockspur-street, to be sold at reduced prices. Going to remove into another line of business. Ladies and Gentlemen have now an opportunity, at a cheap rate, of decorating screens, dressing rooms &c with caricatures of genius, wit and humour, by the first caricaturists from Gillray to Williams.[26]

## THE BELL TOLLS

As William Holland threw in the towel on his print business, Napoleon, too, became fed up of life in exile in Elba. After eleven months on the island, he escaped, arriving back in France on 1 March 1815. The terrible toddler had run away, right under the nose of the mighty powers, and threatened to wreak havoc once more. War-torn, war-weary Europe had no choice but to rally their forces on a monumental scale, determined it would be the final time. Thomas Rowlandson and George Cruikshank made a last-ditch attempt at a spread of satiric volleys.

They blasted the French for having no principles: 'Ye shall kill your King one Day, and Crown his Relative the next.' They scorned Napoleon for being a friend of the Devil. They taunted him with the figure of Death.

But Death had his eyes elsewhere. He'd long been hovering in the threshold of Hannah Humphrey's shop at 27 St James's Street, patient and prepared. It was now five years since Gillray had lost his mind. He was blind and probably drinking heavily. On 1 June 1815, this genius 'was seen for the last time, naked and unshaven at mid-day, standing in the shop where his caricatures were sold'.[27] Hannah Humphrey led him upstairs to his rooms, dressed him and put him to bed. He died later that day.

The following week, on 7 June 1815, a tiny group gathered in the courtyard of St James's, Piccadilly, just around the corner from Hannah Humphrey's print shop. It was a damp, wet June day, the air thick and humid. The red brick and Portland stone of Wren's masterpiece sparkled. As Gillray's strong elm coffin, painted black, was lowered into the damp ground, he was bade goodbye by loyal, loving Hannah Humphrey and his greatest admirer and heir apparent, George Cruikshank.

A man who had once been able to hold the gaze of every Londoner, Gillray's death went unreported and unnoticed. For all eyes were captivated by events across the Channel. Two decades of war in Europe were building to an almighty crescendo. Less than two weeks after Gillray's funeral, the powers of Europe were gathering near Waterloo in Belgium.

Pitted against Napoleon, the Duke of Wellington led a force from the United Kingdom, the Netherlands, Hanover, Brunswick and Nassau. General von Blücher commanded the Prussian Army. It was, according to the Duke of Wellington, 'the nearest-run thing you ever saw in your life'.[28] But Napoleon's luck had finally run out: the Battle of Waterloo was an allied victory. After two decades of tearing Europe apart, and three weeks after Gillray's death, Napoleon Bonaparte was defeated. This time, for good.

London was ablaze with fireworks, illuminations and bonfires, and the streets were filled with the ringing of church bells. 'In the evening we all rode round the streets to see the illuminations for the great victory of the 18th,' wrote John Quincy Adams. But Londoners were spoilt with all these celebratory displays. 'They were not general, nor very magnificent,' Adams complained: 'the whole range of their variety was, "Wellington and Blücher," "Victory," "G.P.R.," and "G.R." The transparencies were very few, and very bad.'[29]

Nevertheless, 7 July 1815 was proclaimed a day of general thanksgiving, and the printseller William Holland was keen to enjoy the conviviality. He headed for the south-eastern corner of the Covent Garden piazza. Here were the Hummums (from the Turkish word *hammam*) or bagnios (from the Italian word *bagno*), both meaning bath house. These were 'a certain kind of house … which are supposed to be baths; their real purpose, however, is to provide persons of both sexes with pleasure'.[30]

Whatever such pleasures were, something overwhelmed William Holland that day. Perhaps it was the vapours of the rising steam, perhaps the shock of seeing so much flesh on display, or perhaps he slipped on a bar of soap. 'At the Hummums Covent-garden,' the *Gentleman's Magazine* reported, 'a few minutes after coming out of the warm bath', disaster struck.[31] Although whatever happened at the baths that day remains a mystery, it would prove fatal. A month after James Gillray's funeral, William Holland died. Yet another body blow to London's greatest generation of satirists.

William Holland was remembered in the papers in the yearly round-up. He was lauded as 'an eminent publisher of caricatures, and patron of Woodward, Rowlandson, Newton, Buck and other artists. He was himself a man of genius and wrote many popular songs, and a volume of poetry, besides being the author of the pointed and epigrammatic words which accompanied most of his caricatures.'[32]

Gillray wasn't given nearly so much praise, having been dead to the world for five years and a reclusive, behind-the-scenes figure. 'June 1,' the report stated, 'in St James's-street, Mr Jas Gillray, the celebrated artist, well known for his numerous engraved works, particularly for his caricatures.'[33] A muted response for the death of one of the greatest artists of the Georgian age.

## THINGS FALL APART, THE CENTRE CANNOT HOLD

As Rowlandson's former comrades and the characters who inspired his work dropped like flies, he seemed to yearn for the familiar comfort of his old friends. 'I met … Bannister at Captn. Gelstons,' he wrote to Henry Angelo. 'He is now [at] South end. On his return to town says he shall take an early opportunity of forming a Jovial Trio – if we three jolly Dogs be – that we may still live and enjoy each other's society is the hearty wish of your Sincere Old Friend.'[34]

But in 1817, Rowlandson was dealt another blow. This time it was his loyal patron, Matthew Mitchell, who was taken by Death's silent hand. He died, probably from obesity, on 28 August 1817, aged 66, laid to rest in the church of St Tudy, Cornwall.[35] A memorial read, 'as a Man his Character stands unimpeached for honor and integrity, a sincere Friend, a true Lover of his Country and a liberal Patron of the Polite Arts'.[36]

Death marched on. In February or March 1818, Hannah Humphrey was taken. She had accrued a small fortune from 30 years of graft, and she left a thriving business to her nephew George, the son of George Humphrey. What's more, in a will created in 1807, Gillray had left everything 'to my dearest friend Hannah Humphrey'. The amount – over £100,000 in today's money – was all 'at her disposal'.[37] So, there was plenty of inheritance for Hannah's sisters-in-law, nieces and great-nieces, and a very generous living for her servant Betty Marshall.

*Am I next?* Rowlandson must have thought. He was still 'living in health of Body and of sound mind and memory'.[38] But Death could appear at any time. On 7 July 1818, a week after Mitchell's collection of Rowlandson prints were sold at Mr Sotheby's, Rowlandson adjusted his will.[39] It was a week before his 61st birthday. All was to go to 40-year-old 'Miss Betsy Winter of the parish of West Wycombe Bucks now residing with me', who, after payment of debts, would have 'the whole rest and residue of my property whether Real or personal my drawings and prints and everything I am possessed whatsoever or wheresoever'.[40]

Britain itself seemed to be spiralling wider and wildly out of control. The end of the war with France brought home swathes of unemployed ex-soldiers and sailors. Things were falling apart. The centre could not hold.

A grim omen had come in 1815, when Indonesia experienced the largest volcanic eruption in recorded history. The world was plunged into a volcanic winter, as volcanic ash and droplets of sulphuric acid and water obscured the sun. The air was choked with ash and dust. Temperatures dropped in the middle of summer, and dry fogs and red snowdrifts were reported across the world. The year of 1816 soon became known as the Year Without a Summer: 'Such an inclement summer is scarcely remembered by the oldest inhabitant of London or its environs.'[41]

Britain, like the rest of Europe was already in a state of 'severe distress' after being ravaged by the Napoleonic Wars, and now it faced the worst harvests in living memory.[42] 'The hay towards the southern counties has been so much injured by the incessant rains,' *The Times* reported, 'that the only alternative left to the proprietor is to convert it into dung for manure.'[43] Food was running scarce, and tensions were rising. The 'minds of the people' were filled with the 'greatest apprehension and alarm'.[44]

Along with harvest failures, there were strikes, riots, marches and armed uprisings. In Suffolk, anarchy was loosed upon the world: workers began smashing threshing machines, burning barns and ransacking local shops, crying: 'Bread or blood!' All the while, the government didn't seem to listen: public money was used to purchase the Elgin Marbles rather than putting bread on the table. 'We don't want Stones,' the satires sang, 'Give us Bread! Give us Bread! Give us Bread!'

The country was filling up with the unemployed, the persecuted and the disenfranchised – only around 10 per cent of adult males had the vote, and with nowhere to air their grievances, violence seemed the only option: 'In the riots and meetings of those troublesome times,' one memoir recalled, 'the mob really meant mischief, had they been accustomed to the use of arms and well drilled, they might have committed as great excesses as the ruffians of 1793 in France.'[45]

Another blow to the country's morale came in 1817, with the news that Princess Charlotte, the heir to the throne and the Prince Regent's only child, had died in childbirth. Charlotte had been a beacon of hope, and now the nation slumped into mourning and the succession was thrown into uncertainty (not one of the Prince Regent's brothers had a legitimate heir).

The rumbling discontent reached a pinnacle on 16 August 1819. The Manchester Patriotic Union organised a gathering in St Peter's Fields for local people to listen to radical speakers. Men, women and children flooded in from nearby towns and villages in their Sunday best. They carried banners reading: 'No Corn Laws', 'Annual Parliaments', 'Universal suffrage' and 'Vote By Ballot'. Between 60,000 and 80,000 people were present, about 6 per cent of the Lancashire population.

But the authorities, gripped by paranoia and terrified of the mob, panicked. After some confusion, cavalry groups began charging and firing straight into the crowd and the Manchester and Salford Yeomanry began 'cutting at every one they could reach'.[46] It was a bloodbath, with innocent people bleeding to death and crushed by crowds.

So, was this what all those years fighting Napoleon had been for? Was this what was meant when the government sang about 'British Liberty'? The Manchester disaster was dubbed the Peterloo Massacre – making mockery of the Waterloo victory four years earlier. 'At Waterloo there was man to man,' an Oldham cloth-worker and veteran of Waterloo remembered, but the events in Manchester were 'downright murder'.[47]

What's more, the Prince Regent not only praised the magistrates in charge, they were also rewarded financially. 'The wicked have drawn out the sword,' quoted the campaigns to raise money for the victims, 'they have cut down the poor and needy and such as be of upright conversation.'[48]

On 29 January 1820, the blind and demented 81-year-old King George III died, bringing his six-decade reign to an end. The country watched on with disdain as the Prince Regent assumed the throne – this rough beast, its hour had come round at last. His first order was to ensure his wife Queen Caroline was banned from his coronation, and he cut her from the *Book of Common Prayer* for good measure. The Queen died three weeks later. The country, it seemed, was ruled by a king who was 'from the crown to the toe, top full of direst cruelty'.[49] It was a bleak outlook for Britain, as she slouched into the 1820s.

## A SPRING MORNING IN COVENT GARDEN

But the nation's woes failed to subdue the perennial jollity of Thomas Rowlandson. He settled into his twilight years, still on the top floor of James Street, and still in the company of his beloved Betsy. Their domestic bliss was probably interrupted by strange noises floating up from downstairs. Below Thomas and Betsy lived an eccentric character, Lieutenant William Pringle Green, who had proudly served at Trafalgar.

While living below Rowlandson's rooms, he entertained himself with the latest technology. He made calculations about how to improve a ship's artillery, the rigging and steerage, the winches and capstans. Next, he got to grips with electricity and magnetism. Soon, there were bangs and smells creeping up from the floorboards. 'Everything all right, Lieutenant?' a concerned Betsy might have called down, to which Pringle Green would emerge with a soot-covered face and frazzled hair.

Rowlandson continued working, but he was in no mood to be learning new techniques or pushing boundaries. Now in his sixties, he was a well-established household name. The work was good; he had a steady stream of commissions, keeping him constantly busy with pencil, reed pen and sketchbook. He sketched old crones selling dead fowl, a woman at her washtub and young ruffians blowing pipe smoke.

In November 1819, after one of his publishers found himself in prison for radicalism, Rowlandson cut all ties with them and never again produced a political satire. As the 1820s pushed on, his output dwindled and the demand for his work began slipping away. But he didn't much mind. He didn't have a name to prove, or a cause to fight. He simply sought to keep a steady income ticking over and enjoy domestic life with Betsy.

As Rowlandson strolled through his city in these final years, it must have felt strangely empty. St James's Street seemed silent without old Hannah Humphrey's bespectacled, kindly face calling out to him across the road. William Holland's Laughing Lounge was boarded up. And never again would the print shops be popping with the latest japes and quips of his old friends Isaac Cruikshank and James Gillray.

And Rowlandson no longer had his raucous gang of bachelors to tear through the town, either. Jack Bannister, once the star of Drury Lane, was now retired, gout-ridden and settled with his wife Elizabeth. They lived at 65 Gower Street in Bloomsbury, kept busy rearing their grandchildren. After an injury, Henry Angelo no longer taught swordsmanship, and from 1822, he moved to Bath to enjoy a quiet life writing his memoirs.

As the vigour and vitality and creativity of his old life wound down, Rowlandson made new acquaintances. Most of these came from his local, the Coal Hole in Fountain Court. It was a pub he shared with a man who was, in many ways, unnervingly similar to himself. A man who had lived a parallel life to Rowlandson, yet who had lived in Rowlandson's shadow. He was the relatively unknown artist William Blake.

Blake and Rowlandson would start and end life in London, four months apart. Blake was born in Soho, Rowlandson in the City. They both trained at the Royal Academy Schools – Blake studied alongside Gillray – and all of them rejected Reynolds's grand manner. Blake, like the satirists, was a total original, reinventing etching and engraving according to his natural inclination. In their thirties, Rowlandson and Blake lived a few doors from one another on Poland Street, and now, in their final years, they were neighbours yet again: Blake was living at 3 Fountain Court, a stone's throw from Rowlandson's rooms at James Street, just along the Strand.

Yet they were never personally close. Blake was a man obsessed with visions of metaphysics and thoughts of the otherworldly. He had written critically of Rowlandson's work in 1799, and probably considered Rowlandson's down-to-earth delight in the ridiculous everyday as silly and pointless. He would have no doubt detested Bannister's pranks. Perhaps it's no surprise that Blake and Rowlandson didn't become close friends. Rowlandson found more jovial company in a new hang-out: the British Museum. He regularly visited the newly built Townley Gallery and, as he climbed the stairs, he would pass the Portland Vase (which Wedgwood had so vigorously studied), then an assortment of coins and medals. Finally, he would push open a heavy iron door.

This was the British Museum Print Room. It was a long, narrow space with thirteen wooden presses and endless piles of boxes. One of these, labelled 'Authorities for Artists', contained sample prints that Rowlandson came to use to study techniques and Old Masters. But before Rowlandson ever took a step into the Print Room, he was most likely greeted by a jolly, booming voice: 'Rowly! Good to have you back!' This was the keeper of prints and drawings, John Thomas Smith, known to friends as 'Antiquity Smith'.

Antiquity Smith was probably the worst archivist the British Museum had ever employed. Firstly, he had absolutely no time to make this a 'quiet study space'. Instead, he seemed to think of it as his own private salon. He greeted every visitor with a barrage of chitter-chatter, delighting in hosting glitzy names; Rowlandson and George Cruikshank were more than welcome. 'What I tell you is the fact,' he would begin, then, with the visitor seated (and trapped), he would continue: 'I'll tell you the whole story.'[50] Good luck getting any work done.

What's more, he was known to be wildly disorganised, which didn't bode well for the collection. His maintenance practices were pretty sketchy, too. The print rooms were often damp, with mildew growing on the collection. Smith's approach for drying off priceless Rembrandt etchings? Wave them vigorously in front of the open fire.[51]

Rowlandson no doubt enjoyed Antiquity Smith's unofficial salon: '[Rowlandson] was a notorious gossip,' a younger artist recalled, 'and I knew ladies who used to go to the Print-room to be amused by his endless and amusing tattle. He was a great retailer of anecdote and scandal, dealt largely in innuendo, and had a keen relish for any story of doubtful propriety.'[52]

On Tuesday 15 June 1824, Antiquity Smith happily set up with his inks and water among the collection and made a charming sketch of Rowlandson at work. With Antiquity Smith's typical loose eye for detail, the sketch was labelled 'Aged 70' (Rowlandson was only 66). He is shown to be a balding, short-sighted, with spectacles balanced on his nose, and a gentle smile on his face. It was the last portrait of Rowlandson.

Thomas Rowlandson by John Thomas Smith, 1824.

From 1825, Rowlandson suffered a 'severe illness of two years'.[53] On 21 April 1827, twelve weeks short of his 70th birthday, Rowlandson went to bed, his beloved Betsy by his side. He never woke up again.

A week later, a small group of glum figures gathered in a courtyard of St Paul's Church in Covent Garden to mark the end of a lifetime of conviviality and veritable madness. It was a sunny, blustery day, and the leaves danced and skipped across the stones. Of course, this church was where Rowlandson's career had begun. For it was in this very spot that Rowlandson had sketched Fox in the spring of 1784, during the Westminster hustings, 43 years before.

And now, Rowlandson said farewell to 'his constant friend and liberal employer, Mr Ackermann', his sister, Elizabeth, and the love of his life, Betsy Winter.[54] There were two old men in attendance, too: one, the greatest fencing masters of his generation, the other, its greatest actor. Rowlandson's 'remains were followed to the grave by the two friends of his youth Mr Bannister and Mr Angelo'.[55] It was the very last meeting of the Three Jolly Dogs.

Once Rowlandson's debts were cleared, Betsy Winter paid the 10 per cent duty and signed for her inheritance on 6 November 1827.[56] This amount – over £200,000 in today's money – was in the form of consolidated funds and bank annuities.

In June, Sotheby's announced the sale of a 'valuable collection' of 'the late distinguished Artist, THOMAS ROWLANDSON, ESQ. So well known for he Humour and Spirit of his Pencil.'[57] Everything went under the hammer: his printing press, his easel, a cabinet writing desk, over 200 etched copperplates and 42 empty picture frames. There was his collection of Rembrandt, Rubens, van Dyck, Carracci and Guido Reni prints. There were stacks of his own etchings. There was the work of Hogarth, Mortimer and Gainsborough. And piles from artists he knew: his original inspiration, Henry Bunbury; his brother-in-law, Samuel Howitt; his drinking companion, Mustard George; and the man who had been there from the start, James Gillray.

Betsy Winter was marked as 'spinster' in the probate document of 5 May 1827.[58] But the rates collector at James Street and the staff at Sotheby's accepted her as Mrs Rowlandson.[59] She moved out of James Street in 1829 and into a cul-de-sac off the Brompton Road, just around the corner from Robert Cruikshank and his family. She died in May 1835, aged 58. But she was buried next to the man who had been the centre of her world – and the centre of London life for decades. She was buried in St Paul's, Covent Garden, next to Thomas, in a gravestone marked 'Betsey Rowlandson'.[60]

# 15

# *Cancelled*

## INTO THE SEWERS

By the 1820s, Britain had gone rotten. It was a nation beset by rapid industrial change and disenfranchised masses, economic doubts and harvest failures; a prime minister was assassinated and a hated king was slowly dying on its throne. The riotous party was over, and now, in the cold light of day, the bleak hangover began. A period of sobriety and restraint was called for.

A puritanical mood swept the country, fuelled by a moral panic surrounding issues such as homosexuality and grave robbery. It was largely pushed by evangelical reformers, a set of earnest middle-class campaigners who made it their duty to fight against alcoholism, prostitution, corruption and whatever else they deemed to be a public vice.

One leading light of the new age was a man named Thomas Bowdler who, in 1818, took the liberty of publishing an adulterated set of Shakespeare's works – without the 'blemishes' that might corrupt a young mind. By the mid-1820s, the verb, 'to bowdlerise' – meaning to remove sensitive or inappropriate material from a text – was in common circulation. Innuendo and unfettered indulgence were out. Earnestness and Christian duty were in.

As the 1820s approached, the excesses of George III's reign seemed increasingly crass and vulgar. It's unsurprising, then, that Gillray and his gang, who delighted in the grotesque, the scurrilous and the scatological, were swiftly relabelled. The prints of Gillray, Rowlandson and Cruikshank were no longer ticklishly amusing. They were considered a dangerous weapon, an encouragement to vice. And a vicious campaign was launched to tread their reputations into the mud.

Firstly, they were recast. They were lumped together with the 'political hirelings' and 'Grub Street scribblers' – amateurs who made a career scratching around unscrupulous gossip and slander. The caricaturist, mused the London literary magazine, the *Athenæum*, in 1831, was 'so disreputable a profession', they were no better than a 'race of vermin'.[1] Indeed, the classical scholar Richard Payne Knight considered caricaturists (whom he called 'sketchers') part of the lowest dregs of society:

> Like maggots hatch'd in summer's noontide hour,
> The filth, which gives them being, they devour …
> Crawl out like bugs, conceal'd in shades of night,
> Unknown to all, but when they stink of bite …
> Thus Pindars, Pasquins, sketchers and reviewers,
> Still rise in shops, to set in common sewers.[2]

Gillray, Rowlandson and Cruikshank were by no means sewer maggots. Their work was a tapestry of political thought and classical allegory. These were extraordinarily technical and highly trained artists. Their prints were passed through gloved hands and displayed in the grandest of stately homes. They even had a place at the breakfast table of Queen Charlotte.

But such truths were ignored by nineteenth-century moralists. A powerful fiction was spun about Gillray's life. This wasn't hard to do, for Gillray was a figure shrouded in mystery. He was a discreet and self-contained individual, and after his death, there was little evidence regarding his private life: 'Neither his model of study nor his mode of life' could be 'disclosed with propriety'.[3] What's more, as an only child with no issue, no next of kin survived to defend his name. He was a blank canvas, which could be blotched and marked to suit any argument. And his posthumous critics were quick to assume the worst: 'Those with whom he commonly associated have hitherto continued silent respecting him,' they noted, drawing the conclusion that 'in silence there is sometimes discretion.'[4] It seems his critics were determined to damn him, whatever the evidence.

The great revelation came when it was made known that Gillray had been the recipient of government payments. When Gillray was briefly arrested in 1796, the line went that 'he was bribed by the Pitt party on the other with the offer of a pension' and the 'cessation of the pending prosecution'.[5] The nineteenth-century critics, who were certain Gillray was a liberal at heart, took this as evidence that his life had been a lie. They cast him as nothing better than a political hireling, paid to express the 'fanatical notions of high toryism'.[6]

Why was this so abominable? This apparent self-betrayal was – in the mind of his critics – akin to military desertion. As William Thackeray put it, the dishonesty made Gillray a fake: 'To be greatly successful as a professional humorist … a man must be quite honest, and show that his heart is in his work.'[7] The radical politician William Cobbett noted that 'this wretch's pension … was paid to the end of his life, which was of that awful description which ought to have made a deep impression on the mind of his profligate prompters and fellow-labourers'.[8]

These damning accusations are based on two assumptions: firstly, that Gillray received a pension beyond 1801, and secondly, that he was, at heart, on the side of the Whigs. Yet, there is no definitive evidence for any of his beliefs, and one could easily conclude he had Tory sympathies, a mixture of sympathies, changing sympathies, or no care for political life at all.

These criticisms echoed through the ages. The Ashmolean Museum in Oxford held a seminar in 2015 entitled 'Caricaturist Without a Conscience?', with the flier accusing him of being 'an unreliable gun for hire' and having 'no moral compass'.[9] Had they considered that Gillray's work might, in fact, not have been an expression of his personal opinion? Or that the whole point was that everyone, across all political parties and walks of life, was vulnerable to a Gillray attack? 'I believe satire is a survival mechanism,' wrote the modern cartoonist Martin Rowson, 'to stop us all going mad at the horror and injustice of it all by inducing us to laugh instead of weep.'[10] Perhaps, for Gillray, his art was nothing more than a coping mechanism. Or, at the very least, a means to put bread on the table.

But the jury was out from the start. Gillray's self-betrayal – the argument went – was so overpowering, and his mind so decayed, that it caused his insanity in 1810. Sermons were preached on the tragedy of his deterioration as a punishment for his depravity. His career was rewritten as a 'melancholy lesson', a story of great talent corrupted by duplicity.[11] He was 'a great genius without principle'.[12] Thackeray pontificated that 'Gillray would have been far more successful and more powerful but for that unhappy bribe which turned the whole course of his humour into an unnatural channel.'[13]

The campaign against Gillray was ruthlessly effective. By 1866, 'his works, once so popular, had fallen so much in fashion ... that the plates were about to be sold for old copper'.[14*] Even Gillray's name had been effectively wiped out: 'Among the artists and professed picture men, few in London, none out, have ever heard his name.'[15]

By the start of the twentieth century, the damage was done. In 1904, historians of caricature looked back at the Napoleonic era, when 'public taste was sufficiently depraved already' and 'Gillray deliberately prostituted his genius to the level of a procurer, to debauch it further'.[16] His reputation as 'a lover of low company and gross mirth, and sensual and impure' had been stamped into the history books.[17] His work, they scorned, was 'characterized by a foulness and an

* Quite remarkable when you consider that the plates – not the prints – are the original artwork.

obscenity which the present generation cannot countenance'. His mind was 'not only unclean, but unbalanced as well'.[18] His prints were considered so repulsive it would 'be absolutely out of the question to reproduce'.[19]

Rowlandson, too, was a victim of Victorian priggishness. If they didn't ignore him altogether, they decried him as slanderous, irreverent and crude: a genius who wasted his talents on scurrilities.

By 1846, Thackeray was jeering at 'the hideous distortions of Rowlandson, who people the picture-books with bloated parsons in periwigs, tipsy aldermen and leering salacious nymphs, horrid to look at'.[20] Two years later, Charles Dickens thought Rowlandson's lifetime's work was 'rendered wearisome and unpleasant by a vast amount of personal ugliness'.[21]

Queen Victoria was forced to censor the royal print collection when Prince Albert discovered a vast quantity of 'most dreadfully obscene'[22] pornographic prints by Rowlandson. These were, Victoria recorded with disgust, 'entirely collected ... by Geo IVth!! Who seemed to delight in them.'[23] Albert immediately had them destroyed.

In 1861, Walter Thornbury, an art writer and biographer of J.M.W. Turner, thought Rowlandson 'loathsomely gross too often'.[24] He was 'a diminutive Swift ... with some of the fun and all of the impurity of the baboon, delighting in filth, and unable to be decent long'.[25] William Bates, who collected Rowlandson's work, wrote in 1869 of the 'recklessness and dissipation of his character, his want of moral purpose, and his unrestrained tendency to exaggeration and caricature'.[26]

The tragedy of Rowlandson's prolific career, thought Joseph Grego in 1880, was that although 'none of the students of the Academy could draw such ludicrous and yet life-like figures', his vanity tripped him up. He was 'recognised as a genius, and was unhappily flattered into becoming a wayward one'.[27] He followed 'his chosen calling of a "free-lance" with a roving commission to work mischief'.[28] He had been, Grego believed, seduced by pleasing the crowd with quick laughs, which came at the expense of what could have been a high-flying portraitist: 'The very excitement of setting the little world wondering, and making the public smile, while his tickled audience accorded him the cheapest popularity by crowding in admiration round his travesties, turned the wilful artist away from serious application.'[29]

By 1904, the line went that, according to the likes of Joshua Reynolds and Benjamin West, Rowlandson 'might have won … a high place among English artists, if he had not turned, through sheer perversity, to satire and burlesque'.[30] By this time, Gillray and Rowlandson were long gone and could not pull their names and reputations from the gutter. And as they died without issue there weren't any relatives to stand in their defence.* It was different, however, for the legacy of Cruikshank.

By the waning years of the Napoleonic Wars, George Cruikshank's career had already eclipsed his father's, and he was lining himself up as Gillray's successor. By the time he was in his twenties, George was a well-known, 'clever, sharp caricaturist'.[31] His brother Robert was working as a professional caricaturist too, most successfully by mocking the dandies – a group of flamboyant men whose 'trade, office and existence consists in the wearing of Clothes'.[32] No doubt Robert – with his years in the navy behind him – would have found the eccentricities of such clothing ridiculous.

The relationship between the Cruikshank brothers was rocky. While they often worked closely together, they shared a pugnacious streak. Their affections were competitive; often they goaded each

* There was no known issue of Gillray or Rowlandson, so there are no known direct descendants. However, I did come across some relatives in a surprising way. While on the dating scene in Edinburgh, I matched on the dating app Bumble with a fellow student who was descended from Gillray's family via a cousin. We arranged to meet at the Wetherspoons on George Street, but alas, during the chaos of the Edinburgh Fringe it never happened. If you know this man, or if you are that man, please get in touch. We must reunite in George Street over a pint of Tennent's.

other. Robert's younger brother lived in the same household as his mother for a long time; Robert considered him very sheltered. The boy 'never went to sea – as I did', argued Robert, and consequently 'knows nothing of the world'.[33] Younger George considered his elder brother 'a perfect savage. Give him a sword, and shield, and he is happy.'[34]

But the Cruikshank brothers faced a far greater challenge than mere brotherly disregard. As they picked up the mantle of their father's craft, great change was afoot. Jibes from a Cruikshank burin had terrorised figures in public life for several decades. High society was reluctant to be mocked by a second generation, however, and they made arrangements to prevent another barrage of satirical comment. In 1820, George Cruikshank was bribed by George IV with £100 to not 'caricature His Majesty in any immoral situation',[35] and the brothers were invited to visit the Royal Pavilion in Brighton. Was this a truce at last?

As the Cruikshanks were being seduced by royal payments, public pressure was mounting on such artists to take a more 'respectable' career path. As commentators rounded on the likes of Gillray for wasting his talents on caricature, they hammered the message home to the next generation to not make the same career mistake. 'It is high time the public should think more than they hitherto done of George Cruikshank,' the critics commented, 'and it is also time that George Cruikshank should begin to think more than he seems to have hitherto of himself.'[36]

In 1823, an essay in *Blackwood's Edinburgh Magazine* insisted that George Cruikshank 'must give up his mere slang drudgery, and labour to what nature has put within his reach – not a caricaturist, but a painter'.[37] It argued that he shouldn't make the same mistake as his forbears: 'Cruikshank may, if he pleases, be a second Gilray; but ... this should not be his ambition. He is fitted for a higher walk ... let him give his days and his nights to labour that Gilray's shoulders were not meant for.'[38]

## A NEW AGE

It wasn't just public comment or changing tastes that pressured George Cruikshank to leave caricature behind. Technology was marching forward and bringing the golden era of satirical prints to a close, too.

The charge was led by Charles Stanhope, a gentleman scientist and brother-in-law of William Pitt.* In 1800, Stanhope built a printing press made entirely of cast iron. It was twice as fast as a standard press, printing 480 pages per hour, and the greatest development in printing since Gutenberg's work almost four centuries earlier.

Stanhope never patented his design, preferring to make it and its advances available to all. So, it was soon developed by a German team – the printer Friedrich Koenig and the engineer Andreas Friedrich Bauer – who *did* patent their model. These steam-powered machines were capable of 1,100 impressions per hour, and soon enough, double-sided pages were flying out.

In 1814, *The Times* bought two Koenig and Bauer printing presses. It heralded a revolution. Now, text and images could be reproduced and printed at rapid speeds and low costs. Illustrated newspapers and periodicals became available to a mass market, and with that came a widespread increase in literacy. There was stiff competition for the bow windows of print shops, which now competed with lively illustrations in newspapers, distributed far and wide. By the 1830s, with caricatures and drawings printed in newspapers, satires displayed in print shop windows had lost their sting. Crowds no longer flocked to the Piccadilly print shops; instead, they flicked through the pages of the latest periodical.

* Stanhope had been the victim of many an attack by Gillray, so it's amusing to suppose he might have developed the press in an elaborate attempt to put Hannah Humphrey out of business and uphold his own reputation.

In 1830, *A Monthly Sheet of Caricatures* was published by Thomas McLean at 26 Haymarket. Then, in 1841, the weekly magazine *Punch*, or *The London Charivari* was founded by the journalist and playwright Henry Mayhew and the wood-engraver Ebenezer Landells. *Punch* would monopolise visual satire in Britain for the rest of the century. The last nail in the print shop's coffin came in 1843: the year the modern cartoon was born.

The word 'cartoon' had been used for centuries by artists such as Michelangelo and Raphael. It was a word that described an artist's preparatory designs or templates, which would be transferred to the plaster on a wall or ceiling to map out a fresco mural. It came from the Italian *cartone*, meaning a sheet of paper or card – the same word which gives us 'carton'.

But in 1834, when a fire ravaged the Palace of Westminster, the meaning of the word was to be altered for ever. This event was immortalised in vivid copper oil paint by Turner. Over the following years, the architect Charles Barry and designer Augustus Pugin began rebuilding it in the Gothic splendour we know today.

As arrays of pointed arches and stained glass were installed in Westminster, the government decided to share the progress with the public. In 1843, an exhibition was opened, showing the preparatory drawings – cartoons – for the decoration of the new palace. It was a badly judged offering. For this was the year Dickens published *A Christmas Carol*, which portrayed a London crawling with shivering street urchins. When Londoners desperately needed clothing, food and medical treatment, the government gave them an art exhibition, one which most couldn't visit because they couldn't afford the one shilling entrance fee.

*Punch* was quick to point this out. The 25-year-old artist John Leech produced a striking satire headed *Cartoon No. 1.* Here were London's starving, bare-footed poor in Westminster Hall, gazing upon the grand cartoons the government had commissioned. The image was well received, and Leech followed it up with a series.

Soon enough, all the illustrations in *Punch* were known as 'cartoons' and their artists as 'cartoonists'. The revolution was complete. The age of the satirical print was over; the age of the newspaper cartoon had begun.

But George Cruikshank never fully delved into the world of cartoons. Instead, he sidestepped into the booming trade of illustration. He was prolific, illustrating countless magazines and periodicals and over 800 books during his lifetime, which totalled nearly 10,000 prints and illustrations. His charming drawings ornamented the novels of Sir Walter Scott and William Ainsworth. He became a close friend of Charles Dickens, providing the visuals for *Sketches by Boz* and *Oliver Twist*. Cruikshank's work was in such demand it was often a greater pull than the text of a novel itself – the *Spectator* described Charles Dickens as 'the CRUIKSHANK of writers'.[39]

His brother, Robert, never reached such success, continuing to produce caricatures and a steady stream of book illustrations and wood engravings. He caught bronchitis in 1856 and died in his modest lodgings at 3 Pleasant Row, Pentonville; he was buried in Highgate Cemetery.

But George Cruikshank lived two decades longer, becoming a well-loved household name, a darling of the nation, a true national treasure. In her early memoirs, the suffragist Dora Montefiore remembered Cruikshank as one of the 'intimates of my parents' home circle',[40] who was a regular visitor to their house, perhaps chattering with her father, a proponent of railway engineering and a driving force behind the 1851 Great Exhibition. 'I can still remember the mischievous delight,' she wrote, 'with which we young ones in the safe seclusion of the schoolroom discussed his eccentricities both of beliefs and personality.'[41] He seemed a natural children's entertainer:

> Old George Cruikshank was practically bald, but he had a long mesh of iron grey hair which he trained across the top of his head

> and kept in its place with a piece of elastic, which arrangement was the delight of us young ones, as it was the only coiffure of that sort we had ever seen.[42]

Cruikshank was not his father's son. Isaac, as we have seen, had a heavy, and ultimately fatal tendency to drink. George became a fanatical campaigner for temperance. Here was a telling generational contrast. The dangerously freewheeling habits of the past gave way to a more controlled, less lethal, and buttoned-up present. From the 1840s, George started illustrating for the National Temperance Society. Dora Montefiore remembered this, too:

> As is well known, he was a rabid teetotaller, and I can remember him taking us children into the hot-houses where the grapes were hanging in rich and ripe bunches, and pointing out to us that nature had provided for each grape an exquisite skin which protected the luscious juice inside from fermentation. This scheme of nature, he averred, was planned with the intention of mankind eating the grape in its unfermented state, but man, with his evil cleverness, had learnt to break and crush that exquisite skin so that the juice of the grape might ferment and turn to alcohol, which was drunk in the form of wine.[43]

This vociferous advocacy of temperance was no game for Cruikshank. It imposed real costs on his life – he would break with Dickens over it. The author argued for moderation, believing that alcoholism originated in 'sorrow, or poverty, or ignorance'.[44] Dickens thought social improvements in education and a living wage would wean the British from their bottles. The illustrator took a harder stance. Sorrow and poverty? These were excuses. Alcoholism was a habit. All that was required to conquer it was willpower. They crossed swords in public, in a spat so vehement that when Dickens died in June 1870, a satisfied Cruikshank declared: 'One of our greatest enemies is gone.'[45]

The following year, Cruikshank even put his own claims on Dickens's work. He wrote a letter to the papers, arguing his rights over *Oliver Twist*:

> When … *Bentley's Miscellany* was first started, it was arranged that Mr Charles Dickens should write a serial and which was to be illustrated by me; and in a conversation with him as to what the subject should be for the first serial, I suggested to Mr Dickens that he should write the life of a London boy, and strongly advised him to do this, assuring him that I would furnish him with the subject and supply him with all the characters, which my large experience of London life would enable me to do. My idea was to raise a boy from a most humble position up to a high and respectable one – in fact, to illustrate one of those cases of common occurrence, where men of humble origin by natural ability, industry, honesty, and honourable conduct, raise themselves to first-class positions in society.[46]

Photograph of George Cruikshank.
Boston Public Library

George Cruikshank died on 1 February 1878, aged 86, at his home at 263 Hampstead Road, London. He was mourned in the papers: 'England is the poorer by what she can ill-spare – a man of genius,' ran *Punch* magazine's obituary. 'Good, kind, genial, honest, and enthusiastic George Cruikshank has passed away,' they wailed.[47]

He embodied the Victorian age, as much as his father had the Georgian: 'There never was a purer, simpler, more straightforward, or altogether more blameless man. His nature had something childlike in its transparency.'[48] In George

Cruikshank, Victorian society saw its highest values reflected back at itself. He was a man as honest and true as could be. Thackeray pointed out that – unlike James Gillray, who was corrupted by self-betrayal – George Cruikshank 'would not for any bribe say what he did not think ... a man of the people if ever there was one'.[49] Thackeray's requiem was Victorian self-satisfaction of the highest grade. A heavy pat on the back. Cruikshank's father's generation, where depravity and drunkenness reigned, had given way to a time of great, honest, self-reliant men, with George heralded as a leading light among them.

Or so they thought. In fact, not long after his death, George Cruikshank's stainless reputation was dirtied when his wife, Eliza, discovered the contents of her husband's will. His money was not destined to support her in her dotage. Instead, every remaining pound and shilling went to another woman: Adelaide Attree, a maid who had once worked for the Cruikshanks years before. Scandalously, it emerged that George had set up Adelaide in a flat around the corner from his own home and supported her financially until his death. What's more, while George Cruikshank never fathered any children with his wife, Eliza, with Adelaide he had eleven.

Isaac's generation had its faults. But hypocrisy on this scale was not one of them. They lived and loved freely, and less cruelly than their sons did. The Victorians, whether it was child prostitution in London, or the inequities of the Poor Law, were good at turning a blind eye to embarrassing truths. So it was with George Cruikshank. Despite his web of lies, he was buried in the grandest plot of the land: alongside his boyhood heroes, Lord Nelson and the Duke of Wellington, in St Paul's Cathedral's sacred national crypt. He was temporarily buried in Kensal Green Cemetery on 9 February until the crypt, then under repair, could be reopened. There, on 29 November 1878, his English oak casket was lowered into the ground.

A memorial still stands at Kensal Green Cemetery today, 'erected by his affectionate' – and *very* forgiving – 'widow, Eliza Cruikshank'.

Eliza immortalised her late husband as an 'Artist, Designer, Etcher, Painter', who was 'for 30 years a total abstainer and ardent pioneer and champion by pencil, word and pen of universal abstinence from intoxicating drinks'.

## AN IMMENSE LEGACY

George Cruikshank was nothing like the artists of his father's generation. A teetotal, moralising Victorian, buried in the vault of St Paul's, he was nothing less than an establishment man. He even claimed ownership of the idea of one of the nation's greatest works of literature, *Oliver Twist*. Along with Reynolds, Nelson, Hogarth and Handel, he had breezed into Britain's historic Club of Respectability, a rooftop bar where the nation's heroes mingled. Cruikshank could use the VIP area, which only those buried in the vault of St Paul's could access.

Of course, Gillray, Rowlandson and Isaac Cruikshank had been kicked out of the club in the 1810s, as the age of Pitt and Fox came to a close. The rules had changed; their jokes about heaving bosoms and their joyously sung drinking ditties were now considered filthily inappropriate. They were erased, deleted, cancelled. Their names had been crossed off the guest list with a black marker, their wristbands had been cut and they'd been booted towards the gutter.

To add insult to injury, the Victorian commentators plucked one of the satirists' direct contemporaries from obscurity and categorised him as one of Britain's greatest artists. Gillray's former Royal Academy Schools classmate and someone who Rowlandson exchanged a few polite words with over a drink in his old age. His name was William Blake.

How did this unknown, who had darted in the shadows of Rowlandson's brilliance, now, in the 1860s, come to be deemed acceptable? Soon, he was the hero of the Pre-Raphaelites and was heralded as a glorious luminary. These Victorians were so sure of their own judgement, they were arrogant enough to declare him 'a man not forestalled by predecessors, nor to be classed with contemporaries, nor to be replaced by known or readily surmisable successors'.[50] Even today, commentators describe Blake as 'far and away the greatest artist Britain has ever produced'.[51]

Meanwhile, Gillray has been spat on as 'the malignant spawn of some forgotten circle of the lower inferno', the creator of 'unshapely figures whose protuberant flesh suggests a tumefied and fungoid growth'.[52] It's a reputation that the satirists are yet to recover from: their names are unknown by all but a select minority of print collectors or history students. Still the satirists are in the gutter. Still we conform to hypocritical Victorian standards.

Despite their sunken reputation, the satirists' genius lives on. Undeniably one of the most powerful forces in Georgian Britain, their prints not only reacted to world events, but propelled political change. They shaped public opinion; they built up careers; they shredded reputations. How many speeches in the House of Commons were tempered to avoid Gillray's criticisms? How many votes were swung by Rowlandson's depictions of the Duchess of Devonshire in the 1784 election? How many nights did the Prince of Wales lie awake, wondering whether another priapic folly would be exposed in Hannah Humphrey's window? How many patriotic young men signed up to fight in Europe, buoyed by images of bloodthirsty *sans-culottes* in Samuel Fores' print shop?

This is nowhere clearer than in the creation of the biggest myths in human history: the misconception that Napoleon was a short man. Napoleon lived an astonishing life marked by truly epic events – the coronation in Notre Dame, the Battle of Austerlitz, the retreat from Moscow – but none of these have landed in the public imagination as effectively as the fiction spun by the British satirists. In fact, the average Briton is more familiar with the character of Little Boney than Napoleon himself. As the critics conceded in 1904: 'No history of Napoleon is quite complete which fails to recognize Gillray as a potent factor in crystallizing public opinion in England.'[53] Napoleon's height might be regarded as one of the biggest myths in history, but with that came one of history's most effective campaigns of visual persuasion.

These were tumultuous years in British history. Madness, revolution and invasion put the very existence of Britain at stake. And yet, with potential national crisis lurking around every corner, satire played a crucial role in releasing pent-up tension and maintaining order. As the nation tossed through perilous seas, satirical prints steadied the hand of Captain Pitt and subdued the ferocity of incoming waves.

Those prints that supported the government, and argued fiercely against radical ideas, persuaded many that a revolution in Britain really wasn't worth it. How many potential revolutionaries resisted the urge to put ideology into action by looking at bountiful 'British Liberty' as opposed to the terrors of the French equivalent? On the other hand, those prints that were critical of those in power eased the pressure, too. Radicals who peered into the print shop windows to see the establishment savagely criticised were placated, knowing that their grievances were given a platform. How many Londoners, furious at the Prince Regent for throwing public money down the drain, were eased of their frustrations by seeing him being publicly ridiculed?

To realise the power of these prints, it's helpful to imagine a Britain where they never even existed at all. Remove the satirists from the picture. A precariously balanced nation may have toppled over into outright destruction.

The political role these satires played is no doubt immense, but we mustn't make the mistake of labelling these artists as purely political. They made images about every aspect of life, and their oeuvre was one of the most widely consumed type of visual entertainment in the country, comparable to the modern-day meme. Everyone from George III to Jane Austen to Olaudah Equiano to Lord Byron lived in a world where daily conversation was peppered with jokes and witticisms from the etching burins of Piccadilly.

It's no surprise that British humour has never been the same since. By 1810, the public were addicted to the satire of Gillray and his gang. We were hooked on innuendo; on pricking the pomposity of the high and mighty; on not taking anyone – or anything – too seriously. Although Victorian commentators may have disliked the idea that the British had a saucy, satirical sense of humour, there was no escaping that Gillray, Rowlandson and Cruikshank had made a permanent mark on the national psyche.

A quick glance through popular culture, and it's easy to see their characters cropping up everywhere. Gillrayic satires on pompous British officers surely played into the mind of the great librettist W.S. Gilbert as he penned the following in the 1870s:

> I grew so rich that I was sent
> By a pocket borough into Parliament.
> I always voted at my party's call,
> And I never thought of thinking for myself at all.
> I thought so little, they rewarded me
> By making me the Ruler of the Queen's Navee!

And Rowlandson's pen-and-ink sketches burst to life in scenes resembling the *Carry On* franchise. A saucy side-eye from Kenneth Williams; a girlish squeal from Barbara Windsor – each could frictionlessly adorn Rowlandson's cheeky satires.

Nowhere is this legacy more pronounced than in the work of recent political cartoonists. For them, the Georgian satires are a visual language, in which they are all fluent. In 2021, the cartoonist Dave Brown declared his admiration in the *Independent*:

> Gillray is, in my opinion, not simply one of the greatest satirical cartoonists to have lived, but one of Britain's greatest artists in any genre. His are the footsteps the rest of us walk in, the shoulders we stand on, the metaphors we still steal.[54]

Flick through any work by any other greats – Gerald Scarfe, Peter Brookes or Steve Bell – and they are jammed with Gillrayic motifs, styles and imagery. Gillray's descendants reuse and reinterpret his ticks: extended speech marks, lewd jokes, lively black outlines, exaggerated forms. Like Gillray, they pinch visual metaphors from great art as well as pop culture. The result is imagery which is bizarre and surreal. How Gillray would delight in Bell's image of Boris Johnson as a giant pimple, or Brookes' Putin bouncing around as an hourglass. While the Georgian satirists used imagery from the classical world, or Reynolds's latest painting, Brookes playfully selects and stretches cultural icons in this way too, basing his satires on Gainsborough's *Blue Boy*, John Tenniel's *Alice's Adventures in Wonderland* illustrations and even the *Jaws* film poster. Very Gillrayic, indeed.

So convinced are modern cartoonists by the electric power of the Georgian satires that they have rehashed entire prints, updating the characters with modern politicians. In 2009, in light of the Parliamentary expenses scandal, Chris Duggan reimagined *A Voluptuary under the horrors of Digestion* for *The Times*. Rather than showing a corpulent Prince George surrounded by evidence of unfettered indulgence propped up by the taxpayer, Duggan gave us *A Select Committee Absentee under the delights of an Expense Account*. And Gillray's *Britannia Between Death and the Doctor's* – a scene where political infighting between Pitt, Fox and Addington distracts them from a real constitutional threat – was reimagined by Dave Brown. He recast the scene with Gordon Brown and Nick Clegg as doctors and David Cameron as Death.

Of course, Gillray's *The Plumb-pudding* has appeared in every guise. According to the cartoonist Martin Rowson, it is 'probably the most famous political cartoon of all time … stolen over and over and over again by cartoonists ever since.'[55] They have delighted in setting the table with Margaret Thatcher, Tony Blair, Theresa May, Nicola Sturgeon, Donald Trump, Vladimir Putin and Angela Merkel, to name just a few. The pudding itself has been reinvented as the

Northern Ireland Protocol, the AstraZeneca Covid vaccine and even a baked bean.

In the 1980s, the cartoonists Roger Law and Peter Fluck brought Georgian satire to the screen with the wildly popular satirical TV series *Spitting Image*. Politicians, celebrities and the royal family were lacerated in sketches acted out by latex puppets. '*Spitting Image* owed a great deal to the great British caricaturist James Gillray,' admitted Roger Law, adding: 'possibly even a royalty payment.'[56] Gillray himself was included as a cameo extra, playing one of the Queen's servants. They knew his influence, though the public did not. Gillray's successors were paying him tribute. The present shook hands with the past and thanked it.

Like the crowds that flocked to Hannah Humphrey's windows, the British watched *Spitting Image* in their millions. Screened on Sunday nights at 10pm, the third series was watched by 15 million viewers, all laughing and guffawing at Gillrayic jokes. It was controversial from the start: for the first time on British television, the Queen and her family were mocked on a weekly basis – just as George III and his family were all those years before. And caricature was the engine that powered it all: just as Gillray reduced Pitt to a toadstool, Thatcherite Education Secretary Kenneth Baker was reduced to a slug.

So *weird*. So *strange*. The Georgian satirists are also owed a chapter in the history of surrealism. They were among the greatest surrealists Britain has ever seen, decades ahead of their time. It's hard to believe that John Tenniel, the illustrator of Lewis Carroll's *Alice's Adventures in Wonderland*, had not registered Gillray's playing with scale or anamorphism. Or think of Lewis Carroll's anthropomorphic playing cards, with human heads, arms and legs. Are these not a complete rip-off of John Nixon's satires of the 1790s, with figures created from hearts, diamonds, clubs and spades? What's more, Salvador Dalí's weird floppy clocks and spindly legged elephants were celebrated as brilliantly cutting-edge, yet Gillray had been stretching and twisting his subjects to the same effect over a century before.

## AN UPROARIOUS SPIRIT

So, why are the names of Gillray, Rowlandson and Cruikshank *still* unknown to most of the British public?

For one thing, they've never received much attention from the academic world. In 1996, Professor Diana Donald opened her study of late Georgian satirical prints with the statement: 'There can be few groups of art works so comprehensively catalogued and yet so seldom discussed as the satirical prints of eighteenth-century England.'[57] She acknowledged the bizarre 'lacuna in scholarship', and that 'a general, critical study of caricature in the so-called "golden age", namely the later Georgian period, has until now been lacking'.[58]

Gross-out, biting, hilarious satire never slotted neatly into other areas of study or research. It fell by the wayside. Historians have been guilty of using prints merely as an illustrative tool: 'A kind of surveillance camera overlooking the major events of the century.'[59] Meanwhile, art historians have never considered caricature as more than a very minor branch of the history of art, 'with little interest in its ideographic and polemical nature'.[60]

Perhaps it's easy to see why satirical prints hold less allure than the famous, glossy paintings that are well established in the art history canon. A print is an image that is endlessly reproduced and duplicated; by its very nature, it has less cachet than a one-of-a-kind oil painting hanging in the sumptuous surroundings of a grand gallery. Even worse, the original artworks from the satirist's hand – the copper plates – have generally been lost or destroyed; those that survive are blackened with ink, the images and text set in reverse.

So, what about books for the general reader? Amazingly there hasn't been a single title on the satirists. There might have been weighty exhibition guides for your coffee table, a few academic books and a pocket guide here and there (Vic Gatrell's wonderful *City of Laughter* is probably the closest) but nothing for the absolute beginner history reader to enjoy on a sunbed in Majorca.* The satirists lead rich lives and produced works worthy of Horace and Juvenal, or Swift and Pope. Yet publishers have been reluctant to pay attention to them.

A quick flick through mainstream history books tells me the satirists are hardly on their radar, either. In Andrew Roberts's epic 900-page biography *Napoleon the Great*, Gillray appears just twice in passing. Gillray, Rowlandson and Cruikshank are absent from the index of William Hague's 600-page biography of William Pitt. Even social histories, such as Lucy Inglis' *Georgian London*, omit the satirists altogether. Ian Mortimer's *The Time Traveller's Guide to Regency Britain* has just one mention of Gillray – despite the image that is used for the front cover being a Gillray print. And of course, none of these books mention the woman at the centre of the whole operation, the person who deserves credit for Gillray's success: the unsung hero Hannah Humphrey.

In truth, the public might be more familiar with the satirists than they realise. Over the past year or so, when friends and family have asked about my book, and I tell them about the satirists, they look blank. But as soon as I pull up the image of the great *Plumb-pudding*, they immediately light up in recognition. They've seen these images many times before, in pretty much every textbook, museum display or documentary regarding George III or the Regency era. Yet, the names of the artists are – more often than not – unknown.

I posed the question while mingling at an event of Gillray enthusiasts at the Cartoon Museum in London in 2021. Why hasn't the average British history enthusiast heard of these satirists? Why aren't these guys national treasures? According to one attendee, the answer is that

* When researching my university dissertation, it struck me that someone needed to write this book. Then the real brainwave came: *I* should write this book.

they aren't particularly trendy, having tended to belong to the realm of stamp-collecting, trainspotting, *Spectator*-reading elderly men. And sure enough, as I glanced at said attendee, and beyond, to the room full of fellow Gillray enthusiasts and experts, this theory was proved correct.

There has been some glimmer of hope in recent years. The artist and cartoonist Dave Brown created a brilliant portrait bust of Gillray in 2021. Two academic books were written on Gillray and the 'Age of Gillray' in 2022. And St James's Church, Piccadilly revealed a new tombstone. Yet still, this great reveal was performed by George Osborne to a crowd of about 30. And the only comment in the mainstream press was a filler entry in the *Spectator Diary* – contributed by myself via WhatsApp (and the write-up was more interested in Osborne than Gillray). So even though there is growing interest, this still resides within the bubble of collectors and cartoonists.

Gillray enthusiasts attend the unveiling of James Gillray's new gravestone, with a VIP appearance from George Osborne.

James Gillray's gravestone in the courtyard of St James's Church, Piccadilly.

Dave Brown and his bronze portrait bust of Gillray. Superb!

In writing this book, I hope to begin to change this. It is my great joy in life to share my passion for history by making it as engaging and entertaining as possible. These satirical prints are a perfect access point to engage the average Brit in their own dramatic and fascinating past. They are the most accessible original sources in British history; these aren't rambling speeches with complex classical references, or long medieval statutes requiring serious enquiry to understand what on earth is going on. These are pictures – pictures that were created to appeal to every type of person, literate and illiterate. They can be understood with a single glance or examined carefully to unravel a puzzle of clever details. What's more, these pictures are humorous. They are – at their root – jokes. Some of which are so vulgar they are bound to appeal to the British public.*

So, the book you are currently reading is, in fact, a joke book. And once you've finished reading it (and passed it on to your friends and relations) my greatest hope is that you'll spend some time learning more about these wonderful prints. There are many prints that I wasn't able to include, so we have only begun to scratch the surface. Take a moment to type 'James Gillray' into Google and trawl through the hilarious, bizarre and shocking images which spring up. Spend a few minutes piecing together the characters and events in question and I guarantee you'll find immense satisfaction from the result. It's even possible to grow your own collection, with original prints sold regularly online near the £100 mark.

And while you are busy pulling down family photos to make way for this new display of caricatures, I sincerely hope other historians, academics, journalists, authors, podcasters, museum curators, TV commissioners and Hollywood producers sit up and pay attention to these visionary artists.

* Even the late Prince Philip – a man famed for his multiple gaffes – acknowledged you need a 'robust' sense of humour to enjoy a Rowlandson print.

The truth is James Gillray, Thomas Rowlandson and Isaac Cruikshank were deleted from the history books by the Victorians, and their reputation has never recovered. And so, in light of this, we are still in the grip of Victorian mores. We are still obediently spoon-fed our heroes according to Victorian priggishness. Still being told who to like. Still being told what to laugh at.

It is time to break free from these restrictions and put Gillray back on the plinth of national treasure. If William Blake has been voted to the top 40 of the 100 greatest Britons, James Gillray has every right to be there, too. Put him on the £20 note. Give him a Netflix series.

Blake may have given us lofty ideas of religion. Reynolds may have created beautiful fantasies of classical grandeur. But none of these transport us back in time. None of these capture the actual experience of our Georgian ancestors. It was the satirists who were able to capture the essence of human nature, to pin down the unchanging foibles and follies that made us who we were then, and still make us who we are now. Their satires allow us to peek through the keyhole and glance at the belly of the beast: to see Georgian Britain as it really was. There is no Photoshopping, here. No touch-ups. This is gritty, raw, real life. Here, we can see the most intimate, vulnerable moments of our ancestors' lives, the faces they made when they took medicine, or how they sleepwalked, or their exclamations of horror as they listened to a ghost story.

Most importantly, these prints did the most powerful of things: they made people laugh. They provoked everything from sniggers, to snorts, to cheerful chuckles, to raucous hysterics. To understand a Gillray etching, a Rowlandson sketch or a Cruikshank engraving is to climb inside the mind of the Georgians. To then laugh at that image is to laugh with our ancestors and pinpoint our common humanity. And as we all stifle a snigger at this bulbous nose or that saucy pun, be assured of one thing: we are still the children of those Piccadilly Mad Men, and we still champion their spirit of UPROAR!

Acknowledgements

There are many people to thank for making this book happen. To the team at Hardman & Swainson, especially Caroline Hardman for believing in me from the start. The team, too, at Icon Books. An enormous thanks must go to my sensational editor, Clare Bullock, for all her hard work in so skilfully shaping this book into what you read today. Thank you also to Thea Hirsi, James Lilford, Emily Cary-Elwes and Andrew Furlow. I am also indebted to the following people for their advice, support and their work on this subject: Jim Sherry, Benjamin Lemer, Tim Clayton, Mathew Crowther, Professor Stana Nenadic and Professor Gordon Pentland.

But there are numerous people and places who, over the years, I am indebted to for encouraging my love of history. To all those history teachers and professors, namely Dr Tullis, for helping me to try and understand the past. To the beautiful cities of Edinburgh and London, for constantly thrilling and inspiring me with your historic secrets (especially the delights of Edinburgh's Hanover Street and London's Dean Street). To the brilliant team at History Hit for everything you've taught me, for always believing in me and giving me the most wonderful opportunities – and making everything such fun. To every one of my followers on TikTok and Instagram – I'm always amazed at your generous support and kind comments, and I look forward to many more years discovering history together.

Thanks too to any friends and family who have ever bought a ticket to a show, watched a documentary, reluctantly dressed up as a medieval peasant, imbibed vast quantities of Tesco cava or come to the pub.

But most importantly, to my parents, for their unwavering support, encouragement and belief in my creative endeavours. Thank you for all those videos you have patiently recorded, the projector screens you have carried, and weird and wacky ideas we have come up with together in the evening sunshine.

And, of course, I must thank James Gillray, Thomas Rowlandson, Isaac Cruikshank and Hannah Humphrey, for providing an endless source of amusement and delight all these years later. Thank you to you, dear reader, for picking up this book. I hope it is as delightful to read as it has been a delight to write.

# *Notes*

## 1: A BENCH OF ARTISTS

1. Mark Bills, *The Art of Satire: London in Caricature* (London: Philip Wilson, 2006), p. 108.

2. Peter Moore, *Endeavour: The Ship and the Attitude that Changed the World* (London: Chatto & Windus, 2018), p. 73.

3. *Gentleman's Magazine*, January 1827.

4. David Morrice, *The Art of Teaching* (London: Lackington, Allen & Co., 1801), p. x.

5. William Barrow, *An Essay on Education* (London: F. & C. Rivington, 1804), vol. 2, pp. 287–289.

6. Old Bailey Proceedings, 27 April 1720, https://www.oldbaileyonline.org/browse.jsp?name=17200427.

7. *Gentleman's Magazine*, January 1827.

8. Instrument of Foundation, Royal Academy Collection: Archive, RAA/IF, https://www.royalacademy.org.uk/art-artists/archive/instrument-of-foundation.

9. Ibid.

10. William Sandby, *The History of the Royal Academy of Arts from Its Foundation in 1768 to the Present Time* (London: Longman & Co., 1862), vol. 2, p. 440.

11. Ibid., p. 452.

12. Geoffrey George Cunningham (ed.), *The English Nation; Or, A History of England in the Lives of Englishmen* (Edinburgh and London: A. Fullarton & Co., 1863), vol. 5, p. 595.

13. Royal Academy of Arts, *Abstract of the Instrument of Institution and Laws of the Royal Academy of Arts in London – Established December 10, 1768*, (London: T. Cadell, 1781), p. 20.

14. 'Ryley, Charles Reuben', *Dictionary of National Biography* (London: Smith, Elder & Co., 1885–1900), vol. 50.

15. Sidney C. Hutchinson, 'The Royal Academy Schools, 1768–1830', *Volume of the Walpole Society*, vol. 38 (1960–62), pp. 123–91, p. 129.

16. Ibid.

17. James Payne and Matthew Payne, *Regarding Thomas Rowlandson, 1757–1827: His Life, Art and Acquaintance* (London: Hogarth Arts: 2010), p. 222

18. Henry Angelo, *Reminiscences of Henry Angelo* (London: Henry Colburn, 1830), vol. 1, p. 238.

19. Ibid., p. 236.

20. Jonathan Glancey, *Architecture* (London: Dorling Kindersley, 2006), p. 309.

21. 'Jean-Baptiste Pigalle', Getty, https://www.getty.edu/art/collection/person/103KZ3.

22. Payne and Payne, *Regarding Thomas Rowlandson*, p. 32.

23. Joseph Grego, *Rowlandson the Caricaturist* (London: Chatto & Windus, 1880). p. 58.

24. Angelo, *Reminiscences of Henry Angelo*, p. 183.

25. Ibid., p. 235.

26. Ibid., p. 70.

27. Ibid.

28. Ibid., p. 235.

29. Ibid., p. 237.

30. Ibid.

31. Ibid.

32. Ibid.

33. Ibid., p. 234.

34. *Gentleman's Magazine*, January 1827.

35. Grego, *Rowlandson the Caricaturist*, pp. 45-6.

36. Stephen Wade, *Rowlandson's Human Comedy* ( Stroud: Amberley Publishing, 2011), p. 30.

37. Angelo, *Reminiscences of Henry Angelo*, p. 233.

38. Ibid., p. 240.

39. John Adolphus, *Memoirs of Jack Bannister*, vol. 1 (London: R. Bentley, 1838) p. 14.

40. Angelo, *Reminiscences of Henry Angelo*, p. 254.

41. Ibid., p. 255.

42. Adolphus, *Memoirs of Jack Bannister*, vol. 1, p. 15.

43. Ibid., p. 15.

44. Angelo, *Reminiscences of Henry Angelo*, p. 233.

45. Grego, *Rowlandson the Caricaturist*, p. 13.

46. William Hogarth, *Anecdotes of William Hogarth* (London: J.B. Nichols & Son, 1833), p. 12.

47. Angelo, *Reminiscences of Henry Angelo*, p. 233.

48. Ibid., p. 234.

## 2: PUTRID MASQUERADES AND TWITTERY

1. Patrick Crotty (ed.), *The Penguin Book of Irish Poetry* (London: Penguin Classics, 2018).

2. Draper Hill, *Mr Gillray the Caricaturist: A Biography* (London: Phaidon Press, 1965), p. 12.

3. Anita McConnell and Simon Heneage, 'Gillray, James', *Oxford Dictionary of National Biography* (Oxford: Oxford University Press, 2004): https://doi.org/10.1093/ref:odnb/10754.

4. Angelo, *Reminiscences of Henry Angelo*, p. 383.

5. Ibid.

6. Hill, *Mr Gillray the Caricaturist*, p. 15.

7. Angelo, *Reminiscences of Henry Angelo*, p. 384.

8. Ibid.

9. Ibid.

10. *The Statutes at Large*, vol. 12 (London: Charles Eyre & William Strahan, 1776), p. 307.

11. 'A brief history of the RA': https://www.royalacademy.org.uk/page/a-brief-history-of-the-ra.

12. *Morning Post*, 6 May 1780, in Martin Postle, '1780: Trouble with the Tribuna at the "Temple of Priapus", in Mark Hallett, Sarah Victoria Turner and Jessica Feather (eds), *The Royal Academy of Arts Summer Exhibition: A Chronicle, 1769–2018* (London: Paul Mellon Centre for Studies in British Art, 2018).

13. *Morning Post* and *Daily Advertiser*, 15 May 1780, ibid.

14. *Morning Post* and *Daily Advertiser*, 25 May 1780, ibid.

15. Royal Academy Council Minutes, vol. C, 1768–84, I, f286; Martin Postle, 'Flayed for Art: The Ecorché Figure in the English Art Academy', *British Art Journal*, vol. 5, no. 1 (2004), p. 60.

16. Royal Academy Summer Exhibition Catalogue 1780: https://chronicle250.com/1780#catalogue.

17. Angelo, *Reminiscences of Henry Angelo*, p. 411.

18. Kenneth D. Keele and Jane Roberts, *Leonardo da Vinci: Anatomical Drawings from the Royal Library, Windsor Castle* (New York: The Metropolitan Museum of Art, 1983), p. 66.

19. Leonardo da Vinci, *The Notebooks of Leonardo da Vinci*, vol. 1 (New York: Dover Publications, 2012), p. 171.

20. Edward MacCurdy, *The Notebooks of Leonardo da Vinci Arranged, Rendered into English and Introduced*, vol. 2 (London: Jonathan Cape, 1950), p. 891.

21. Nina Edwards, *Darkness: A Cultural History* (London: Reaktion Books, 2018), p. 89.

22. James Hall, 'Kenneth Clark: Looking for Civilisation', *Tate Etc.*, 25 June 2019: https://www.tate.org.uk/tate-etc/issue-31-summer-2014/rescue-civilisation-man.

23. Müntz, Eugéne, *Michelangelo* (New York: Parkstone International, 2005), foreword.

24. Angelo, *Reminiscences of Henry Angelo*, p. 393.

25. 'Caricature', *Oxford Learner's Dictionaries*: https://www.oxfordlearnersdictionaries.com/definition/american_english/caricature_1.

26. Jonathan Greenberg, *The Cambridge Introduction to Satire* (Cambridge: Cambridge University Press, 2019), p. 11.

27. 'Satire', *Oxford English Dictionary*: https://www.oed.com/viewdictionaryentry/Entry/171207.

28. Bills, *The Art of Satire*, p. 18.

29. Greenberg, *The Cambridge Introduction to Satire*, p. 3.

30. Bills, *The Art of Satire*, p. 19.

31. John Trusler, *The Works of Mr Hogarth Moralized*, vol. 1 (London: J. Goodwin, 1821), p. 177.

32. Henry Fielding, *The History of the Adventures of Joseph Andrews and of his Friend Mr Abraham Adams*, vol. 1 (London, 1742), pp. ix–x.

33. E.H. Gombrich and Ernst Kris, *Caricature* (Harmondsworth: Penguin, 1940), pp. 11–12, quoted in Mark Bryant, 'Drawing the Line', *The British Art Journal*, vol. 20, no. 2 (2019), pp. 42–52.

34. Jenny Uglow, *William Hogarth: A Life and a World* (London: Faber & Faber, 2011), p. 31.

35. Ibid., pp. 31–2.

36. Angelo, *Reminiscences of Henry Angelo*, p. 410.

37. Douglas Fordham, *British Art and the Seven Years' War: Allegiance and Autonomy* (Philadelphia: University of Pennsylvania Press, 2010), p. 75.

38. William Feaver, *Masters of Caricature* (London: Weidenfeld & Nicolson, 1981), p. 43.

39. Ibid.

40. Angelo, *Reminiscences of Henry Angelo*, p. 410.

41. Mary Darly, *A Book of Caricaturas* (London: Mary Darly, 1769).

42. Clayton, T. Darly, Matthias (*c.* 1720–1780), designer and printseller. *Oxford Dictionary of National Biography*. Retrieved 18 Nov. 2022, from https://www.oxforddnb.com/view/10.1093/ref:odnb/9780198614128.001.0001/odnb-9780198614128-e-7161.

43. Aileen Ribeiro, 'Meet the Macaronis', *History Today*, 31 July 2019: https://www.historytoday.com/miscellanies/meet-macaronis.

44. *Oxford Magazine*, 1770, in Joseph Twadell Shipley, *The Origins of English Words: A Discursive Dictionary of Indo-European Roots* (Baltimore: Johns Hopkins University Press, 1984).

45. Oliver Goldsmith, *She Stoops to Conquer*, in *The British Theatre; or, a Collection of Plays, Which Are Acted at the Theatres Royal, Drury Lane, Covent Garden, and Haymarket*, vol. 17 (London: Longman, Hurst, Rees & Orme, 1808), p. 59.

46. Feaver, *Masters of Caricature*, p. 44

47. Ibid.

48. *General Post*, May 1776.

49. *Morning Chronicle* and *London Advertiser*, 2 July 1776.

50. Bills, *The Art of Satire*, p. 24.

51. Angelo, *Reminiscences of Henry Angelo*, p. 410.

52. Ibid., p. 392.

## 3: A KINGDOM TRUSTED TO A SCHOOL-BOY'S CARE

1. William Hague, *William Pitt the Younger* (London: HarperCollins, 2004), p. 76.

2. Grego, *Rowlandson the Caricaturist*, p. 13.

3. John Hayes, 'Rowlandson, Thomas', *Oxford Dictionary of National Biography*: https://www.oxforddnb.com/view/10.1093/ref:odnb/9780198614128.001.0001/odnb-9780198614128-e-24221.

4. Angelo, *Reminiscences of Henry Angelo*, p. 392.

5. Ian Mortimer, *The Time Traveller's Guide to Regency Britain* (London: Bodley Head, 2020), p. 41.

6. Angelo, *Reminiscences of Henry Angelo*, p. 249.

7. Ibid., pp. 249–50.

8. M. Dorothy George, *Hogarth to Cruikshank: Social Change in Graphic Satire* (London: Allen Lane, 1967), p. 141.

9. Ibid.

10. Metropolitan Museum of Art: https://www.metmuseum.org/art/collection/search/744566.

11. Dick Leonard and Mark Garnett, *Titans: Fox vs. Pitt* (London: I.B. Tauris, 2019), p. 34.

12. Loren Reid, *Charles James Fox: A Man for the People* (London: Longmans, 1969), p. 16.

13. *The World*, 3 February 1787.

14. Leslie George Mitchell, *Charles James Fox* (Oxford: Oxford University Press, 1992), p. 8.

15. Ibid., p. 9.

16. Andrew Roberts, *George III: The Life and Reign of Britain's Most Misunderstood Monarch* (London: Penguin Books, 2021), p. 404.

17. Christopher Hibbert, *Redcoats and Rebels: The American Revolution Through British Eyes* (New York: Norton, 1990), p. 86.

18. Ibid., p. 86.

19. Susan Ratcliffe, *Oxford Essential Quotations*, 4th edn (Oxford: Oxford University Press, 2016).

20. George III's memorandum of abdication, 1782. RA GEO/MAIN/4555, Royal Archives/© His Majesty King Charles III 2022.

21. Roberts, *George III*, p. 465.

22. Peter Ackroyd, *Revolution: The History of England*, vol. 4 (London: Macmillan, 2016), p. 250.

23. Roberts, *George III*, p. 464.

24. Ibid., p. 464.

25. Philip Henry Stanhope, *Life of the Right Honourable William Pitt*, vol. 1 (London: John Murray, 1861), p. iii.

26. William Roberts, *Memoirs of the Life and Correspondence of Mrs Hannah More* (London: Seeley, 1834), p. 181.

27. Reginald Jacobs, *Covent Garden: Its Romance and History* (London: Simpkin, Marshall & Co., 1913), p. 54.

28. Michael Macdonagh, *The Book of Parliament* (London: Isbister & Co., 1897), p. 8.

29. Roberts, *George III*, p. 470.

30. Ibid., p. 470.

31. Jo Pugh, 'The World According to Pitt', *Public Domain Review*, 1 October 2013: https://publicdomainreview.org/essay/the-world-according-to-pitt.

32. Ibid.

33. Ibid.

34. Ibid.

35. Ibid.

36. Ibid.

37. Hague, *William Pitt the Younger*, p. 30.

38. Ibid.

39. Jeremy Black, *Pitt the Elder* (Cambridge: Cambridge University Press, 1992), p. 299.

40. Dick Leonard, *Nineteenth-Century British Premiers* (London: Palgrave Macmillan, 2008), p. 8.

41. Hague, *William Pitt the Younger*, p. 64.

42. Horace Walpole, W.S. Lewis, Grover Cronin, Jr, Charles H. Bennett, *Horace Walpole's Correspondence*, vol. 2 (New Haven: Yale University Press, 1955), p. 116.

43. Hague, *William Pitt the Younger*, p. 67.

44. Ibid.

45. Ibid., p. 66.

## 4: A STILLNESS THE MOST UNCOMMON

1. Roberts, *George III*, p. 473.

2. Ibid.

3. Ibid.

4. Ibid.

5. 'Print; trade-card', British Museum: https://www.britishmuseum.org/collection/object/P_Heal-3-8.

6. Hill, *Mr Gillray the Caricaturist*, p. 27.

7. Payne and Payne, *Regarding Thomas Rowlandson*, p. 107.

8. Mortimer, *The Time Traveller's Guide to Regency Britain*, p. 81.

9. Payne and Payne, *Regarding Thomas Rowlandson*, p. 107.

10. Ibid., p. 108.

11. Ibid., p. 109.

12. Mortimer, *The Time Traveller's Guide to Regency Britain*, p. 300.

13. Ibid.

14. Matthew White, 'Crime and punishment in Georgian Britain', British Library, 14 October 2009: https://www.bl.uk/georgian-britain/articles/crime-and-punishment-in-georgian-britain.

15. Ibid.

16. E.B. Krumbhaar, *Isaac Cruikshank, A Catalogue Raisonné, with a Sketch of His Life and Work* (Philadelphia: University of Pennsylvania Press, 1966), p. 15.

17. Edward Topham, *Letters from Edinburgh; Written in the Years 1774 and 1775* (London: J. Dodsley, 1776), pp. 272–3.

18. Robert Patten, 'Cruikshank, George', *Oxford Dictionary of National Biography*: https://www.oxforddnb.com/view/10.1093/ref:odnb/9780198614128.001.0001/odnb-9780198614128-e-6843.

19. Roberts, *George III*, p. 506.

20. Ibid., p. 506.

21. Ibid., p. 507.

22. Ibid.

23. Ibid., p. 510.

24. Ibid., p. 511.

25. Ibid.

26. Ibid., p. 512.

27. Hodgman, Charlotte, HistoryExtra, 14 March 2022, https://www.historyextra.com/period/georgian/history-explorer-the-decline-of-george-iii/.

28. Roberts, *George III*, p. 505.

29. Ibid., p. 516.

30. Ibid., p. 527.

31. Ibid., p. 510.

32. Edmund Burke, *The Correspondence of Edmund Burke* (Chicago: University of Chicago Press, 1958), p. 39.

33. Charles James Fox and John Wright, *The Speeches of the Right Honourable Charles James Fox* (London: Longman & Co., 1815), p. 201.

34. Ibid., p. 400.

35. Ibid.

36. Duke of Buckingham, *Memoirs of the Court and Cabinets of George the Third*, vol. 2 (Project Gutenberg, 2009), p. 25.

37. Charles James Fox, *Memorials and Correspondence of Charles James Fox*, vol. 2 (London: Richard Bentley, 1854), p. 300.

38. John Wesley Derry, *The Regency Crisis and the Whigs 1788–9* (Cambridge: Cambridge University Press, 1963), p. 89.

39. Payne and Payne, *Regarding Thomas Rowlandson*, p. 120.

40. John Ashton, *Florizel's Folly* (London: Chatto & Windus, 1899), ch. 6.

41. Ibid.

42. Ibid.

43. Payne and Payne, *Regarding Thomas Rowlandson*, p. 120.

44. Roberts, *George III*, p. 526.

45. Mark Brown, 'Letters shed light on lovelorn prince who became George IV', *Guardian*, 23 October 2019: https://www.theguardian.com/uk-news/2019/oct/23/letters-prince-george-iv.

46. Roberts, *George III*, p. 526.

47. Ibid., p. 529.

48. Nicholas Rogers, *Crowds, Culture, and Politics in Georgian Britain* (Oxford: Clarendon Press, 1998), p. 186.

49. Roberts, *George III*, p. 533.

50. Bills, *The Art of Satire*, p. 13.

## 5: NOW THAT'S WHAT I CALL SATIRE!: 1789

1. Diana Donald, *The Age of Caricature: Satirical Prints in the Reign of George III* (New Haven: Yale University Press, 1996), p. 28.

2. Stephen A. Smith, *Freedom of Expression: Foundational Documents and Historical Arguments* (Oxford: Oxbridge Research Associates, 2018), p. 65.

3. John Locke, *Locke: Political Essays* (Cambridge: Cambridge University Press, 1997), p. 331.

4. Roberts, *George III*, p. 495.

5. Donald, *The Age of Caricature*, p. 2.

6. Thomas Wright (ed.), *The Works of James Gillray, the Caricaturist: With the Story of his Life and Times* (London: Chatto & Windus, 1873), p. 12.

7. Roberts, *George III*, p. 495.

8. Philip Dormer Stanhope and Bonamy Dobrée (ed.) *The Letters of Philip Dormer Stanhope, 4th Earl of Chesterfield*, vol. 3 (London: Eyre & Spottiswoode, 1932), pp. 114–18.

9. Ibid., pp. 1379–82.

10. Christiane Banerji and Diana Donald (eds), *Gillray Observed: The Earliest Account of his Caricatures in London and Paris* (Cambridge: Cambridge University Press, 2009), p. 144.

11. Hill, *Mr Gillray the Caricaturist*, p. 31.

12. *Gentleman's Magazine*, 1816, in Nicholas K. Robinson, *Edmund Burke: A Life in Caricature* (New Haven: Yale University Press, 1996), p. 6.

13. Ibid.

14. Donald, *The Age of Caricature*, p. 4.

15. James Caulfield, *Calcographiana: The Printseller's Chronicle and Collectors Guide to the Knowledge and Value of Engraved British Portraits* (London: G. Smeeton, 1814), p. 6.

16. Bills, *The Art of Satire*, p. 32.

17. Ibid.

18. Simon Turner, 'Fores, Samuel', *Oxford Dictionary of National Biography*, https://www.oxforddnb.com/view/10.1093/ref:odnb/9780198614128.001.0001/odnb-9780198614128-e-63093.

19. Tim Clayton, 'The London Printsellers and the Export of English Graphic Prints', in Anorthe Kremers and Elisabeth Reich (eds), *Loyal Subversion? Caricatures from the Personal Union Between England and Hanover (1714–1837)* (Gottingen: Vandenhoeck & Ruprecht, 2014), p. 154.

20. Maria Edgeworth, *Life and Letters of Maria Edgeworth*, vol. 2 (London: Arnold, 1894), pp. 66–7.

21. Hill, *Mr Gillray the Caricaturist*, p. 29.

22. Mortimer, *The Time Traveller's Guide to Regency Britain*, p. 265.

23. Ibid., p. 265.

24. Simon Turner, '"I will not alter an Iota for any Mans Opinion upon Earth": James Gillray's Portraits of William Pitt the Younger', in Tessa Murdoch et al., *Burning Bright: Essays in Honour of David Bindman* (London: UCL Press, 2015), p. 204.

25. Joseph Monteyne, *Media Critique in the Age of Gillray: Scratches, Scraps, and Spectres* (Toronto: University of Toronto Press, 2022), p. 83.

26. Julie L. Mellby, 'Printmaker's abbreviations', Graphic Arts, Princeton University, 6 February 2009: https://www.princeton.edu/~graphicarts/2009/02/printmakers_abbreviations.html.

27. Angelo, *Reminiscences of Henry Angelo*, p. 390.

28. Ibid.

29. Bills, *The Art of Satire*, p. 33.

30. Ibid.

31. Ibid.

32. Kate Heard, '"I Only Got One Little Peep": George III's Family and Satirical Prints', Royal Collection Trust, p. 10: https://www.rct.uk/sites/default/files/Transcript%20I%20only%20got%20one%20little%20peep_1.pdf.

33. Donald, *The Age of Caricature*, p. 4.

34. Heard, '"I Only Got One Little Peep"', p. 9.

35. Wright (ed.), *The Works of James Gillray, the Caricaturist*, p. 13.

36. Bills, *The Art of Satire*, p. 34.

## 6: THE FOULEST AND MOST ATROCIOUS DEED

1. Caroline Alexander, *The Bounty: The True Story of the Mutiny on the Bounty* (London: Harper Collins, 2003), pp. 154–6.

2. *The Times*, 20 July 1789.

3. Ibid.

4. Fox, *Memorials and Correspondence of Charles James Fox*, vol. 2, p. 361.

5. Fox and Wright, *The Speeches of the Right Honourable Charles James Fox*, p. 219.

6. Mark Philp, 'Britain and the French Revolution', BBC History, 17 February 2017: https://www.bbc.co.uk/history/british/empire_seapower/british_french_rev_01.shtml.

7. Thomas Paine, *Rights of Man: Being an Answer to Mr Burke's Attack on the French Revolution* (London: H.D. Symonds, 1792), p. 72.

8. Ibid., p. 16.

9. Simon Sebag Montefiore, *Voices of History: Speeches that Changed the World* (London: Orion, 2019), p. 184.

10. *The Times*, 10 September 1792.

11. Ibid.

12. *St James's Chronicle or British Evening Post*, 11 September 1792.

13. *The Times*, 12 September 1792.

14. Ibid.

15. M. Dorothy George, 'Catalogue of Political and Personal Satires in the British Museum', VI, 1938, British Museum: https://www.britishmuseum.org/collection/object/P_1868-0808-6242.

16. Tim Clayton and Sheila O'Connell, *Bonaparte and the British: Prints and Propaganda in the Age of Napoleon* (London: British Museum Press, 2015), p. 25.

17. Payne and Payne, *Regarding Thomas Rowlandson*, p. 164.

18. Ibid.

19. Ibid.

20. Ibid., p. 177.

21. John Hostettler, *Thomas Erskine and Trial by Jury* (Hook: Waterside Press, 2010), pp. 94–5.

22. Mark Crosby, 'The Voice of Flattery *vs* Sober Truth: William Godwin, Thomas Erskine and the 1792 Trial of Thomas Paine for Sedition', *Review of English Studies*, vol. 62, no. 253 (February 2011), pp. 90–112, p. 92.

23. William Cobbett, *The Parliamentary History of England from the Earliest Period to the Year 1803*, vol. 30 (London: Longman & Co., 1817), p. 90.

24. Margarette Lincoln, *Trading in War: London's Maritime World in the Age of Cook and Nelson* (New Haven: Yale University Press, 2018), p. 182.

25. *The Times*, 25 January 1793.

26. 'Past Prime Ministers: William Pitt "The Younger"', UK Government: https://www.gov.uk/government/history/past-prime-ministers/william-pitt.

27. Adolphus, *Memoirs of Jack Bannister*, p. 300.

## 7: A BULLET WHIZZES TO CATCH THE PHIZZES

1. Hill, *Mr Gillray the Caricaturist*, p. 49.

2. Ibid.

3. George, *Hogarth to Cruikshank: Social Change in Graphic Satire*, p. 141.

4. Hill, *Mr Gillray the Caricaturist*, p. 50.

5. Ibid., p. 51.

6. Ibid., p. 50.

7. Angelo, *Reminiscences of Henry Angelo*, p. 381.

8. Ibid., p. 382.

9. Ibid.

10. Ibid., p. 383.

11. Ibid.

12. Ibid.

13. 'The Prince of Saxe-Coburg', James Gillray: Caricaturist: http://www.james-gillray.org/pop/saxe-coburg.html.

14. Ibid.

15. Hill, *Mr Gillray the Caricaturist*, p. 53.

16. The Treason Act: https://www.legislation.gov.uk/apgb/Geo3/36/7/1991-02-01/data.xht?view=snippet&wrap=true.

17. Hill, *Mr Gillray the Caricaturist*, p. 30.

18. Michael T. Davis, *Radicalism and Revolution in Britain 1775–1848: Essays in Honour of Malcolm I. Thomis* (Basingstoke: Macmillan, 2000), p. 112.

19. Ibid.

20. Jane Austen, *Northanger Abbey* (London: Penguin Classics, 1972), p. 199.

21. Stanhope, *Life of the Right Honourable William Pitt*, vol. 1, p. 328.

22. Joseph Fitzgerald Molloy, *Court Life Below Stairs; or, London Under the First Georges, 1714–1760* (London: Hurst & Blackett, 1885), p. 140.

23. Bills, *The Art of Satire*, p. 17.

24. Davis, *Radicalism and Revolution in Britain 1775–1848*, p. 114.

25. Daniel Defoe, *Moll Flanders* (London: Penguin, 1978), p. 258.

26. 'Building plan of Newgate Prison', British Library: https://www.bl.uk/collection-items/building-plan-of-newgate-prison.

27. 'Henry Delahay Symonds', British Museum: https://www.britishmuseum.org/collection/term/BIOG118822.

28. Ibid.

29. Mark Pottle, 'Newton, Richard', *Oxford Dictionary of National Biography*: https://www.oxforddnb.com/view/10.1093/ref:odnb/9780198614128.001.0001/odnb-9780198614128-e-20065.

30. John Britton, *The Auto-Biography of John Britton* (London: John Britton, 1850), p. 87.

31. Banerji and Donald (eds), *Gillray Observed*, p. 246.

32. Hill, *Mr Gillray the Caricaturist*, p. 47.

33. Kate Heard, *High Spirits: The Comic Art of Thomas Rowlandson* (London: Royal Collection Trust, 2018), p. 18.

34. Robert William Buss, *English Graphic Satire and Its Relation to Different Styles of Painting, Sculpture and Engraving* (London: Robert Buss, 1874), p. 118.

35. Angelo, *Reminiscences of Henry Angelo*, pp. 385-6.

36. Hill, *Mr Gillray the Caricaturist*, p. 47.

37. Angelo, *Reminiscences of Henry Angelo*, p. 388.

38. Ibid., p. 385.

39. Martin Rowson, 'Satire, sewers and statesmen: why James Gillray was king of the cartoon', *Guardian*, 21 March 2015: https://www.theguardian.com/artanddesign/2015/mar/21/satire-sewers-and-statesmen-james-gillray-king-of-cartoon.

40. Angelo, *Reminiscences of Henry Angelo*, pp. 387–8.

41. Ibid., p. 368.

## 8: FRUGAL MEALS AND HORRORS OF DIGESTION

1. Mark Overton, 'Agricultural Revolution in England 1500–1850', BBC History, 17 February 2017: https://www.bbc.co.uk/history/british/empire_seapower/agricultural_revolution_01.shtml.

2. Roberts, *George III*, p. 485.

3. Ibid.

4. Ibid.

5. Marilyn Morris, 'Princely Debt, Public Credit, and Commercial Values in Late Georgian Britain', *Journal of British Studies*, vol. 43, no. 3 (July 2004), pp. 339–65.

6. Roberts, *George III*, p. 450.

7. Ibid., p. 449.

8. Morris, 'Princely Debt, Public Credit, and Commercial Values in Late Georgian Britain'.

9. Roberts, *George III*, p. 449.

10. Jane Austen, *Pride and Prejudice* (London: Penguin Classics, 1996), p. 12.

11. Morris, 'Princely Debt, Public Credit, and Commercial Values in Late Georgian Britain', p. 342.

12. Roberts, *George III*, p. 494.

13. Morris, 'Princely Debt, Public Credit, and Commercial Values in Late Georgian Britain', p. 342.

14. Ibid.

15. Roberts, *George III*, p. 484.

16. Mortimer, *The Time Traveller's Guide to Regency Britain*, p. 64.

17. Ibid.

18. Ibid.

19. Donald, *The Age of Caricature*, p. 101.

20. Roberts, *George III*, p. 470.

21. Mark Ford (ed.), *London: A History in Verse* (Cambridge, Massachusetts: Harvard University Press, 2015), p. 510.

22. Bills, *The Art of Satire*, p. 35.

23. Ibid., p. 15.

24. *Morning Post Gazetteer*, 17 April 1802.

25. Rachel E. Cowgill, 'Billington [*née* Weichsel], Elizabeth', *Oxford Dictionary of National Biography*: https://www.oxforddnb.com/view/10.1093/ref:odnb/9780198614128.001.0001/odnb-9780198614128-e-2397.

26. *London Chronicle*, 6 October 1801.

27. George, *Hogarth to Cruikshank: Social Change in Graphic Satire*, pp. 138-9.

28. Ibid., p. 138.

29. Ibid., p. 139.

30. Hazel Jones, *Jane Austen and Marriage* (London: Continuum, 2009), p. 100.

## 9: WHAT A PICTURE OF *LIFE* WAS THERE!

1. James Boswell, *The Life of Samuel Johnson*, vol. 2 (London: Henry Baldwin, 1791), p. 286.

2. Vic Gatrell, *The First Bohemians: Life and Art in London's Golden Age* (London: Penguin Books, 2003), p. 310.

3. Ibid.

4. Ibid., p. 311.

5. Ibid., p. 5.

6. *Hatters' Gazette*, 16 January 1797, in 'The first top hat causes a commotion', The British Newspaper Archive, 15 January 2014: https://blog.britishnewspaperarchive.co.uk/2014/01/15/the-first-top-hat-causes-a-commotion/.

7. Horace Walpole and George Vertue, *Anecdotes of Painting in England*, vol. 2 (London: H. G. Bohn, 1849), p. 413.

8. Mortimer, *The Time Traveller's Guide to Regency Britain*, p. 263.

9. R.J.S. Stevens and Mark Argent (ed.), *Recollections of R.J.S. Stevens: An Organist in Georgian London* (London: Macmillan, 1992), p. 25.

10. *Morning Chronicle*, 25 January 1798, in 'The Loyal Toast', James Gillray: Caricaturist: http://www.james-gillray.org/pop/loyal.html.

11. *True Briton*, 26 January 1798, ibid.

12. Angelo, *Reminiscences of Henry Angelo*, p. 240.

13. *Gentleman's Magazine*, April 1827.

14. Bills, *The Art of Satire*, p. 107.

15. Adolphus, *Memoirs of John Bannister*, vol. 1, p. 289.

16. Angelo, *Reminiscences of Henry Angelo*, p. v.

17. Ibid., p. 380.

18. Gatrell, *The First Bohemians*, p. xxii.

19. Bills, *The Art of Satire*, p. 110.

20. Ibid., p. 109.

21. Donald, *The Age of Caricature*, p. 10.

22. Ibid.

23. Ibid., pp. 10-11.

24. Wright (ed.), *The Works of James Gillray, the Caricaturist*, p. 13.

25. Benjamin Moseley, *An Oliver for a Rowland; or, A Cow Pox Epistle to the Reverend Rowland Hill* (London: Longman, Hurst, Rees, and Orme, 1807), p. 5.

26. Banerji and Donald (eds), *Gillray Observed*, p. 126.

27. Benjamin Douglas Perkins, *The Influence of Metallic Tractors on the Human Body* (London: J. Johnson and Ogilvy & Son, 1798), p. 11.

28. William Snow Miller, 'Elisha Perkins and His Metallic Tractors', *Yale Journal of Biology and Medicine*, vol. 8, no. 1 (October 1935), pp. 41–57.

29. Banerji and Donald (eds), *Gillray Observed*, p. 126.

30. Gatrell, *The First Bohemians*, p. 28.

31. Bills, *The Art of Satire*, p. 123.

32. Payne and Payne, *Regarding Thomas Rowlandson*, p. 169.

33. Ibid.

34. Ibid., p. 182.

35. Ibid., p. 184.

36. Ibid.

37. Banerji and Donald (eds), *Gillray Observed*, p. 35.

38. Ibid., p. 35.

39. Angelo, *Reminiscences of Henry Angelo*, p. 368.

40. Ibid., p. 389.

41. Ibid., p. 388.

42. Ibid.

43. Donald, *The Age of Caricature*, p. 31.

44. Hill, *Mr Gillray the Caricaturist*, p. 39.

45. Ibid.

46. Ibid.

47. Ibid.

48. Robert Patten, 'Cruikshank, Isaac', *Oxford Dictionary of National Biography*: https://www.oxforddnb.com/view/10.1093/ref:odnb/9780198614128.001.0001/odnb-9780198614128-e-6844.

## 10: A WONDERLAND OF DELIGHTS

1. Grego, *Rowlandson the Caricaturist*, p. 10.

2. Angelo, *Reminiscences of Henry Angelo*, p. 274.

3. Hill, *Mr Gillray the Caricaturist*, p. 57.

4. Ibid., p. 56.

5. Ibid., p. 58.

6. Ibid. p. 59.

7. Ibid., p. 61.

8. Ibid, p. 60.

9. Ibid., p. 61.

10. Ibid.

11. *Evening Mail*, 22 January 1796, in 'The Presentation, or The Wise Men's Offering', James Gillray: Caricaturist: http://www.james-gillray.org/pop/presentation.html.

12. Hill, *Mr Gillray the Caricaturist*, p. 62.

13. Ibid.

14. Sir John Dalrymple, *Consequences of the French Invasion* (London: Dalrymple, 1798), p. v.

15. Ibid., p. vi.

16. Ibid.

17. *Quarterly Review*, January and April 1874.

18. J. E. Thomas, *Britain's Last Invasion: Fishguard 1797* (Barnsley: The History Press, 2007), p. 67.

19. 'Political-ravishment, or the Old Lady of Threadneedle Street in Danger!', LBMA: https://www.lbma.org.uk/wonders-of-gold/items/political-ravishment-or-the-old-lady-of-threadneedle-street-in-danger.

20. Richard Brinsley Sheridan, *The Speeches of the Right Honourable Richard Brinsley Sheridan*, vol. 3 (London: Henry G. Bohn, 1842), p. 164.

21. George, *Hogarth to Cruikshank: Social Change in Graphic Satire*, p. 147.

22. Payne and Payne, *Regarding Thomas Rowlandson*, p. 189.

23. Ibid.

24. Matthew White, 'Popular politics in the 18th century', British Library, 14 October 2009: https://www.bl.uk/restoration-18th-century-literature/articles/popular-politics-in-the-18th-century.

25. Henry Wigstead, *Remarks on a Tour to North and South Wales, in the Year 1797* (London: J. Bateson, 1800), pp. v–vi.

26. Ibid., p. 7.

27. Ibid., p. 14.

28. Ibid.

29. William Wordsworth, *The Poetical Works of Wordsworth* (London: J.W. Lovell Company, 1881), p. 590.

30. Ibid.

31. Ibid., p. 589.

32. Wigstead, *Remarks on a Tour to North and South Wales, in the Year 1797*, p. 20.

33. Ibid., p. 69.

34. Bills, *The Art of Satire*, p. 26.

35. Angelo, *Reminiscences of Henry Angelo*, p. 468.

36. Ibid., p. 431.

37. Ibid., p. 432.

38. Payne and Payne, *Regarding Thomas Rowlandson*, p. 244.

39. Banerji and Donald (eds), *Gillray Observed*, p. 45.

40. Ibid., p. 26.

41. Bills, *The Art of Satire*, p. 28.

42. Banerji and Donald (eds), *Gillray Observed*, p. 8.

43. Ibid., p. 69.

44. Ibid., p. 22.

45. Ibid., p. 35.

46. Ibid., p. 27.

47. Ibid., p. 35.

## 11: THE FIRST KISS THIS TEN YEARS

1. James Boswell, *An Account of Corsica: The Journal of a Tour to that Island; and Memoirs of Pascal Paoli* (London: Edward and Charles Dilly, 1768), p. 25.

2. Andrew Roberts, *Napoleon the Great* (London: Allen Lane, 2014), p. 3.

3. Ibid., p. 6.

4. Ibid., p. 7.

5. Ibid., pp. 27–8.

6. Ibid., p. 11.

7. Ibid., p. 14.

8. Ibid., p. 12.

9. Ibid., p. 3.

10. David G. Chandler, *The Campaigns of Napoleon* (London: Folio Society, 1995), p. 7.

11. Ibid.

12. Roberts, *Napoleon the Great*, p. 16.

13. 'Authentic Account of the Important Battle of the Nile', 1800, p. 3: https://digital.nls.uk/street-literature-about-napoleons-wars/archive/74458559#?c=0&m=0&s=0&cv=2&xywh=-1631%2C0%2C5761%2C4326..

14. Robert Southey, *The Life of Nelson* (New York: J. & J. Harper, 1833), p. 132.

15. 'Authentic Account of the Important Battle of the Nile', p. 4.

16. James Watt, 'The injuries of four centuries of naval warfare', *Annals of the Royal College of Surgeons of England*, vol. 57 (1975).

17. Felicia Hemans, 'Casabianca' (1826), Poetry by Heart: https://www.poetrybyheart.org.uk/poems/casabianca/.

18. Cahal Milmo, 'Horatio's unknown heroes', *Independent*, 19 April 2005: https://www.independent.co.uk/news/uk/this-britain/horatio-s-unknown-heroes-2397.html.

19. Banerji and Donald (eds), *Gillray Observed*, p. 68.

20. Ibid., p. 68.

21. Clayton and O'Connell, *Bonaparte and the British*, p. 75.

22. Banerji and Donald (eds), *Gillray Observed*, pp. 68-9.

23. McConnell and Heneage, 'Gillray, James', *Oxford Dictionary of National Biography*.

24. Thomas Smith, *A Topographical and Historical Account of the Parish of St Mary-le-Bone* (London: J. Smith, 1833), p. 204.

25. Ibid., p. 203.

26. Ibid., p. 204.

27. Ibid.

28. Isaac Cruikshank, *An Aerial Excursion*, 1802, British Museum: https://www.britishmuseum.org/collection/object/P_1851-0901-1359.

29. *Quarterly Review*, January and April 1866.

30. Clayton and O'Connell, *Bonaparte and the British*, p. 110.

31. John Sugden, *Nelson: A Dream of Glory* (London: Random House, 2011), p. 135.

## 12: MANIAC RAVINGS AND LOW SCURRILITIES

1. Patten, 'Cruikshank, Isaac', *Oxford Dictionary of National Biography*.

2. W. Hamilton Reid, *Memoirs of the Public and Private Life of Napoleon Bonaparte* (London: Sherwood, Gilbert & Piper, 1826), p. 289.

3. 'Napoleon's planned invasion of England: what went wrong', HistoryExtra: https://www.historyextra.com/period/georgian/napoleon-invasion-england-when-why-fail/.

4. Clayton and O'Connell, *Bonaparte and the British*, p. 109.

5. Mark Bryant, *Napoleonic Wars in Cartoons* (London: Grub Street, 2015), p. 7

6. Donald, *The Age of Caricature*, p. 7.

7. Clayton and O'Connell, *Bonaparte and the British*, p. 119.

8. James Gillray, *Buonaparte, 48 Hours after Landing!*, British Museum: https://www.britishmuseum.org/collection/object/P_J-3-30.

9. *London Courier and Evening Gazette*, 23 January 1805.

10. *The Times*, 15 February 1805.

11. 'Defence of the Country, Volume 3: debated on 21 February 1805', Hansard: https://hansard.parliament.uk/Commons/1805-02-21/debates/bed96a6a-572c-4ccb-a612-abe420057fe4/DefenceOfTheCountry.

12. Banerji and Donald (eds), *Gillray Observed*, p. 215.

13. Ibid., p. 216.

14. Ibid., p. 217.

15. Ibid., p. 219.

16. Ibid.

17. Robert Justin Goldstein, *Censorship of Political Caricature in Nineteenth-Century France* (Kent, Ohio: Kent State University Press, 1989), p. 97.

18. Bryant, *Napoleonic Wars in Cartoons*, p. 8.

19. Thomas Rowlandson, *The Progress of the Emperor Napoleon*, 1808: https://www.metmuseum.org/art/collection/search/744096.

20. Roberts, *Napoleon the Great*, p. 4.

21. Bryant, *Napoleonic Wars in Cartoons*, p. 65.

22. Sam Willis, 'Tales from Nelson's Navy', HistoryExtra, 1 March 2013: https://www.historyextra.com/period/georgian/tales-from-nelsons-navy/.

23. Ibid.

24. Hague, *William Pitt the Younger*, p. 565.

25. Ibid.

26. J.P.W. Ehrman and Anthony Smith, 'Pitt, William', *Oxford Dictionary of National Biography*: https://www.oxforddnb.com/view/10.1093/ref:odnb/9780198614128.001.0001/odnb-9780198614128-e-22338.

27. Joshua White, *Supplement to the Life of the Late Horatio Lord Viscount Nelson*, vol. 2 (London: 1806), p. 12.

28. Ibid.

29. Ibid.

30. *Monthly Mirror*, January 1806.

31. Ibid.

32. Ibid.

33. Patten, 'Cruikshank, Isaac', *Oxford Dictionary of National Biography*.

34. *Monthly Mirror*, January 1806.

35. Ibid.

36. Ibid.

37. Patten, 'Cruikshank, George', *Oxford Dictionary of National Biography*.

38. Hague, *William Pitt the Younger*, p. 573.

39. Ibid., p. 574.

40. Ibid., p. 578.

41. Ibid.

42. Ibid., p. 571.

43. Ehrman and Smith, 'Pitt, William', *Oxford Dictionary of National Biography*.

44. James Gillray, *More Pigs than Teats*, 1806, British Library: https://www.bl.uk/collection-items/more-pigs-than-teats-by-gillray.

45. Mitchell, *Charles James Fox*, p. 227

46. Ibid., p. 235.

47. 'How did the slave trade end in Britain?', Royal Museums Greenwich: https://www.rmg.co.uk/stories/topics/how-did-slave-trade-end-britain.

48. Charles James Fox, *The Speeches of the Right Honourable Charles James Fox in the House of Commons* (London: John Wright, 1815), p. 659.

## 13: ADVANTAGES OF WEARING MUSLIN DRESSES

1. *Morning Post*, 28 November 1810.

2. Grego, *Rowlandson the Caricaturist*, p. 59.

3. Payne and Payne, *Regarding Thomas Rowlandson*, p. 246.

4. Ibid., p. 247.

5. Ibid., p. 246.

6. Ibid., p. 260.

7. William Henry Pyne, *Wine and Walnuts, Or, After Dinner Chit-Chat*, vol. 2 (London: Longman & Co., 1823), p. 323.

8. John Thomas Smith, *A Book for a Rainy Day: Or, Recollections of the Events of the Years 1766–1833* (London: Richard Bentley, 1861), p. 103.

9. Ibid.

10. Payne and Payne, *Regarding Thomas Rowlandson*, p. 254.

11. Smith, *A Book for a Rainy Day*, p. 103.

12. Pyne, *Wine and Walnuts*, p. 323.

13. Ibid., p. 324.

14. Ibid.

15. Ibid., p. 329.

16. Donald, *The Age of Caricature*, p. 4.

17. Payne and Payne, *Regarding Thomas Rowlandson*, p. 285.

18. Ibid.

19. Ibid., p. 263.

20. James Beresford, *The Miseries of Human Life* (London: William Miller, 1806).

21. Ibid.

22. Ibid.

23. Payne and Payne, *Regarding Thomas Rowlandson*, p. 263.

24. Ibid.

25. Ibid., p. 266.

26. Ibid.

27. Bills, *The Art of Satire*, p. 114.

28. Payne and Payne, *Regarding Thomas Rowlandson*, p. 281.

29. Ibid., p. 281.

30. Ibid., p. 282.

31. Ibid., p. 283.

32. Ibid.

33. Ibid., p. 284.

34. Henry Curwen, *A History of Booksellers: The Old and the New* (London: Chatto & Windus, 1874), p. 389.

35. James J. Barnes and Patience P. Barnes, 'Reassessing the Reputation of Thomas Tegg, London Publisher, 1776–1846', *Book History*, vol. 3 (2000), p. 47.

36. Ibid.

37. Donald, *The Age of Caricature*, p. 5.

## 14: THE CREW TO PLUTO'S REALM

1. Thomas Rowlandson, *A Parliamentary Toast.*, 1809, British Museum: https://www.britishmuseum.org/collection/object/P_1868-0808-7741.

2. Grego, *Rowlandson the Caricaturist*, p. 28.

3. Thomas Rowlandson, *A Parliamentary Toast.*, 1809, British Museum: https://www.britishmuseum.org/collection/object/P_1868-0808-7741.

4. Thomas Rowlandson, *Original Plan for a Popular Monument to be Erected in Gloucester Place*, 1809, British Museum: https://www.britishmuseum.org/collection/object/P_1868-0808-7802.

5. Patten, 'Cruikshank, George', *Oxford Dictionary of National Biography*.

6. Ibid.

7. Payne and Payne, *Regarding Thomas Rowlandson*, p. 245.

8. McConnell and Heneage, 'Gillray, James', *Oxford Dictionary of National Biography*.

9. Payne and Payne, *Regarding Thomas Rowlandson*, p. 277.

10. Ibid., p. 280.

11. Ibid.

12. Angelo, *Reminiscences of Henry Angelo*, p. 469.

13. Ibid., p. 432.

14. Ibid.

15. Ibid., p. 392.

16. Christopher Hibbert, *George III: A Personal History* (London: Basic Books, 2000), p. 394.

17. Roberts, *George III*, p. 652.

18. Mortimer, *The Time Traveller's Guide to Regency Britain*, p. 64.

19. Donald, *The Age of Caricature*, p. 43.

20. Payne and Payne, *Regarding Thomas Rowlandson*, p. 286.

21. Donald, *The Age of Caricature*, p. 4.

22. Gordon Pentland, 'The assassination of prime minister Spencer Perceval; what happened and was it a popular murder?' HistoryExtra: https://www.historyextra.com/period/georgian/assassination-british-prime-minister-spencer-perceval-how-why-shot-reaction.

23. Grego, *Rowlandson the Caricaturist*, pp. 25–6.

24. Ibid.

25. George Cruikshank, *The Allied Bakers or: The Corsican Toad in the Hole*, 1814, British Museum: https://www.britishmuseum.org/collection/object/P_1978-U-826.

26. *Morning Post*, 16 February 1815.

27. *Athenæum*, 1 October 1831.

28. 'Waterloo', Cambridge Digital Library: https://cudl.lib.cam.ac.uk/collections/waterloo/1.

29. John Quincy Adams and Charles Francis Adams (eds), *Memoirs of John Quincy Adams, Comprising Portions of His Diary From 1795 to 1848*, vol. 3 (Philadelphia: J.B. Lippincott & Co., 1874), p. 231.

30. Johann Wilhelm von Archenholz in Fergus Linnane, *London: The Wicked City: A Thousand Years of Vice in the Capital* (London: Robson, 2003), p. 104.

31. *Gentleman's Magazine*, July 1815.

32. Ibid.

33. Ibid.

34. Payne and Payne, *Regarding Thomas Rowlandson*, p. 310.

35. Ibid., p. 321.

36. Ibid.

37. McConnell and Heneage, 'Gillray, James', *Oxford Dictionary of National Biography*, and 'Will of James Gillray of Saint James Westminster, Middlesex', 17 June 1815, National Archives, TNA: PRO, PROB 11/1569, fol. 313.

38. Payne and Payne, *Regarding Thomas Rowlandson*, p. 325.

39. Ibid.

40. Ibid., p. 325 and p. 351.

41. *St James's Chronicle*, 20 July 1816.

42. Ibid.

43. *The Times*, 20 July 1816.

44. Ibid.

45. Mortimer, *The Time Traveller's Guide to Regency Britain*, p. 95.

46. *Peterloo Massacre, Containing a Faithful Narrative of the Events which Preceded, Accompanied, and Followed the Fatal Sixteenth of August, 1819* (Manchester: J. Wroe, 1819), p. 178

47. Stephen Bates, 'The bloody clash that changed Britain', *Guardian*, 4 January 2018: https://www.theguardian.com/news/2018/jan/04/peterloo-massacre-bloody-clash-that-changed-britain.

48. British Museum: https://www.britishmuseum.org/collection/object/C_M-5625.

49. William Hone, *The Divine Right of Kings to Govern Wrong!*, 3rd edn (London: William Hone, 1821), p. 60.

50. Payne and Payne, *Regarding Thomas Rowlandson*, p. 348.

51. Ibid.

52. Ibid.

53. Ibid., p. 350.

54. *Gentleman's Magazine*, July 1827.

55. Ibid.

56. Payne and Payne, *Regarding Thomas Rowlandson*, p. 351.

57. Ibid., p. 352.

58. Ibid., p. 354.

59. Ibid.

60. Ibid.

## 15: CANCELLED

1. Donald, *The Age of Caricature*, p. 23.

2. Ibid.

3. Ibid.

4. Wright (ed.), *The Works of James Gillray, the Caricaturist*, p. 25.

5. *Athenæum*, 15 October 1831.

6. Donald, *The Age of Caricature*, p. 43.

7. Ibid.

8. Ibid.

9. Rowson, 'Satire, sewers and statesmen', *Guardian*.

10. Ibid.

11. Donald, *The Age of Caricature*, p. 43.

12. Ibid.

13. Ibid.

14. *Quarterly Review*, January and April 1866.

15. Wade, *Rowlandson's Human Comedy*, p. 13.

16. Arthur Bartlett Maurice and Frederic Taber Cooper, *The History of the Nineteenth Century in Caricature* (London: Grant Richards, 1904), p. 21.

17. Donald, *The Age of Caricature*, p. 43.

18. Bartlett Maurice and Taber Cooper, *The History of the Nineteenth Century in Caricature*, p. 21.

19. Ibid.

20. Payne and Payne, *Regarding Thomas Rowlandson*, p. 355.

21. Ibid.

22. Heard, '"I Only Got One Little Peep"', p. 11.

23. Ibid.

24. Payne and Payne, *Regarding Thomas Rowlandson*, p. 355.

25. Ibid.

26. Ibid.

27. Grego, *Rowlandson the Caricaturist*, p. 13.

28. Ibid.

29. Ibid.

30. Payne and Payne, *Regarding Thomas Rowlandson*, p. 22.

31. Donald, *The Age of Caricature*, p. 27.

32. Robert Patten, 'Cruikshank, (Isaac) Robert', *Oxford Dictionary of National Biography*: https://www.oxforddnb.com/view/10.1093/ref:odnb/9780198614128.001.0001/odnb-9780198614128-e-6845.

33. Patten, 'Cruikshank, Isaac', *Oxford Dictionary of National Biography*.

34. Ibid.

35. Donald, *The Age of Caricature*, p. 27.

36. Robert Patten, 'Lectures on the Fine Arts No. 1 On George Cruikshank', *Blackwood's Edinburgh Magazine*, vol. 4, 1823.

37. Ibid.

38. Ibid.

39. Patten, 'Cruikshank, George', *Oxford Dictionary of National Biography*.

40. Dora Montefiore, *From a Victorian to a Modern: An Autobiography* (London: E. Archer, 1927), p. 26.

41. Ibid., p. 28.

42. Ibid., p. 29.

43. Ibid., p. 28.

44. Charles Dickens to John Forster, 2 September 1847, in Madeline House and Graham Storey (eds), *The Letters of Charles Dickens*, vol. 5 (Oxford: Clarendon, 1980), pp. 156–7.

45. Paul Schlicke, *The Oxford Companion to Charles Dickens* (Oxford: Oxford University Press, 2011), p. 148.

46. 'The Origins of "Oliver Twist"', *Birmingham Mail*, 30 December 1871.

47. 'Obituary', *Punch*, 9 February 1878.

48. Ibid.

49. Donald, *The Age of Caricature*, p. 43.

50. William Michael Rossetti (ed.), *The Poetical Works of William Blake: Lyrical and Miscellaneous* (London: George Bell and Sons, 1890), p. xiii.

51. Jonathan Jones, 'Blake's heaven', *Guardian*, 25 April 2005: https://www.theguardian.com/culture/2005/apr/25/williamblake.

52. Draper Hill (ed.), *The Satirical Etchings of James Gillray* (London: Constable, 1976), p. xxix.

53. Bartlett Maurice and Taber Cooper, *The History of the Nineteenth Century in Caricature*, p. 22.

54. Dave Brown, 'Modern cartoonists can still learn from the famous James Gillray – that's why I've chosen to honour him', *Independent*, 17 November 2021: https://www.independent.co.uk/voices/cartoonists-dave-brown-james-gillray-b1959488.html.

55. Martin Rowson speaking on *The Secret of Drawing*, episode 2, BBC Two, 15 October 2005.

56. Roger Law, 'Puppet masters: The creator of iconic TV satire *Spitting Image* on whether we still have our sense of humour', *Index on Censorship*, vol. 46, issue 1 (April 2017), pp. 82–4.

57. Donald, *The Age of Caricature*, p. vii.

58. Ibid.

59. Ibid.

60. Ibid.

# *Bibliography*


Ackroyd, Peter, *Revolution: The History of England*, vol. 4 (London: Macmillan, 2016)

Adams, John Quincy, and Adams, Charles Francis (eds), *Memoirs of John Quincy Adams, Comprising Portions of His Diary From 1795 to 1848*, vol. 3 (Philadelphia: J.B. Lippincott & Co., 1874)

Adolphus, John, *Memoirs of Jack Bannister*, vol. 1 (London: R. Bentley, 1838)

Alexander, Caroline, *The Bounty: The True Story of the Mutiny on the Bounty* (London: HarperCollins, 2003)

Angelo, Henry, *Reminiscences of Henry Angelo*, vol. 1 (London: Henry Colburn, 1830)

Ashton, John, *Florizel's Folly* (London: Chatto & Windus, 1899)

Austen, Jane, *Northanger Abbey* (London: Penguin Classics, 1972)

Austen, Jane, *Pride and Prejudice* (London: Penguin Classics, 1996)

Banerji, Christiane, and Donald, Diana (eds), *Gillray Observed: The Earliest Account of his Caricatures in London and Paris* (Cambridge: Cambridge University Press, 2009)

Barrow, William, *An Essay on Education*, vol. 2 (London: F. & C. Rivington, 1804)

Bartlett Maurice, Arthur, and Taber Cooper, Frederic, *The History of the Nineteenth Century in Caricature* (London: Grant Richards, 1904)

Beresford, James, *The Miseries of Human Life* (London: William Miller, 1806)

Bills, Mark, *The Art of Satire: London in Caricature* (London: Philip Wilson, 2006)

Black, Jeremy, *Pitt the Elder* (Cambridge: Cambridge University Press, 1992)

Boswell, James, *An Account of Corsica: The Journal of a Tour to that Island; and Memoirs of Pascal Paoli* (London: Edward and Charles Dilly, 1768)

Boswell, James, *The Life of Samuel Johnson*, vol. 2 (London: Henry Baldwin, 1791)

Britton, John, *The Auto-Biography of John Britton* (London: John Britton, 1850)

Bryant, Mark, *Napoleonic Wars in Cartoons* (London: Grub Street, 2015)

Buckingham, Duke of, *Memoirs of the Court and Cabinets of George the Third*, vol. 2 (Project Gutenberg, 2009)

Burke, Edmund, *The Correspondence of Edmund Burke* (Chicago: University of Chicago Press, 1958)
Buss, Robert William, *English Graphic Satire and Its Relation to Different Styles of Painting, Sculpture and Engraving* (London: Robert Buss, 1874)
Caulfield, James, *Calcographiana: The Printsellers Chronicle and Collectors Guide to the Knowledge and Value of Engraved British Portraits* (London: G. Smeeton, 1814)
Chandler, David G., *The Campaigns of Napoleon* (London: Folio Society, 1995)
Clayton, Tim, and O'Connell, Sheila, *Bonaparte and the British: Prints and Propaganda in the Age of Napoleon* (London: British Museum Press, 2015)
Cobbett, William, *The Parliamentary History of England from the Earliest Period to the Year 1803* (London: Longman & Co., 1817)
Crotty, Patrick (ed.), *The Penguin Book of Irish Poetry* (London: Penguin Classics, 2018)
Cunningham, Geoffrey George (ed.), *The English Nation; Or, A History of England in the Lives of Englishmen*, vol. 5 (Edinburgh and London: Fullarton & Co., 1863)
Curwen, Henry, *A History of Booksellers: The Old and the New* (London: Chatto & Windus, 1874)
da Vinci, Leonardo, *The Notebooks of Leonardo da Vinci*, vol. 1 (New York: Dover Publications, 2012)
Dalrymple, John, *Consequences of the French Invasion* (London: Dalrymple, 1798)
Darly, Mary, *A Book of Caricaturas* (London: Mary Darly, 1769)
Davis, Michael T., *Radicalism and Revolution in Britain 1775–1848: Essays in Honour of Malcolm I. Thomis* (Basingstoke: Macmillan, 2000)
Defoe, Daniel, *Moll Flanders* (London: Penguin Classics, 1978)
Derry, John Wesley, *The Regency Crisis and the Whigs 1788–9* (Cambridge: Cambridge University Press, 1963)
Donald, Diana, *The Age of Caricature: Satirical Prints in the Reign of George III* (New Haven: Yale University Press, 1996)
Edgeworth, Maria, *Life and Letters of Maria Edgeworth*, vol. 2 (London: Arnold, 1894)
Edwards, Nina, *Darkness: A Cultural History* (London: Reaktion Books, 2018)
Feaver, William, *Masters of Caricature* (London: Weidenfeld & Nicolson: 1981)
Fielding, Henry, *The History of the Adventures of Joseph Andrews and of his Friend Mr Abraham Adams*, vol. 1 (London: A. Millar, 1742)
Fitzgerald Molloy, Joseph, *Court Life Below Stairs; or, London Under the First Georges, 1714–1760* (London: Hurst & Blackett, 1885)

Ford, Mark (ed.), *London: A History in Verse* (Cambridge, Massachusetts: Harvard University Press, 2015)

Fordham, Douglas, *British Art and the Seven Years' War: Allegiance and Autonomy* (Philadelphia: University of Pennsylvania Press, 2010)

Fox, Charles James, *Memorials and Correspondence of Charles James Fox*, vol. 2 (London: Richard Bentley, 1854)

Fox, Charles James, and Wright, John, *The Speeches of the Right Honourable Charles James Fox* (London: Longman & Co., 1815)

Fox, Charles James, *The Speeches of the Right Honourable Charles James Fox in the House of Commons* (London: John Wright, 1815)

Gatrell, Vic, *The First Bohemians: Life and Art in London's Golden Age* (London: Penguin Books, 2003)

Gatrell, Vic, *The First Bohemians: Life and Art in London's Golden Age* (London: Penguin Books, 2003).

George, M. Dorothy, *Hogarth to Cruikshank: Social Change in Graphic Satire* (London: Allen Lane, 1967)

Glancey, Jonathan, *Architecture* (London: Dorling Kindersley, 2006)

Goldsmith, Oliver, *She Stoops to Conquer*, in *The British Theatre; or, a Collection of Plays, Which Are Acted at the Theatres Royal, Drury Lane, Covent Garden, and Haymarket*, vol. 17 (London: Longman, Hurst, Rees & Orme, 1808)

Goldstein, Robert Justin, *Censorship of Political Caricature in Nineteenth-Century France* (Kent, Ohio: Kent State University Press, 1989)

Gombrich, E.H., and Kris, Ernst, *Caricature* (Harmondsworth: Penguin, 1940)

Greenberg, Jonathan, *The Cambridge Introduction to Satire* (Cambridge: Cambridge University Press, 2019)

Grego, Joseph, *Rowlandson the Caricaturist* (London: Chatto & Windus, 1880)

Hague, William, *William Pitt the Younger* (London: Harper Collins, 2004)

Hallett, Mark, Turner, Sarah Victoria, and Feather, Jessica (eds), *The Royal Academy of Arts Summer Exhibition: A Chronicle, 1769–2018* (London: Paul Mellon Centre for Studies in British Art, 2018)

Heard, Kate, *High Spirits: The Comic Art of Thomas Rowlandson* (London: Royal Collection Trust, 2018)

Hibbert, Christopher, *George III: A Personal History* (New York: Basic Books, 2000)

Hibbert, Christopher, *Redcoats and Rebels: The American Revolution Through British Eyes* (New York: Norton, 1990)

Hill, Draper, *Mr Gillray the Caricaturist: A Biography* (London: Phaidon Press, 1965)

Hill, Draper (ed.), *The Satirical Etchings of James Gillray* (London: Constable, 1976)

Hogarth, William, *Anecdotes of William Hogarth* (London: J.B. Nichols & Son, 1833)
Hone, William, *The Divine Right of Kings to Govern Wrong!*, 3rd edn (London: William Hone, 1821)
Hostettler, John, *Thomas Erskine and Trial by Jury* (Hook: Waterside Press, 2010)
House, Madeline, and Storey, Graham (eds), *The Letters of Charles Dickens*, vol. 5 (Oxford: Clarendon, 1980)
Jacobs, Reginald, *Covent Garden: Its Romance and History* (London: Simpkin, Marshall & Co., 1913)
Jones, Hazel, *Jane Austen and Marriage* (London: Continuum, 2009)
Keele, Kenneth D., and Roberts, Jane, *Leonardo da Vinci: Anatomical Drawings from the Royal Library, Windsor Castle* (New York: The Metropolitan Museum of Art, 1983)
Krumbhaar, E.B., *Isaac Cruikshank, A Catalogue Raisonné, with a Sketch of His Life and Work* (Philadelphia: University of Pennsylvania Press, 1966)
Leonard, Dick, *Nineteenth-Century British Premiers* (London: Palgrave Macmillan, 2008)
Leonard, Dick, and Garnett, Mark, *Titans: Fox vs. Pitt* (London: I.B. Tauris, 2019)
Lincoln, Margarette, *Trading in War: London's Maritime World in the Age of Cook and Nelson* (New Haven: Yale University Press, 2018)
Linnane, Fergus, *London: The Wicked City: A Thousand Years of Vice in the Capital* (London: Robson, 2003)
Locke, John, *Locke: Political Essays* (Cambridge: Cambridge University Press, 1997)
MacCurdy, Edward, *The Notebooks of Leonardo da Vinci, Arranged, Rendered into English and Introduced*, vol. 2 (London: Jonathan Cape, 1950)
Macdonagh, Michael, *The Book of Parliament* (London: Isbister & Co., 1897)
Mitchell, Leslie George, *Charles James Fox* (Oxford: Oxford University Press, 1992)
Montefiore, Dora, *From a Victorian to a Modern: An Autobiography* (London: E. Archer, 1927)
Monteyne, Joseph, *Media Critique in the Age of Gillray: Scratches, Scraps, and Spectres* (Toronto: University of Toronto Press, 2022)
Moore, Peter, *Endeavour: The Ship and the Attitude that Changed the World* (London: Chatto & Windus, 2018)
Morrice, David, *The Art of Teaching* (London: Lackington, Allen & Co., 1801)
Mortimer, Ian, *The Time Traveller's Guide to Regency Britain* (London: Bodley Head, 2020)

Murdoch, Tessa, et al., *Burning Bright: Essays in Honour of David Bindman* (London: UCL Press, 2015)

Paine, Thomas, *Rights of Man: Being an Answer to Mr Burke's Attack on the French Revolution* (London: H.D. Symonds, 1792)

Payne, James, and Payne, Matthew, *Regarding Thomas Rowlandson, 1757–1827: His Life, Art and Acquaintance* (London: Hogarth Arts: 2010)

Perkins, Benjamin Douglas, *The Influence of Metallic Tractors on the Human Body* (London: J. Johnson and Ogilvy & Son, 1798)

*Peterloo Massacre, Containing a Faithful Narrative of the Events which Preceded, Accompanied, and Followed the Fatal Sixteenth of August, 1819* (Manchester: J. Wroe, 1819)

Pyne, William Henry, *Wine and Walnuts, Or, After Dinner Chit-Chat*, vol. 2 (London: Longman & Co., 1823)

Ratcliffe, Susan, *Oxford Essential Quotations*, 4th edn (Oxford: Oxford University Press, 2016)

Reid, Loren, *Charles James Fox: A Man for the People* (London: Longmans, 1969)

Reid, W. Hamilton, *Memoirs of the Public and Private Life of Napoleon Bonaparte* (London: Sherwood, Gilbert & Piper 1826)

Roberts, Andrew, *George III: The Life and Reign of Britain's Most Misunderstood Monarch* (London: Penguin Books, 2021)

Roberts, Andrew, *Napoleon the Great* (London: Allen Lane, 2014)

Roberts, William, *Memoirs of the Life and Correspondence of Mrs Hannah More* (London: Seeley, 1834)

Robinson, Nicholas K., *Edmund Burke: A Life in Caricature* (New Haven: Yale University Press, 1996)

Rogers, Nicholas, *Crowds, Culture, and Politics in Georgian Britain* (Oxford: Clarendon Press, 1998)

Rosner, Lisa, *Vaccination and Its Critics: A Documentary and Reference Guide* (Santa Barbara, California: Greenwood, 2017)

Rossetti, William Michael (ed.), *The Poetical Works of William Blake: Lyrical and Miscellaneous* (London: George Bell & Sons, 1890)

Royal Academy of Arts, *Abstract of the Instrument of Institution and Laws of the Royal Academy of Arts in London – Established December 10, 1768* (London: T. Cadell, 1781)

Sandby, William, *The History of the Royal Academy of Arts from Its Foundation in 1768 to the Present Time*, vol. 2 (London: Longman & Co., 1862)

Schlicke, Paul, *The Oxford Companion to Charles Dickens* (Oxford: Oxford University Press, 2011)

Sebag Montefiore, Simon, *Voices of History: Speeches that Changed the World* (London: Orion, 2019)

Sheridan, Richard Brinsley, *The Speeches of the Right Honourable Richard Brinsley Sheridan*, vol. 3 (London: Henry G. Bohn, 1842)

Smith, John Thomas, *A Book for a Rainy Day: Or, Recollections of the Events of the Years 1766–1833* (London: Richard Bentley, 1861)

Smith, Stephen A., *Freedom of Expression: Foundational Documents and Historical Arguments* (Oxford: Oxbridge Research Associates, 2018)

Smith, Thomas, *A Topographical and Historical Account of the Parish of St Mary-le-Bone* (London: J. Smith, 1833)

Southey, Robert, *The Life of Nelson* (New York: J. & J. Harper, 1833)

Stanhope, Philip Dormer, and Dobrée, Bonamy (ed.), *The Letters of Philip Dormer Stanhope, 4th Earl of Chesterfield*, vol. 3 (London: Eyre & Spottiswoode, 1932)

Stanhope, Philip Henry, *Life of the Right Honourable William Pitt*, vol. 1 (London: John Murray, 1861)

*The Statutes at Large, From the Thirteenth Year in the Reign of King George the Third to the Sixteenth Year in the Reign of King George the Third*, vol. 12 (London: Charles Eyre & William Strahan, 1776)

Stevens, R.J.S., and Argent, Mark (ed.), *Recollections of R.J.S. Stevens: An Organist in Georgian London* (London: Macmillan, 1992)

Sugden, John, *Nelson: A Dream of Glory* (London: Random House, 2011)

Thomas, J.E., *Britain's Last Invasion: Fishguard 1797* (Barnsley: The History Press, 2007)

Topham, Edward, *Letters from Edinburgh; Written in the Years 1774 and 1775* (London: J. Dodsley, 1776)

Trusler, John, *The Works of Mr Hogarth Moralized*, vol. 1 (London: J. Goodwin, 1821)

Twadell Shipley, Joseph, *The Origins of English Words: A Discursive Dictionary of Indo-European Roots* (Baltimore: Johns Hopkins University Press, 1984)

Uglow, Jenny, *William Hogarth: A Life and a World* (London: Faber & Faber, 2011)

Wade, Stephen, *Rowlandson's Human Comedy* (Stroud: Amberley Publishing, 2011)

Walpole, Horace, and Vertue, George, *Anecdotes of Painting in England*, vol. 2 (London: H.G. Bohn, 1849)

Walpole, Horace, Lewis, W.S., Cronin Jr, Grover, and Bennett, Charles H. (eds), *Horace Walpole's Correspondence*, vol. 2 (New Haven: Yale University Press, 1955)

White, Joshua, *Supplement to the Life of the Late Horatio Lord Viscount Nelson*, vol. 2 (London: James Cundee, 1806)

Wigstead, Henry, *Remarks on a Tour to North and South Wales, in the Year 1797* (London: J. Bateson, 1800)

Wordsworth, William, *The Poetical Works of Wordsworth* (London: J.W. Lovell Company, 1881)

Wright, Thomas (ed.), *The Works of James Gillray, the Caricaturist: With the Story of his Life and Times* (London: Chatto & Windus, 1873)

## NEWSPAPERS AND PERIODICALS

*Athenaeum*
*Birmingham Mail*
*General Post*
*Gentleman's Magazine*
*London Chronicle*
*London Courier and Evening Gazette*
*Monthly Mirror*
*Morning Chronicle*
*Morning Post*
*Punch*
*Quarterly Review*
*St James's Chronicle*
*The Times*
*True Briton*
*The World*

## DATABASES AND WEBSITES

British Library
British Museum
Cambridge Digital Library
Getty
Hansard
James Gillray: Caricaturist – www.james-gillray.org
Metropolitan Museum
National Archives
National Library of Scotland
Old Bailey Proceedings
Oxford Dictionary of National Biography
Oxford English Dictionary
Oxford Learner's Dictionaries
The Printshop Window – https://theprintshopwindow.wordpress.com
Public Domain Review
Royal Academy Collection

Royal Academy of Arts
Royal Academy Summer Exhibition Catalogue
Royal Archives
Tate
UK Government

## ARTICLES AND ONLINE RESOURCES

Barnes, James J., and Barnes, Patience P., 'Reassessing the Reputation of Thomas Tegg, London Publisher, 1776–1846', *Book History*, vol. 3 (2000)

Bates, Stephen, 'The bloody clash that changed Britain', *Guardian*, 4 January 2018: https://www.theguardian.com/news/2018/jan/04/peterloo-massacre-bloody-clash-that-changed-britain

Brown, Dave, 'Modern cartoonists can still learn from the famous James Gillray – that's why I've chosen to honour him', *Independent*, 17 November 2021: https://www.independent.co.uk/voices/cartoonists-dave-brown-james-gillray-b1959488.html

Brown, Mark, 'Letters shed light on lovelorn prince who became George IV', *Guardian*, 23 October 2019: https://www.theguardian.com/uk-news/2019/oct/23/letters-prince-george-iv

Bryant, Mark, 'Drawing the Line', *The British Art Journal*, vol. 20, no. 2 (2019)

Clayton, Tim, 'The London Printsellers and the Export of English Graphic Prints', in Kremers, Anorthe, and Reich, Elisabeth (eds), *Loyal Subversion? Caricatures from the Personal Union Between England and Hanover (1714–1837)* (Gottingen: Vandenhoeck & Ruprecht, 2014)

Crosby, Mark, 'The Voice of Flattery *vs* Sober Truth: William Godwin, Thomas Erskine and the 1792 Trial of Thomas Paine for Sedition', *Review of English Studies*, vol. 62, no. 253 (February 2011)

Hall, James, 'Kenneth Clark: Looking for Civilisation', *Tate Etc.*, 25 June 2019: https://www.tate.org.uk/tate-etc/issue-31-summer-2014/rescue-civilisation-man

Heard, Kate, '"I Only Got One Little Peep": George III's Family and Satirical Prints', Royal Collection Trust: https://www.rct.uk/sites/default/files/Transcript%20I%20only%20got%20one%20little%20peep_1.pdf

Hemans, Felicia, 'Casabianca' (1826), Poetry by Heart: https://www.poetrybyheart.org.uk/poems/casabianca/

'House of Lords Library: Gillray Collection', House of Lords, February 2017: https://www.parliament.uk/globalassets/documents/lords-library/SpecialCollections/Library-Gillray-Collection.pdf

'How did the slave trade end in Britain?', Royal Museums Greenwich: https://www.rmg.co.uk/stories/topics/how-did-slave-trade-end-britain

Hutchinson, Sidney C., 'The Royal Academy Schools, 1768–1830', *Volume of the Walpole Society*, vol. 38 (1960–62)

Jones, Jonathan, 'Blake's heaven', *Guardian*, 25 April 2005: https://www.theguardian.com/culture/2005/apr/25/williamblake

Law, Roger, 'Puppet masters: The creator of iconic TV satire *Spitting Image* on whether we still have our sense of humour', *Index on Censorship*, vol. 46, issue 1 (April 2017)

Mellby, Julie L., 'Printmaker's abbreviations', Graphic Arts, Princeton University, 6 February 2009: https://www.princeton.edu/~graphicarts/2009/02/printmakers_abbreviations.html

Miller, William Snow, 'Elisha Perkins and His Metallic Tractors', *Yale Journal of Biology and Medicine*, vol. 8, no. 1 (October 1935)

Milmo, Cahal, 'Horatio's unknown heroes', *Independent*, 19 April 2005: https://www.independent.co.uk/news/uk/this-britain/horatio-s-unknown-heroes-2397.html

Morris, Marilyn, 'Princely Debt, Public Credit, and Commercial Values in Late Georgian Britain', *Journal of British Studies*, vol. 43, no. 3 (July 2004)

'Napoleon's planned invasion of England: what went wrong', HistoryExtra, https://www.historyextra.com/period/georgian/napoleon-invasion-england-when-why-fail/

Overton, Mark, 'Agricultural Revolution in England 1500–1850', BBC History, 17 February 2017: https://www.bbc.co.uk/history/british/empire_seapower/agricultural_revolution_01.shtml

'Past Prime Ministers: William Pitt "The Younger"', UK Government: https://www.gov.uk/government/history/past-prime-ministers/william-pitt

Pentland, Gordon, 'The assassination of prime minister Spencer Perceval: what happened and was it a popular murder?' HistoryExtra: https://www.historyextra.com/period/georgian/assassination-british-prime-minister-spencer-perceval-how-why-shot-reaction/

Philp, Mark, 'Britain and the French Revolution', BBC History, 17 February 2017: https://www.bbc.co.uk/history/british/empire_seapower/british_french_rev_01.shtml

'Political-ravishment, or the Old Lady of Threadneedle Street in Danger!', LBMA: https://www.lbma.org.uk/wonders-of-gold/items/political-ravishment-or-the-old-lady-of-threadneedle-street-in-danger

Postle, Martin, 'Flayed for Art: The Ecorché Figure in the English Academy', *British Art Journal*, vol. 5, no. 1 (2004)

Pugh, Jo, 'The World According to Pitt', *Public Domain Review*, 1 October 2013: https://publicdomainreview.org/essay/the-world-according-to-pitt

Ribeiro, Aileen, 'Meet the Macaronis', *History Today*, 31 July 2019: https://www.historytoday.com/miscellanies/meet-macaronis

Rowson, Martin, 'Satire, sewers and statesmen: why James Gillray was king of the cartoon', *Guardian*, 21 March 2015: https://www.theguardian.com/artanddesign/2015/mar/21/satire-sewers-and-statesmen-james-gillray-king-of-cartoon

*St James's Chronicle or British Evening Post*, 11 September 1792

*The Secret of Drawing*, episode 2, BBC Two, 15 October 2005

'The Top-Hat in 1797', *Huddersfield Chronicle*, 24 January 1899: https://blog.britishnewspaperarchive.co.uk/2014/01/15/the-first-top-hat-causes-a-commotion/

Watt, James, 'The injuries of four centuries of naval warfare', *Annals of the Royal College of Surgeons of England*, vol. 57 (1975)

White, Matthew, 'Crime and punishment in Georgian Britain', British Library, 14 October 2009: https://www.bl.uk/georgian-britain/articles/crime-and-punishment-in-georgian-britain

White, Matthew, 'Popular politics in the 18th century', British Library, 14 October 2009: https://www.bl.uk/restoration-18th-century-literature/articles/popular-politics-in-the-18th-century

Willis, Sam, 'Tales from Nelson's Navy', HistoryExtra, 1 March 2013: https://www.historyextra.com/period/georgian/tales-from-nelsons-navy/

# *Index*

Page references in *italics* indicate images.

This book was brought to you through the team effort of the following people at Icon Books and our wonderful freelancers.

**Editorial**
Duncan Heath
Clare Bullock

**Sales**
Matt Boxell
Annalise Peters

**Marketing and Publicity**
Emily Cary-Elwes
Hamza Jahanzeb

**Typesetting and Internal Design**
Marie Doherty

**Cover Design**
Kid Ethic

**Production**
Simon Colverson
Thea Hirsi

**Copy Editor**
James Lilford

**Proof Reader**
Alice Brett